RAISING CUBBY

ALSO BY JOHN ELDER ROBISON

Look Me in the Eye

Be Different

RAISING CUBBY

A FATHER AND SON'S ADVENTURES
WITH ASPERGER'S, TRAINS, TRACTORS,
AND HIGH EXPLOSIVES

JOHN ELDER ROBISON

CROWN PUBLISHERS

NEW YORK

Library of Congress Cataloging-in-Publication Data

Robison, John Elder.
Raising Cubby : a father and son's adventures with Asperger's, trains,
tractors, and high explosives / John Elder Robison. — First edition.
Summary: "The comic memoir of an Aspergian father raising his
Aspergian son, by the bestselling author of Look Me in the Eye"—
Provided by publisher.
 1. Asperger's syndrome—Patients—Family relationships.
 2. Asperger's syndrome in children—Patients—Life skills guides.
 3. Asperger's syndrome in children—Patients—United States—
Biography. 4. Parenting. 5. Robison, John Elder. I. Title.
RC553.A88R6355 2013
616.85'8832—dc23   2012033979

ISBN 978-0-307-88484-8
eISBN 978-0-307-88486-2

PRINTED IN THE UNITED STATES OF AMERICA

Jacket design by Oliver Munday
Jacket photograph: Comstock Images

1 3 5 7 9 10 8 6 4 2

First Edition

For Little Bear, Cubby's mom

I may be the one who wrote this book, but Cubby's mom deserves credit for much of the hard work of kid raising, especially when he was small.

I worked to support our fledgling family, took Cubby on many fun adventures, and taught him useful skills. Meanwhile, Little Bear nursed him, changed his diapers, carried him to the doctor, and escorted him to school. She was the one who was there for all those firsts in his life: walking, talking, and peeing on a parent. Later, when he floundered in school, it was Little Bear who grabbed hold of the school system, shook hard, and made them accommodate our kid.

Lest you think I was the only one who did fun things, she also took him to Mexico, won awards with him at science fiction conventions, introduced him to fireworks and rockets, and served as a leader for his Cub Scout troop.

Even though we have not been married to each other for many years, her achievement in raising our son is not to be minimized. To the extent that he is a prizewinning specimen, she is in large part responsible.

CONTENTS

RAISING CUBBY

1

EVERY PARENT'S WORST NIGHTMARE

Anyone who willfully, intentionally and without right, by the explosion of gunpowder or of any other explosive, unlawfully damages property or injures a person, shall be punished by imprisonment in the state prison for not more than twenty years." [Massachusetts General Laws; Felonies 266.101]

That's the state's definition of "malicious explosion," the destruction of property with an explosive device. It's a serious felony, on a par with armed robbery or deadly assault. My teenage son was charged with three counts. If convicted, he would face up to sixty years in state prison. The charges made him sound like a pretty scary guy.

Just in case that wasn't enough, the Commonwealth of Massachusetts had also charged him with one count of "possessing explosives with the intent to harm people or property." I guess that was their backstop—if they couldn't prove he harmed people or destroyed property, they wanted to prove he meant to. That was worth a few years in prison if the first charges weren't enough to send him away forever.

Until that point, people charged with malicious explosion in

Massachusetts had mostly been outlaw bikers, Mafia hit men, drug dealers, or vicious thugs. Their explosions were obvious and unmistakable: pipe bombs in clubhouses, firebombs in churches, car bombs under Cadillacs, maybe a hand grenade tossed through a window. Most of the time, someone was killed, or at least seriously injured. The idea that my son would be lumped together with people like that was just crazy. He wasn't a violent criminal; he was a bright, geeky teenager who'd dropped out of high school so he could study chemistry in college at age sixteen. Now he was fighting for his life over one question: Was he a budding scientist or a mad bomber?

All this had happened because Jack, whom I call Cubby, had gotten interested in the physics and chemistry of explosives at a time when most kids are still learning multiplication and division. He had made experimental explosive compounds from common and legal chemicals and set them off on the ground in the woods where we live. No one was hurt. No property was damaged. No one even complained. He just wanted to see if his concoctions would really explode, and they did. Sometimes. He'd filmed his experiments and put them on YouTube for others to see and discuss.

To me, he was just a smart kid with a love of science. When Cubby's interest in chemistry turned serious at age twelve, it was no surprise he had explored homemade explosives. I could not expect him to be interested in industrial chemistry at his age, and he knew about fireworks from the time he had spent in Mexico, where his mom was studying for her doctorate. I was proud of his knowledge, though I wasn't too happy about where it had led us.

My son's explosions hadn't looked very scary to me—not much more than firecrackers tossed on the ground. Ten-second videos showed capfuls of explosive blowing half-cups of dirt into the air. A few of the blasts were larger, but they were still in the big-rock-tossed-in-a-pond category. Unfortunately, they were enough to set the DA on the warpath.

"It's the scary times we live in," people told me. I remembered my own childhood on a farm in Georgia, where I'd go to the local hardware store, buy dynamite, and use it to blow up stumps and rocks in our fields. I'd done that when I was Cubby's age, and no one had cared at all. Farm kids everywhere did the same back then. I did not fully understand how much things had changed—how fearful and jumpy people had become in the wake of 9/11.

And of course we didn't live on a farm anymore. My parents had moved from rural Georgia to western Massachusetts when I was a little boy. When I grew up, I stayed in the area and Cubby had spent his life in the suburbs around Amherst.

A different teenage boy might have hidden his newfound hobby, but Cubby was proud of what he achieved, and it never occurred to him that anyone would question his intent. You see, Cubby's brilliant, but he has Asperger's syndrome, a mild form of autism, which makes it hard for him to see how others might perceive his interests. I've got Asperger's too, so I know firsthand what it means. Everyone who knows my son would tell you how gentle he is, but because of the Asperger's, he's often oblivious to what's going on around him. Unfortunately, that obliviousness made him an easy target for a narrow-minded, publicity-seeking prosecutor. When she heard about his home chemistry lab and his experiments, she went after him with everything she had, quickly securing a grand jury indictment. My son could not believe anyone would prosecute him for his interest in chemistry. He had no idea what to do, or why he was under siege. You can imagine how I felt, with my only child being attacked by a public official who had never even spoken to either one of us.

Now we were in the superior courtroom of the Hampshire County Courthouse, in Northampton, Massachusetts. In Massachusetts, superior court is reserved for the biggest cases; everyone else is processed in district court or the magistrate's office. The year before, of the thousands of cases in our county's court system, only fifteen made it all the way to superior court trials, and most of those ended in conviction. The room was air-conditioned, but sweat beaded on my forehead as I pondered my son's odds. I rocked back and forth on the hard courtroom bench, thinking and worrying. All the witnesses had come and gone. Closing arguments were over, and the judge had finished reading the instructions to the jury. A few minutes before, I had watched them file slowly out of the room, to begin their deliberations. It was all up to the jury. They were eleven women and one man, strangers to one another and to me. What would they decide?

Ten feet in front of me, my son sat at the defense table between his lawyers. To his right, the prosecutor shuffled her papers and looked toward the empty jury box. The judge gazed down on all of us from her bench, and armed bailiffs guarded the flanks. My son looked so young and vulnerable among all those serious-looking adults. He wore a grown man's suit, but underneath he was still my little boy, skinny as a rail, with only a wisp of beard. My heart hurt for him.

Meanwhile, I had my own deliberations going on. I wanted to understand how my kid's science experiments had led to felony criminal charges. My son was still a teenager, with no history of breaking the law. He'd never even been in a fight. He wasn't in trouble in school. He wasn't any kind of renegade. Everyone who knew him was struck by two things: his kindness and his intelligence.

So why was he on trial? Had he really done something terrible, something I did not comprehend? Could it be that I was blind to the true nature of my only child? Was he in trouble because of the way I had raised him, as some commenters had suggested in the local newspaper's online forum? *Perhaps it all came down to being different,* I thought. *Now we might have to pay a high price for our nonconformity.* My Asperger's had made me feel like a social isolate, and I knew my son felt the same way. Both of us wanted to be a part of society; we just didn't always know quite how.

Sitting there in court, neither of us had any idea how the jurors felt or what they might do. Would they protect an eccentric but harmless member of the community or fall for the prosecutor's fear-mongering? As I waited anxiously for the verdict, I could not help but reflect on my choices as a dad and our tumultuous father-son journey of the past eighteen years.

FROM DROPOUT TO EXECUTIVE

The story began thirty years ago, before there was even the idea of a Cubby. I was twenty-some years old, a newly minted adult with a serious girlfriend. We were talking of marriage and possibly even a family.

I might have flunked out of high school a few years before, but I'd truly graduated from teenager to grown-up. Having made such a momentous change, I figured I should stop doing the kind of things kids did and start doing what adults did. I looked around for some sample adults, to get a sense of what came next.

I knew that having kids was something most grown-ups do. But when should we embark on that journey, and how? I was still new to dating and sex. To me, kids were a feared consequence, as in, *Uh-oh . . . do you think you might be pregnant?* Fatherhood, for young adults like me, was the unwanted result of the ultimate dating success. Luckily, I was not introduced to parenting via that pathway.

I followed the more traditional route, starting with dropping out of school. It began when my girlfriend, Mary Trompke, left me in tenth grade. "I don't ever want to speak to you again," she said one day, and I didn't even know why. At the same time, my home life

turned nasty. "You're never going to amount to anything," my father would shout at me in drunken rages. "You're going to end up
pumping gas or sweeping floors!" At the time, none of us knew that
I had Asperger's, so I had no way of understanding my difficulties
fitting in and doing well in school. I was inclined to believe what
the grown-ups said—that I was just lazy and no good. Depressed
and angry, I quit school and went out on my own. Luckily, I had
a marketable skill—electronics—and a plan for putting myself to
work. My teenage fascination with music and circuitry turned into
a budding career as local musicians began looking to me to repair
their broken instruments and amplifiers. To me, the choice was
clear: *I was a failure in school, but I had a future in music.* I decided to
go where I was wanted.

Of course, not everyone agreed with my decision to quit school,
and they didn't embrace my choice of career either. "Dropping out
isn't going to lead you anywhere, boy," my grandfather, Jack, told
me. His own father had been the first Robison to graduate from college, so school meant a lot to him. "Those musicians are all starving
freaks," my father added. "How can you expect to make a living
from them?"

I don't know what my mother thought. After a recent psychotic
break and a violent and endless divorce from my dad, she had her
own problems to deal with. Once I left home, she and my father
were so wrapped up in their own worlds, they hardly paid any attention to me at all. It cut both ways; after a rough and tumultuous
childhood, I didn't want much to do with either parent. It would be
some years before my feelings toward them changed.

So there I was, a sixteen-year-old dropout in need of a job and a
home. I jumped at the chance to become the newest crew member
of Fat, a local rock and blues band. For eighty bucks a week and a
room in the rambling farmhouse where they lived, I set up and took
down their equipment. I even drove the truck back and forth to the
clubs where we played. We worked five nights a week and spent

the other two days fixing anything that broke. In my spare time I continued to repair amplifiers and instruments for other musicians and I kept studying as much as I could.

Over the next few years, as my skills developed, the nature of my work changed. Instead of fixing old equipment, more and more of my time was spent making old designs better, and building new things I dreamed up from thin air. It felt good, creating things and seeing them work. I was on my own, on my way up, and feeling proud and defiant because my family's threats hadn't come true. *I'd show them!* The bands I worked for got bigger and bigger, as performances in barrooms morphed into concerts in stadiums. Even my father grudgingly conceded I'd done okay.

Over the next few years, two girlfriends came and went, and then I got back together with Mary. But I didn't call her that. I've always had a tendency to make up my own names for the people, pets, and things I especially like. Growing up, I called my little brother Varmint because he was such a pest, and when I got to feeling sick, I called University Health Services the Repair Center. I don't know why, but I've often had trouble with the names other people have chosen. My girlfriend's mother called her Mary Lee, just the way my own parents used my middle name, John Elder. I called her Little Bear because she was stocky and tenacious, at times even belligerent. I liked her a lot. She was my best friend.

We always had a lot in common, and what we shared often seemed pretty weird to other people. Trains had always been one of my great loves, and she walked the tracks with me, collecting stray insulators from abandoned telegraph poles. I'd climb twenty feet up the poles, unscrew the old insulators, and lower them carefully so she could stow them in her backpack. If I said, "Let's sneak into the passage under the university's student union and explore the steam tunnels," she would be right there with me. Instead of asking if I was crazy, she would say, "Do you think we'll need extra batteries for the flashlight?" No challenge was too strange.

We were both logical and sensible, though that wasn't always obvious by our actions. Both of us loved to read, especially science fiction. We never ran out of things to say to each other. Sometimes we talked about our families and life at home. We didn't do that too often, though, because growing up hadn't been much fun. Both of us had left home in a hurry, and we weren't moving back.

Seen from the perspective of middle age, it's obvious how messed up and crazy both our childhoods were. At the time, however, neither of us knew any other way of growing up. The best thing you could say was that our parents showed us what we didn't want in a family, and we took that lesson to heart, especially when it came to liquor. Our dads were both drinkers, the kind that seem real nice to their friends but are actually mean as hell to the kids. My only brother was eight years younger and lived in a commune with my mother's crazy shrink. Mary's brothers and sister were all older, and they'd gone as far from home as they could get. Big sister was in Florida, getting divorced. Brother Ted was in Oregon, contemplating law school. Paul had joined the navy and headed for the Philippines on a submarine. Danny had gone the farthest. I was shocked and saddened when he froze to death in the winter of 1976, camped out alone in the woods.

While I was establishing myself in the music business, Little Bear enrolled at the University of Massachusetts at Amherst. If she was going to stay in school, that seemed like the most practical choice. It was right in town, and she'd grown up prowling the campus, so she knew her way around. The school assigned her to a dorm, but after her first year she moved to an apartment about ten miles north, in Sunderland. There were two roommates in the apartment already—fellow science fiction aficionados. One was into insects, and the other was a jolly nearsighted gnome whose entire world revolved around comic book artwork, imaginary creatures, superheroes, and a sometime girlfriend.

The most charitable word I could use to describe the apartment structure itself would be *deteriorated*. An abandoned Volkswagen sat on four flat tires in the front yard. Inside, the halls were lined with rotten, peeling plasterboard, and the thin walls were insulated with vast stacks of paperback books. When I moved in after we got back together, the place went from crowded to untenable. The sink was already overflowing with dirty dishes, and the shelves in the bathroom sagged from the load. There was no room for my stuff, and when I used their towels and soaps, they complained. After a month, Little Bear and I rented a house of our own in South Hadley and worked harder to pay for it.

By that time I had parlayed my love of music and electronics into something pretty substantial. I'd left the local music scene for New York City and an engineering gig with Britannia Row Audio, the sound company Pink Floyd had formed a few years before. The Floyd owned a vast array of sound equipment, and when they weren't touring they rented it out to other touring bands. They had a big studio on 45th Road in Long Island City that was filled with gear they'd shipped from England. My job was to keep it all running and build whatever esoteric devices we could think up to keep our sound systems the best in the world. It was a heady job for a twenty-one-year-old geek, for sure. I'd drive there and work a few days, then bring home with me whatever I couldn't finish.

Little Bear was floundering at UMass, and she seized the chance to jump into electronics. We made a good team; I designed the circuits and she assembled them. In addition to being my girlfriend, she became a technician and a partner in the stuff we created.

Our first musical collaboration was for the Canadian supergroup April Wine. We spent a few weeks with them crisscrossing eastern Canada as we patched together a reliable sound system for their First Glance tour. That was followed by a whirlwind of shows back in America as we set up sound systems for the Kinks, Roxy Music, Phoebe Snow, Rick James, Dan Hill, Talking Heads, and Blondie. The next year I got hired by KISS, where we made Ace Frehley's signature fire-breathing, rocket-firing, and disco-lighted guitars. It was a good life, but unpredictable. We'd be busy and flush with cash one month, and idle and destitute two months later. It seemed like everyone in the music business lived hand to mouth, and I wanted more than that.

I thought I'd find it in a regular job, and I was incredibly lucky to find one for which I was truly the perfect candidate, at toy and game maker Milton Bradley, just half an hour's drive away in East Longmeadow, Massachusetts. My experience designing sound systems for musicians landed me a role creating special effects for their newest electronic games. I became a staff engineer, a pretend executive commuting from the suburbs. It looked like easy work: I had designed circuits on napkins when I worked for bands; Milton Bradley was offering a lab, reference books, and even state-of-the-art computers. All I had to do was look the part.

The superficial change from grungy rock and roller to corporate drone was virtually instantaneous. I trimmed my hair a full six inches, bought a new Oxxford suit, and reported for work at the required hour. But though my appearance was dramatically altered, I was exactly the same person I'd been before. So was Little Bear. A few months earlier, we'd been freaks in an overcrowded apartment in a college town. Now I was supposed to be a responsible executive, building a family in the suburbs of Springfield. It was only fifteen miles by road, but it was light-years away from anything I had known before. The transformation looked successful to me, but there must have been chinks in my armor. I knew that because the older redneck engineers called me a hippie freak.

A few years passed as we practiced looking like a nice, middle-class suburban couple. It worked. The rednecks stopped calling me names. I drifted away from music, and did my best to be the young executive my managers wanted me to be. Pretending made me miserable, but I had to do it—I wanted to be accepted by polite society. I wanted a job where I felt safe and secure. It was a means to an end:

I saw families all around me, and I knew I eventually wanted one of my own.

Little Bear found a job as a technician at a local electronics firm and pondered her own future. After a lot of thought and discussion she decided to become an anthropologist, specializing in colonial New England. The following fall she returned to college. She was determined that at least one of us was going to get a legitimate education. She had flunked out the first time, but the second time around she was earning top marks.

As we both got more settled, the notion of fatherhood appealed to me more and more. It seemed like the right thing to do sometime in the future. But the operative word remained *future*. I always wanted a kid, just not *then*. At twenty-one, my excuse was simple and socially acceptable: I wasn't married. That excuse evaporated when we tied the knot after three years of living together, at the age of twenty-five.

Even then, I still wasn't ready to rush into parenthood. I felt like I was just getting started at working life, and I didn't have any safety net. There was always the risk of getting laid off or even fired. After all, jobs in electronics were far from stable. My job at Milton Bradley had only lasted two and a half years. By the time we got married, I was with a company called Simplex Time Recorder in Gardner. The new job paid more but came with even more pressure to conform, and a three-hour round-trip commute. When I took the job, I thought I'd made a smart move, with a 50 percent increase in pay and a fancy new title. Once I got there, I realized I'd traded the laid-back atmosphere of a fast-growing toy company for a management grind in a stodgy old factory. I'd gone from an airy cubicle and lab in a brand-new building to a windowless work space filled with ancient furniture on the fourth floor of an old New England mill. As I trudged past security and climbed the stairs to my office, I could feel the rumble of machinery from the factory floors below.

It was a world totally alien to anything I had known. My grandfather Jack had the best advice for the situation. "Son," he said, "just keep your mouth shut, look serious, and watch close." Jack was glad I'd left the music world behind, but I wasn't so sure this corporate job was really a step up. In my new workplace, the factory boss was king, and music and sound effects were something to be discussed after hours, if at all.

There was no way I was ready for a kid during the first year I worked at Simplex. "We're the world leader in time clocks and fire alarms," my new boss said, beaming. I just winced. Compared to Milton Bradley, the Simplex factory felt like a blacksmith shop. For the first year, all my energy was directed toward fitting in and making a success of myself in The Big Corporation. The second year, I went into debt to purchase the trappings of executive life, so I still couldn't afford a kid. I did have a closetful of (to me) shockingly expensive suits, and after learning that the factory boss kept a baseball bat behind his desk, I'd gotten myself a more cultured head cracker: a spiffy walking stick with a heavy brass knob on top. But everyone around me had kids, and none of my possessions would play with me in the sandbox. Still, I held off. I don't remember what the third year's excuse was, but that fall I got laid off, and I surely could not consider having a kid while collecting $199 a week in unemployment and drowning in debt. Fine clothes weren't much help to me then either.

When I'd worked in music I'd had plenty of experience with feast and famine. I assumed I'd left that behind with my so-called executive job. Boy, was I wrong! All it took was someone a bit higher up the corporate food chain to nod his head, and I was on the street. *What am I going to do now?* I wondered. Whatever it was, I knew I had to act fast. Otherwise I'd go broke and lose everything.

Luckily, I had a backup skill: automobile repair. I'd actually supported myself for a short time by fixing cars, and I still tinkered with them even while working for the electronics firms. It was a fun weekend activity that made money too. Not only that, my efforts allowed me to drive neat old cars. My colleagues had always admired my vintage Mercedes, BMW, and Porsche chariots as they parked their practical but boring Camrys and Tauruses in the company parking lot. As I pondered my newly unemployed status my thoughts kept circling back to the thousand dollars I could make selling a ten-year-old Benz. That cash would double my unemployment income for five whole weeks. *What if I could do that regularly?*

Till then, I had been buying old, tired cars and fixing them up because I liked to tinker, but I decided to treat car sales as a job, not as a hobby. Looking at the car dealers around me, I concluded I should be buying newer and nicer merchandise. I sifted through the listings in the Boston *Auto Trader* and settled on a five-year-old Mercedes 300SD.

It was a big leap, buying a car like that. For one thing, it cost a lot more than any of the old beaters I'd purchased before. It was a full decade newer than my last Mercedes, top of the line and much more sophisticated.

To my surprise it was easier to get that car ready for sale than any of the old junks I'd been messing with before, and once I'd cleaned it up, it sold right away. I bought another as fast as I could, and another after that. My new business was off and running.

Just then, I found a new job. That was a big relief, but it meant I had to push my fledgling business into the background just as I was getting it moving. I was back on the treadmill, commuting three hours each day to a management job at Candela, a big laser manufacturer in suburban Boston. Once again, I was an electronics executive, or so my employers believed. This time, though, I had a backstop—an income stream of my own. The car business was turning into a profitable little sideline with the potential to be a whole lot more.

My thirtieth birthday came and went, another milestone. The older I got, the more I was torn by a combination of fear and anticipation. My focus was still on attaining financial security, but I knew the clock was ticking, and I didn't want to end up with a toddler at the age of fifty. And it seemed like all my coworkers had kids. Not only that, their children were five, six, even ten years old. I realized I had missed the boat in terms of timing. Everyone else must have faced the same threats and worries as me, but somehow they had found the time or courage, or perhaps the babies "just happened."

And then there was Little Bear. Throughout the ups and downs of married life, she expressed a steady and increasing desire to become a mother. So I felt pressure everywhere I turned, from within and without. The closer I got to taking the plunge, the more scared I became. *Would I get a good kid? Could I be a good dad? Could I afford to raise a child?*

I tried to break down the situation and evaluate it logically, as I am wont to do. When you look at kid acquisition from the outside, the hidden joys of parenthood may escape you. I strongly suspected there would be a good and fun side to raising a child, but I could not be sure. At the same time, there was no avoiding the stories my colleagues told of private school costs, uninsured doctor visits, and even more esoteric expenses like toddler yoga.

Then there was the risk of birth defects. I figured the odds were high that my kid would be all right, but what if he wasn't? What if he was born with brain damage, a bad heart, or three arms? One-in-a-thousand odds sound long and safe in a casino, where all you can lose is the cash in your pocket. In the kid lottery, a thousand-to-one long shot might condemn me to something I could not even conceive of, beyond the vague suspicion that life could become really hard for a very long time. I wondered whether that was a legitimate worry or an irrational one.

And of course there was the memory of my own bad childhood. No one could deny the reality and ugliness of that. No one who knew, at least, because I kept that shameful secret carefully hidden.

Could I be a good dad despite the example of my own father? I tried to break that down logically too, and when I did, it always came down to the influence of liquor. My dad drank, and when he got drunk, he turned mean. I didn't drink. Still, I could not be sure that I would not be mean too. Perhaps meanness was inherited. That's what my grandmother said.

"Them Robison boys all have a mean streak, they surely do," she'd say. I was never certain if that applied to me, or just the generations before. If it was true, it was scary.

All those fears kept me firmly committed to *later,* whenever Little Bear and I talked about having a baby. Yet we were getting older; I knew something had to happen soon, if it was going to happen at all. Sure enough, it did. In the summer of 1989, I resigned from my electronics job to focus on my fledgling automobile company. A few weeks later, Little Bear found out she was pregnant. She had gotten pregnant a few times before, but each time, the pregnancy ended just as soon as it began. That made me wonder if this one would last, but as the weeks passed, it became clear that it would.

Little Bear went to work preparing a nest. We decided the baby could live in the rear bedroom, which I'd been using for an office. We moved my desk and papers to the basement and she began decorating the room for our kid. The traditional white walls vanished, to be replaced with train wallpaper. Magazines and books on parenting appeared. I even read some of them.

I was both terrified and excited. The idea of being a dad sounded really fun. The notion of running my own business was pretty attractive too. At the same time, I wasn't sure I could do it all. I had to get my company moving, and fast. There would soon be a tyke to pay for.

AN INCIPIENT BEAR CUB

I'd always loved cars, and I was now testing the notion that I could turn that love into a living. A few weeks before, I'd been an engineering manager at a high-tech laser manufacturer. Now I was a one-man show. I was the buyer, the mechanic, and the salesman, traveling New England, buying high-end cars, fixing them up, and selling them to anyone I could. My former colleagues thought I was crazy, but I just couldn't handle the corporate life anymore.

If you'd asked me at the time, that's all I could have said by way of explanation. Today, I realize that my autism made the complex social dynamics of a corporate workplace nearly impossible to navigate. People were forever saying one thing and meaning another and expecting me to follow subtle social cues that I did not even know existed. I'd been a star engineer, but I was a failure as an executive, because I was blind to what I needed to see. In retrospect, starting my own small business was probably the smartest thing I could have done.

My new business needed a name, and I wanted something clever. The problem was, carmakers trademarked their brands, so I couldn't call myself John Robison, Mercedes Magician or John,

Lord of Land Rovers. When I looked at dealerships, which set the standard for respectability in the car business, I saw that many were named after their owners, like Bob Baker Motors. After careful consideration, I decided to do the same and my company became J E Robison Service. Armed with a brand of my own, I told everyone who would listen that my company was the best place in all of New England to buy or repair a used Mercedes, Jaguar, or Land Rover. I hadn't started with much, but I was determined to make the words true. After hearing me talk, my first clients may have been a little shocked to find me operating out of the garage behind our little South Hadley home.

There were some unexpected benefits from going out on my own. While I worked the corporate job, my asthma had become almost uncontrollable. It had gotten so bad that I was using up a one-month albuterol inhaler every seven days, and the drug was making me jumpy, shaky, and tense. My inhaler wasn't enough anymore—I'd made four or five trips to the emergency room over the past few years. The last time, I couldn't even walk, and Little Bear had to roll me in from the car with a wheelchair.

My doctor looked at me like a disobedient child and said, "You have chronic asthma. You have to stay on the regular medicine and take the steroids when you feel worse. It's not going away." He was wrong. When I removed the stress of a job I hated and stopped trying to be someone I wasn't, my asthma receded. The inhaler I had in my pocket that final day at work lasted a month, and the next one lasted three months. I was on the road to recovery. I knew I'd need the energy, because that kid was looking more real every day. Little Bear had expanded, and her doctor said the baby was coming along fine.

As she got bigger, I worked harder. I didn't know how much time a baby would take, and I didn't know how much money a baby would cost. Plenty of both, I thought. So I was buying as many cars as I could find and selling upward of twenty a month. Unfortunately, simply selling cars wasn't enough. I had to do it *profitably*. That was proving a lot harder than I had expected. Our bank account was dwindling despite my best efforts.

The problem was, the economy had taken a nosedive in the fall of 1989, just as I was going out on my own. Lots of businesses were hurting, but I hadn't really noticed the decline because I was new on the scene. With the economy in free fall, the changes became painfully obvious as cars I bought for ten grand sold a few months later for seven.

I was just about busted, and I hadn't even completed my first year in business. I was on the edge of panic. With the baby's arrival getting closer every day, I didn't know what to do. When I complained to Little Bear, she just told me what a hard time she was having with the pregnancy. Things had started smoothly enough, but the longer the pregnancy went on, the sicker she became. Finally, the doctors decided she had stomach ulcers. When I heard that, I got scared that she wasn't really pregnant at all! Maybe there was something else growing in there—cancer or worse. The stress I thought I'd left behind returned with a vengeance. Nothing was going right.

I think the thing that frightened me the most about Little Bear's illness was that it didn't end. *What did that mean?* Having read a lot of history, I knew moms could die having babies, and being sick surely increased the odds of death. Not only would I lose my mate, I would be left to care for a kid and a new business all by myself. There was no way I could do that. The mere thought was terrifying.

When I'd worked at Milton Bradley, one of the other engineers had developed a stomach ulcer. He learned he was sick when he threw up blood all over the bathroom at work and was rushed to the hospital. The guy almost died. I was terrified the same thing might happen to Little Bear and I wondered what that might portend for the baby.

I tried to tell myself everything would be okay, but she didn't get better. That meant I stayed anxious. Gradually, my fears evolved. Instead of worrying that she would die, I became afraid her sick, lethargic state would become her permanent way of being. That would be even worse, in a way. I was doing my best to be a good husband and a good pre-dad, but I didn't know what to do. I'd never been involved with a pregnancy or a new baby before and couldn't tell if her situation was exceptional. Nothing I read mentioned any association between pregnancy and ulcers, and the doctors were no help.

"Sometimes these things happen," they said, as if those words would reassure me. *Sometimes moms die in childbirth,* was all I could think in reply, so I just kept quiet. It was clear that they had no hard facts to share, just opinion and vague hope.

Some guys might have asked their friends, but I didn't have many friends, and I was too insecure to ask anyway. I wasn't comfortable talking to my parents, and my little brother was barely full grown and living in Chicago, which was no help at all. In the end, I kept my fears to myself. The more my wife complained, the more worried I got. Every new problem made me more afraid the healthy baby I was hoping for would never arrive. If she was "broken," as I thought of it, and the kid was growing inside her, I was afraid he would be broken too.

Little Bear saw the situation very differently. She was convinced that her pregnancy was the hardest one a mother had ever endured, but she found it bearable because she believed it would result in the world's most wonderful baby. She thought I was an ungrateful SOB for not believing and not being more considerate. Now I realize she just wanted me to be supportive and reassuring, but back then I was so terrified that there was nothing I could do for her.

That put me in a terrible fix. Little Bear wanted me to acknowledge her sickness, but the more I conceded she was having a difficult time, the more scared I got for her and the baby.

The most constructive thing I could do was work to ensure we had some financial security no matter what happened. Unfortunately, with every passing week, I was sliding closer to insolvency, borrowing from one credit card to pay another.

Then, just when I thought I was finished, salvation appeared in the most unlikely form. I sold a blue Mercedes convertible to an old fellow with a foreign accent. We got to talking, and he made me a proposition.

"This is a good business you have here. All you need is working capital. I can put up some money," he said, "and you can expand your car buying. We'll split what we make fifty-fifty. You do the work, and I'll provide the cash. What do you think?"

And if that wasn't enough, he had more to offer.

"I have an extra garage at my construction company in Springfield. You need room to expand. Why don't you move out of your backyard and set up in the city? That's where all the customers are." What he said was true. I knew I could only go so far working from home.

Feeling it might be too good to be true, but hopeful anyway, I moved my business to Springfield in the winter of 1989. The baby was due in April, so I had to work fast. I used the last of my money to buy a hydraulic lift so I could work under cars without lying on my back. I drove all over the area putting flyers on cars, advertising my new business. Anywhere I saw a Mercedes, BMW, or other high-end car, I left my little ad. After that, I crossed my fingers and prayed.

Meanwhile, I kept driving to the big dealerships near Boston, looking for cars I could buy. That was getting harder and harder to do. When I had started out, it seemed like easy money. I'd buy a car for ten thousand dollars and sell it a few days later for ten five. The profits weren't huge, but they were steady. If only that had lasted. When the economy tanked, every car in my inventory collapsed in value. I broke even on a few but lost thousands on most. Demand had dried up.

My new partner was expecting the bankroll he put into cars to grow. It didn't. It was shrinking at an alarming rate. Like a fellow with a gambling addiction, I doubled my bets by buying even more cars. I thought I'd bought them so cheap I couldn't lose, but I was wrong. My partner's money evaporated as quickly as my own. That's when he turned nasty. Actually, *nasty* is too nice a word. He became downright dangerous.

I mentioned my situation to someone at work, and he said, "Don't you know? Your new landlord's family is in the rackets. You don't want to mess with them." I asked what that meant and got a five-minute description of the Mafia in New England. They were not people to cross. I felt sick.

The money he had invested in cars was not really an investment at all. It was a loan, one I had to pay back even though it was all lost. I had no choice but to find a way out of the mess. It was simple, I told myself. I just had to make a lot of money and pay my partner back. And I had to do it with the added complication of baby preparation, and soon, baby management. That hadn't turned out too well so far, but tomorrow was a new day.

4

NAMES

While I was losing my shirt in the car business, Little Bear was working on the house. She had a million things to do to make room for a baby. There was a crib to acquire, furniture to set up, and diapers and blankets to stockpile. She did most of those things herself, but there was one important task we did together: thinking of a name for our soon-to-be baby.

We didn't know if we would have a boy or a girl, so we decided to be prepared with names for either. I was shocked and mildly amused to find that there was actually a thriving industry selling guides to baby naming. I did everything on my own, so the idea that we'd buy a baby name in a bookstore seemed vaguely ridiculous to me. Yet there the books sat, prominently displayed in the parenting section. I looked at a few of those published suggestions, but they weren't for me. I sensed that the best names were not in books at all.

For example, if we ended up with a girl, I favored naming her Thugwena, because I knew a girl named Thugwena would be tough and not hassled by bullies. Thugwena is a strong, forceful name. Germanic, even. Lillian or Anne had nothing on Thugwena. In fact, if they were to meet Thugwena in a dark alley one night far in the future, they would surely turn and run.

Little Bear didn't like that idea much at all. "That sounds like a truck driver's name," she said. I wondered what was wrong with truck drivers. She preferred a name from our family tree, like Mary, Alice, or Carolyn. I thought those choices were too common. But most of all, I thought we should have a boy, and to encourage that, I concentrated on male names. After all, I was a man, and I assumed my kid would be a little version of me. I never even considered that Little Bear might feel exactly the same way and expect a little girl. I decided to proceed with positive thinking and plan for the arrival of a son.

As everyone knows, the male version of Thugwena is Thugwald, but Little Bear rejected that fine manly name out of hand just as quickly. She also rejected Butch, Spike, Godfrey, and Bertrand. Fine country monikers like Zeke or Juke were unacceptable to her too. I wanted a strong, self-reliant sort of name, like Zeus or Thor, but she didn't like those either. It seemed like we couldn't agree on anything.

She even rejected my functional choices. He would outgrow Baby pretty fast, but Kid seemed perfectly suitable, and admirably descriptive, to me. She wouldn't even consider it. "What about Boy?" I suggested. "You can't name a kid Boy," she said without ever telling me why.

From my perspective, refined names like Ascot, Geoffrey, or Clive were nonstarters. Luckily, Little Bear didn't have any more enthusiasm for those names than me. We thought about John or Ed, our own fathers' names, but we both rejected them. Our rocky childhoods were a little too clear in memory for either of us to honor our fathers in that way. And neither of us liked Wyman, my maternal grandfather's name.

But there was one name we both liked: Jack, my dad's father's name. He had died a few years before and he'd meant a whole lot to me. He was always the one person who'd believed in me as a kid, and he'd taught me about many things, including fine clothes and cars. When I was learning to drive, my parents grudgingly let me drive their Chevy Vega. Jack let me drive his Cadillac. He taught me how to work a shotgun and how to operate farm machinery. While everyone else said I was a failure, he was proud of me and said I was special.

Little Bear knew all that, and she liked Jack too. We'd both been sad when he died. Finally, we had a name we could agree on. We would have a boy, and we would name him Jack. And that was what happened. But I could not leave well enough alone. Before the ink was even dry on the birth certificate, I had renamed our tyke.

I knew Kid was unacceptable, and Child was no good either because he would outgrow it in short order. Luckily, I had one name in reserve, and it proved perfect: Bear Cub. I called his mom Little Bear in recognition of her shape, disposition, and pugnacity. She was used to that. How could she object when I called her offspring Bear Cub? So that's what he became. The Bear Cub.

I took him everywhere and held him up in people's faces. "Look," I would exclaim. "Bear Cub!" They would generally nod and smile without any prompting, but if they didn't, I would repeat myself, louder, until they got the idea. By the time he was one year old, he was known far and wide—or at least in every good restaurant, bookstore, and auto parts wholesaler in western Massachusetts—as Bear Cub. Cubby for short.

But I'm getting ahead of myself. Before I could take him places and show him off, he had to be born, and that's what happened next. . . .

HATCHING TIME

Hatching time arrived just before midnight on April 11, 1990. When Little Bear told me it was time, I loaded her into our gray Jaguar sedan and headed for Cooley Dickinson Hospital, half an hour away in Northampton.

Some people would have doubted the reliability of an old British car at a time like that, but I was confident. How could I be otherwise? I had staked everything on my ability to rebuild and resell vintage British and German motorcars. If I couldn't trust my handiwork to deliver my own wife to the hospital, where would I be? Walking a newborn baby to the hospital and sending an ambulance to pick up his mom by the roadside, I guess. In any event, the car came through and my ability to deliver my own baby by the roadside was not tested. It was usually a thirty-minute drive, but I made it in twenty, traveling at a briskly illegal but not felonious rate of speed. It was the time of night when solid citizens are all in bed and the bars have not yet closed, filling the road with drunks, and the streets were virtually empty the whole way there.

I had called the hospital before leaving home, and two nurses were waiting at the emergency-room door when we arrived. "Let's get you into this chair and off to delivery," they said. They had the door open and Little Bear in a wheelchair before she could blink. Then they turned and rolled her out of sight, jogging fast. *They take this baby stuff seriously,* I thought. I stayed behind a few minutes to park the car properly and sign the admission and insurance papers.

Now that the financial future of the hospital had been secured, another nurse led me to the delivery room. It was past midnight by then. They made me wash up and put on a clean gown. I wondered what would happen. *Would there be lots of blood? Would the baby emerge with three arms or two heads?* Luckily, I did not have much time to ruminate and worry. Some baby deliveries drag on for hours, but this wasn't one of them.

Cubby was born less than twenty minutes later. Unlike me, he came out in the normal way, with no need for scalpels or pliers. When I was born the doctor had grabbed my head with forceps and squashed it hard as he pulled me out. According to my mother, I emerged looking like an early Conehead. Seeing my misshapen skull, she thought I must have brain damage. The doctor told her I'd be fine, but she always thought that was why I ended up kind of different. Nothing like that happened to Cubby. The doctor dangled him by the feet, and he made a little yell of protest. Everyone smiled except for Cubby, though he wasn't called Cubby yet. He just frowned and made squally noises.

One of the first things they did was put Cubby onto the scale. Six pounds, six-tenths of an ounce, or half the weight of Small Animal, our pet cat. I'd caught bigger bass when I was fourteen. He was a little bit shorter than my forearm, wet, and red. He was also bald, and roaring steadily. Everyone had smiled at the first howl, and his mom still looked happy, but after a few minutes of steady roar some of the hospital staff looked like they were starting to wonder where the off switch was located.

They swaddled our newborn son in a blanket and handed him to Little Bear, who admired him for a moment and then passed him to me. Between us, he settled down. I wasn't sure if the handoff was part of a ritual, but I thought not, because I knew Mom didn't have any more baby experience than me. Ritual or not, I wanted to be sure the baby I brought home was the same one I was holding that very moment in the delivery room.

The truth was, I had a fear of baby swapping. Like most people, I had read news stories of baby exchanges (usually, but not always, accidental) with some sense of amusement. But now that I faced the possibility of a personal swap experience I did not find it funny at all. Prior to hatching time, I had studied the layout and operation of the standard baby spaces in hospitals. Armed with that knowledge, I'd made a plan.

The first and most important step was to get a positive ID on him. A nurse had slipped a name bracelet around his arm, but I knew that could be pulled off and swapped as fast as she'd put it on. I wanted something more personal and I was ready. When the doctor handed me our new hatchling, I quickly but discreetly wiped off his foot and tagged him with a Sharpie permanent marker. He was now the only baby anywhere with a little black triangle on his foot: a delta, the Greek symbol that signifies uncertainty and change. Whatever else he did, he would certainly bring us that.

With his ID assured, I smiled and handed him to his mom. We were safe. Even if other people carried him away for testing or evaluation, we could be sure of getting the same baby back.

The doctors and nurses looked at me a bit funny, but I didn't care. I had not inspected the baby-holding facility at Cooley Dickinson Hospital before that night; for all I knew it was just a big open pen, like the Sunderland fish hatchery. There was no way you'd tell one fish from another without a slime-proof marker. I had looked at the other kids in the ward, and none of them were solidly tagged. Did baby swaps happen often? For all I knew, depraved nurses shuffled babies for entertainment. That was something I might do if I was a bored maternity nurse late at night. Once when I was a teenager, a group of us did that with cars, swapping identical-looking red Toyotas and watching the confusion as their owners tried to figure out how their cars had mutated overnight. (We took advantage of the fact that the key to Doug's dad's Toyota fit a number of other vehicles.)

I have never trusted authority. To me, the idea the hospital would keep track of him was just ridiculous.

I was surprised to discover that few people shared my point of view. Some of them actually questioned my actions. "You wrote on your baby?" Their tone of voice suggested they could not believe I would mark my kid, but why not? At work I marked my tools to keep them from getting stolen. All I could figure was, those people had never looked at a sea of babies basking under baby warmers and tried to pick out the one that was theirs. Also, the nurses had given Little Bear some awfully powerful painkillers, and if Cubby was taken away and mixed in with other newborns, I doubted that she could recognize him either. The fact is, identifying a baby can be a lot more difficult than identifying someone older. I knew that intuitively. Babies don't have many distinguishing marks; they are too young for scars and tattoos. Furthermore, they change fast. You can look at two newborns, one bald and the other speckled, and their hair might grow in to look exactly the same a week later. Given all that, marking a brand-new kid seemed like a no-brainer.

It is possible that I have a particular difficulty in recognizing people I have just met. Neurologist Oliver Sacks has that problem; he's written about it in *The Mind's Eye* and other books. My poor recognition capacity might have made me unusually fearful about identifying my own kid. Then again, maybe I am just wiser and more cautious than most. After all, the onus of baby recognition was entirely on me. There was no way the baby would know me from Adam, and even if he did, he couldn't say so.

As it turned out, the markings were not really needed, because no one tried to take Cubby away from us. Mom held him tight as they rolled her to a room where they could rest. After that, she retained possession of him until they were both released the following day. I had him in my sight all the way home, and within a week, when my mark wore off, I had gotten sufficiently familiar with him that I felt confident that I could recognize him anywhere. Thanks to my Sharpie, I have no regrets, and a strong sense of confidence in Cubby's origins.

6

A PROUD, SCARED DAD

After our baby was born, I followed Little Bear to her room and sat with them as long as I could. Finally I had to go to sleep. I wished there was a place I could lie down too, but there wasn't. I headed home to bed, excited and scared at the same time. I was thrilled at the thought of a new baby, but worried about my ability to be a good dad and the possibility that Cubby might be damaged or nonfunctional, or even that he wouldn't survive.

My brother and my parents told me my fears were ridiculous and that Cubby would be just fine. I heard their words, but I was convinced they were just saying them to make me feel better. They were not in the room, looking at Cubby. Even if they had been, they had no knowledge of medicine or statistics, the two things that might have offered solid comfort to a logical guy like me.

I knew the odds of an ordinary, viable infant were in my favor, but I couldn't help being worried. Psychologists call that thought pattern catastrophizing: imagining disaster at every turn of events. Today I know that's an Aspergian trait. However, I didn't know about Asperger's back then; I just knew my new baby was one more thing to be worried about.

A few of my male friends offered advice based on their own experience as parents. "We all worry we won't be good dads. All we can do is do our best." That was a practical acknowledgment that I could accept.

The broken-baby fears were less easily allayed. My newborn baby didn't talk, and I had no test data. In the electronics world, we called that flying blind, and sometimes our creations blew up when we did it. Yet I saw no alternative. One encouraging sign was visible in his mom: Her ulcers went away once he was born. As she got healthier, I felt better about Cubby's chances.

Other people acted horrified when I expressed doubt that Cubby would remain alive and functional. Why? When someone goes to the hospital with a heart attack people wonder exactly the same thing, and they say the odds improve with every day of survival. I figured the same was true for a baby. Being born was surely as big a deal as having a heart attack, so every day a baby lived meant the odds for long-term survival increased. *What was horrible about that?* Other people's attitudes seemed strange to me.

Then there was my basic insecurity—my inability to believe that he was really with us to stay. To combat those feelings, I began telling people about my new baby boy right away. For some reason, the act of describing Cubby to others made him seem less ethereal and more real to me.

Little Bear carried him around with her much of the time when he was new. He slept on top of her or next to her on the bed. Sometimes I would place him on the bed next to me and we'd both fall asleep. I was always afraid I'd roll over and suffocate him, but that never happened. Still, we knew he needed a place of his own. We didn't have much money, so we lined a nice yellow laundry hamper with a soft blanket and he was in hog heaven.

One of the problems with babies is that they howl, at high volume and at inopportune times. If some of the accounts I've read are to be believed, an energetic baby can make sleep for the parents just about impossible. Cubby wasn't all that bad, but he sure had his moments. Most of the time, Little Bear would soothe him with nursing or rocking. When her techniques failed to work, I resorted to my own secret baby-management measures.

First I picked him up, bounced him a bit, and trotted him around the house. That often worked, but his mom always watched me and said, "Be careful with him. His little brain is fragile." He didn't seem all that fragile to me, but I was cautious anyway. He still had a soft spot on his head, and there was no telling how mushy the brains inside might be.

I wondered about things like that a lot. I didn't want to make any mistakes with this dadhood thing. I knew some new dads had prior experience raising gerbils, hamsters, or snakes, and others had read lots of books or gone to classes. I hadn't been able to do much at all, and now that he was here, I had to work twelve hours a day to keep my new business alive to support him. I tried remembering what my little brother had been like, but that was many years ago and it didn't do much good now. So I just did the best I could.

Cubby would cling to me pretty well if I gave him a chance, but the rest of him was floppy. His head was the floppiest part of all. It seemed pretty big relative to the rest of him, and he usually had trouble holding it steady. When we rode in the car, it would bob around like those springy toys they sell, as we went over bumps or around corners. I could never tell if he was too little to hold himself steady or if he just let it roll because he liked the motion. I was that way myself at times. Bobbing and rocking has always been a comfort, and people used to say I looked like a bobblehead. Maybe he was the same.

I suggested that to Little Bear, but she dismissed it out of hand. "He hasn't developed the muscles in his neck," she said. I wondered where she got that particular idea, since she didn't have any more parenting experience than me. I realized she must have been reading baby how-to manuals while I was away at work.

When bouncing Cubby around the house failed to settle him down, we moved to plan B: We went for a ride. That always worked. Cubby went right to sleep in the car. That made him a good traveler most of the time, and it inspired me to take him places. Wherever we went, he found new things to look at and interesting objects to stuff in his mouth.

The older he got, the farther we ranged. It was good for Cubby to see the world, I reasoned. He was going to have to learn his way around one day, and I figured he might as well start now. I told him the names of streets and described the interesting places we passed. Even though he didn't answer, I knew he was paying attention. He sat there in his car seat, chewing placidly and watching the world go by.

I knew how important reading was, so I started showing Cubby words as soon as he was able to sit up in the seat. The words we saw were on billboards, on vehicles, and in the windows of gas stations. Anytime I saw a glowing sign with simple language I read it to my son. "Trucks," I would say, as I pointed to the sign leading to the truck parking area at the local diner. In that way, he learned the language of commercialism. When he learned to talk, he began with what he heard in ads and what I read him from signs—words like *Bud, diesel, bathroom,* and *food.* I didn't smoke or drink, and neither did he, but we knew all the language thanks to roadside America.

All babies love to chew, and he was no exception. He had pacifiers and traditional baby rings, but he wasn't a picky chewer. He'd stick anything in his mouth at least once. If I let my fingers stray close he would even gnaw on me. When that happened, I would yell, and he snorted with delight. Obviously, he knew what he was doing.

"No bite!" I would tell him. Often as not, he would bite me again.

He would even attempt to eat metal if given the chance. He would also try and feed me the drool-covered objects of his attention, something I found particularly revolting even though he was just being companionable.

I had loved the taste of wooden Tinker Toys when I was a kid. Wood is nice and chewy, with a definite flavor. Beavers love it. Cubby loved wood too. He found his in the form of Brio wooden trains and wooden track sections. They were perfect for a toddler—tasty enough to provide hours of enjoyment, yet tough enough to remain basically unmarked by his emerging baby teeth.

He grew pretty fast and learned new tricks every day. I watched him follow objects with his eyes and make noises and expressions in response to what he saw or heard. He smiled at his mom and me, and reached out his little paws to be picked up. It was remarkable how quickly he learned to manipulate us to do his bidding without saying a single word. He did that better than any cat or dog.

We set about feeding him, changing diapers, and watching him grow. We both took to the task with gusto and enthusiasm. More so his mom than me, when it came to diapers. As I saw it, my job was to entertain him, make him think, and help him understand the world. I began pondering ways to do that.

THE KING OF EVERYTHING

Excited as we were with our newborn baby, we could not help but see that Cubby had some challenges. We noticed the first one before he was even old enough to walk. It started with a triumph—the realization that he was doing something I could seldom do when I was young.

Cubby mirrored our expressions.

If I smiled at him, he would smile back. It was automatic. When I came in the door, we smiled at each other every time. I don't know that I've ever felt a connection like that with anyone else in my life.

Some people might have taken that for granted. Not me. I remembered my early days very clearly, when my parents and their friends picked me up and made faces at me. Now I know the adults were expecting me to smile back when they made those big smiley faces, but at the time I was just scared and confused. I had no idea what was happening; for all I knew, those big toothy mouths meant that I was about to be eaten. When I didn't respond as expected, they turned away as if I had something wrong with me. Even now I remember the sting of that rejection.

The inability to automatically mirror other people's expressions is very common in people with autism, and I'm still that way to some extent today. My mother certainly remembers my lack of response to her smiles. When I was older, she said my serious demeanor made her worry that I didn't like her. I liked her fine, but I don't think I ever smiled about it.

My maternal grandmother had the hardest time with my lack of response. She would pick me up and make faces at me while holding me at arm's length. After a moment, when I didn't do what she wanted, she plopped me on the floor. "You're just a mean little boy," she would tell me, waddling off down the hall. Luckily for me, my other grandmother liked me better.

Cubby was totally different. He smiled all the time. I can see the difference instantly when I compare pictures of us. Old photos of me show a stern, serious tyke. Images of Cubby show a happy, grinning toddler. Smiles were one way Cubby had me beat, and it delighted me to see that.

But although Cubby mirrored smiles right away, he was not so quick to imitate behavior. Little Bear found that out when she tried to play patty-cake with him. I never did stuff like that, because I thought it was foolish, but Little Bear was very enamored of such inane baby entertainments. She'd spend hours on the floor with Cubby, touching her palms to his while reciting the patty-cake rhyme. The idea, of course, was for him to follow her lead. He never did. He just sat there on the floor, giggled, and let his mom touch her paws to his and sing to him. The idea that he was supposed to do the same thing just didn't seem to sink in.

The problem was not lack of interest; she could see how much he liked having her arrange his little forelegs for the game. He grinned and babbled with delight whenever she did patty-cake. He just didn't do it himself. It was as if he enjoyed watching rather than participating.

I wondered if he was like me in that regard. When I was little, I watched the other kids play and never joined in. There were all sorts of reasons: I didn't know how, or I wasn't invited, or I tried and failed. Whatever the explanation, I spent my toddlerhood alone, watching the other kids play from the sidelines. Now I worried that Cubby might be headed in the same direction.

He wasn't sad or troubled. We could see him smiling and bouncing. He just didn't take an active role and play along. What did that mean? We didn't have any other babies to compare him to. My own social skills were not very good, and it simply did not occur to me to look outside my own family for answers. I pondered the situation without reaching any definite conclusion. So did his mom.

"Maybe he needs glasses, like us," said Little Bear. She thought he might be nearsighted because we were, and when things passed before him he didn't respond. I didn't agree, because there were times he'd see something go by and grab it right away, and I knew vision troubles didn't come and go.

My secret fear was that his behavior meant that his brain did not have enough computing power. Maybe he was seeing fine but not figuring out what he should do next. Could a game like that exceed a baby's cognitive powers? Was a baby smarter than a puppy? Dogs didn't play patty-cake, not even smart poodles. I considered ways to evaluate his intelligence, but in the end I made no progress because I knew of no standards for baby brainpower.

I thought back to my own childhood and how important being smart was to me. When I recalled the things people said about me, most were negative. I didn't do this and I didn't do that. Because of my Asperger's, my social skills were almost nonexistent. When you can't read the unspoken messages in other people's faces and bodies, how can you know how to respond? We know a lot more about autism today, but back then grown-ups just assumed I was poorly behaved. The one complimentary thing they said was, "You're a really smart little boy." The idea that Cubby might not share my best and most important attribute was very scary.

What is smart in a baby? I continued to wonder. *How do you recognize it?* I watched him play with the toys we gave him. When left to his own devices, he was very inquisitive. He figured out how to stack rings from large to small and small to large. He knew how to make cubes, lines, and even buildings from his blocks, and he knew all the different colors. We gave him wooden puzzles with pieces that had to be placed into a tray in a certain way to make a pattern. He figured them out all by himself. If I tried to do them with him, he often took the toys away from me so he could do them on his own.

Cubby was a very opinionated tyke. When I got down on the floor and played with him, it quickly became clear that he had definite ideas about how his blocks and rings should be arranged and which pieces went where. He was too young to voice those opinions in words, but if I deviated from his play plan, he would make his displeasure known by howling loudly. In fact, he had no trouble expressing his wishes even before he could talk. I couldn't always tell exactly what he wanted, because he didn't utter words that made sense. However, there was no mistaking when my response made him happy or annoyed; words were not needed to send those signals. He did that with great emphasis and at high volume.

All those things told me his brain was working somewhat normally, though he wasn't much of a team player. I wasn't a team player either as a kid, so I didn't make too much of that.

He kept getting bigger and figuring out more puzzles, but he never mastered patty-cake. Actually, *mastered* is the wrong word. He never even tried. That particular game just passed him by. Even after months of practice, he just sat still, watched his mom's hands, and smiled. I found his behavior perplexing, and so did his mom.

As he got older, Cubby became steadily more aware. He looked at mobiles we hung over his head, and he picked up and played with anything in his reach. Soon he learned to crawl, and overnight he was on his way, grabbing anything he could see and sticking his fingers anywhere they would fit and some places they wouldn't.

He shrieked like he was being eaten alive when he became stuck, but when he got in the groove, he just played and played. I brought him into the garage with me, and he'd stay busy for hours, chewing the car parts I'd left on the floor. His mom would find him out there and bring him back inside, hoping to keep him clean. Whenever I got an interesting car in for service, I'd bring him out and set him behind the wheel. If there was a camera handy, I might even take his picture. By the time his birthday rolled around, he had driven a Gull Wing Mercedes, a Ferrari Testarossa, an Aston Martin DB5, and more Porsches than we could count. His favorite—or so I told him—was a Shelby Cobra with an electric blue finish and an engine that rumbled like a WWII fighter plane. He'd grip their steering wheels with his little paws and stare at the gauges as I wondered what he was thinking.

The most peculiar thing was Cubby's lack of interest in others of his kind. When we put him in a playpen with other babies, he mostly just ignored them. I would have thought a real live kid would be more interesting than a Playskool ring puzzle, but Cubby didn't agree. He paid no attention to the child as he dominated the puzzle.

Today I realize that behavior is another marker of autism. When we are small, our limited ability to sense the inner feelings or even just the proximity of other people causes us to ignore them, even though we want very much to have friends. How I wish I'd known that when my son was growing up! My own version of autism—Asperger's syndrome—entered the diagnostic lexicon in 1994, when Cubby was four years old, and it took some time for that knowledge to percolate down to me. His diagnosis was still far in the future.

In the meantime, like all hopeful parents, we glossed over his struggles and told ourselves he was better than us. He seemed happy and healthy, so we encouraged him when we could and hoped for the best.

I never did figure out how to ascertain intelligence in infants, but the bigger he got, the less I worried. Instead, I thought about the bigger questions, like whether he would join me at work someday and what he might become when he was full grown. One day we were playing in the backyard and I announced, "I am the King of Bees and Rodents!" Cubby just laughed. Later, when he could talk, he remembered that and said, "I will be King of Everything. Even you!" He laughed even louder at that. I snorted, but I liked the size of his ambition.

TWO-WHEEL DRIVE

For the first few months we managed parenthood by ourselves. Little Bear took care of Cubby while I was working, and she tended him at night. In between those times, I brought him interesting places and showed him things to occupy his mind. His mom would say she did all the work and I had all the fun, but I don't think it was that black and white. I certainly gave Cubby many unique and stimulating experiences. In fact, like most dads, I believe I taught him every useful thing he knows.

When Cubby was five months old, Little Bear returned to school. She had gotten her bachelor's before Cubby was born, but that wasn't enough to get her a teaching job, so she had applied to and gotten accepted into grad school in anthropology at the University of Massachusetts. She'd started the program before getting pregnant and figured Cubby could just tag along for the rest of it. This ought to tell you how little experience either of us had with babies.

At first she brought Cubby with her to class, but he made noises, acted in a loud and unruly manner, aggravated the teachers, and distracted the students. When he started hollering he could disrupt a hundred people, maybe more. The commotion he created at college was way out of proportion to his size. The only thing Little Bear could do was take him outside and hope he calmed down. Bouncing and jollying usually worked, but it always took a while and made attending school essentially unworkable. Seeing what happened when she took an infant to college helped me understand why colleges don't recruit kids until they are teenagers. By then they are somewhat more manageable.

Things went a little better when Mom went into the lab or the field. Cubby accompanied her and picked up many arcane skills of the anthropologist's trade, even before he could read and write. He could assemble a dog skeleton from a dusty box of bones, and he knew all about early American glassware from excavating Colonial outhouses and trash pits in historic Deerfield. He had no idea where we lived, but he could describe all the buildings and roads on a map of Deerfield, where his mom was working on her master's thesis.

On days when Little Bear couldn't take Cubby with her, I tried bringing him to work with me. That didn't work out very well, because I couldn't watch him and he couldn't stay still. An inquisitive baby was an amusing or annoying distraction at school, but there was nothing there to hurt him. The situation was very different in a dirty auto-repair shop. We knew grease was unhealthy to eat, and we were really trying to keep him clean. On the days I had Cubby I could not do any useful work because I was forever washing my hands and tending him. Cubby, on the other hand, reveled in filth. He grabbed every opportunity to escape his hamper and crawl across a greasy floor just to put both paws into a big tub of diesel fuel. He would have eaten old car parts, too, if I hadn't caught him. There's something irresistible about a nice, chewy fan belt.

I was also concerned that Cubby would get squashed if he got loose in the yard. My neighbor owned several front-end loaders, and he drove the giant machines back and forth past my doors several times a day. It's hard to see close up when you're driving a loader, and I didn't want my new baby getting squashed.

Then there was my fellow tenant, Pete the Paver. I took an immediate liking to Pete. Some days, he'd come back from work with hot pavement left in his trucks, and he'd dump it steaming on the driveway by my shop and roll it onto the ground. The trouble was, if Cubby got in front of Pete's steamroller, he'd be flattened like Wile E. Coyote.

That made me look out for him real close.

Before long, the need for a kid-management plan was painfully apparent. We knew there were commercial storage options, but they were costly and their quality was uncertain. We did not want to leave him with a smiling nanny only to discover that we had entrusted our kid to some fiend who chained him to a pipe in the basement and passed the day with her boyfriend upstairs. You never know with some of those places. They seem safe, until you see them on the evening news. Our thoughts returned to my mother, who liked Cubby a lot. We knew we could trust her, she was home, and she always wanted Cubby around. She had not been the best mom when I was little, but she'd mellowed with age and doted on her new grandchild.

Also, my mother really liked Little Bear. I think she saw her as the daughter she had never had. So they made a deal. Little Bear would bring Cubby, his diapers, and his other paraphernalia over to my mother's house in the morning. Then she'd go to school and return to pick him up in the afternoon.

My mother was in that first year of recovery from her stroke, and Cubby's need for constant attention turned out to be good for her. He kept her awake and active as she chased him through the house in her wheelchair. The two of them even learned to walk together. My mother had to figure out how to get up and use a cane, and Cubby had to learn to get onto his hind legs and walk. Both of them were determined to succeed.

I can't remember when my mother started walking again, but I can say with certainty that Cubby walked on his first birthday. It was a Friday, and his grandmother had come to our house in South Hadley. I was at work.

He had been self-propelled for a while, but only in four-wheel drive. We had talked about using two-wheel drive, hind legs only, but Cubby had been resistant. I say we talked about it, but I really don't know how he perceived those exchanges. We expressed our thoughts and wishes to him, but he was too little to answer in a comprehensible fashion. Still, I knew he was thinking about walking, because I'd see him pull himself up on the legs of the kitchen table, stand erect, and gaze thoughtfully across the vast ten-foot gulf of living room carpet. At the other side, the sofa offered a soft landing, but the distance was daunting. Christopher Columbus probably felt much the same, gazing across the Atlantic Ocean in 1492. Everything looks huge when you're two feet tall.

His birthday was the day he finally found the courage to cross the mounds and ridges of carpet and reach the safety of the couch on his hind legs only. He was standing, holding on to the table leg, when my mother held out her arms and called him from the sofa. He let go, took a step, and went. He made it all the way at a run, crashing into his grandmother with a grin and some babble. His mom and GrandMargaret—as he learned to call her—were amazed and thrilled and called me right away.

I hoped he'd repeat the feat when I got home. I even picked him up and set him on his hind legs to activate walk mode, but he just sat back down. He refused to walk again. He must have been shocked and terrified by his success.

The experience had given him a lot to think about. Four-wheel drive was, after all, the only means of locomotion he'd ever known. Could he leave it behind? The benefits of navigating on one's hind legs were obvious to me. Greater speed, elevated vantage point, and the ability to use one's forelegs for other purposes, like pushing.

Two weeks passed as he crawled and pondered. Every day I'd pick him up and set him on his feet, hoping he'd take the cue. He didn't. When I was at work, Little Bear would do the same.

Then, one afternoon, Cubby made a decision. He started walking, then running, and he never looked back. Unless I chased him.

TELL ME WHAT YOU WANT

One of my greatest challenges as a new dad was determining what my kid wanted or needed. Even though I got better at empathy following Cubby's arrival, it remained hard for me to figure him out much of the time. He seemed to get distressed and yell for no reason, but I knew there must be one—I just couldn't discern it. *Things will get better once he learns to talk.* I reassured myself with that platitude, but it did not really come to pass. The biggest problem was Cubby himself: Even after he could talk, he could not be counted on to reliably articulate his needs. People had always said I should take responsibility for my actions, and I assumed the same was true for him. That assumption turned out to be wrong.

I did my best to anticipate his needs, but I didn't get a whole lot better at it. "I'm not a mind reader," guys sometimes say to the women in their lives. "It's up to you to tell me what you want." While I could say that to a grown-up, I was somehow expected to figure out a kid, even though he was more inscrutable than most adults.

Some gestures were unmistakable. A single arm outstretched and accompanied by yelling meant, *Give that toy back to me!* Both arms outstretched meant, *Pick me up!* Arms outstretched while rocking side to side meant, *Toss me in the air and catch me!* At least, that's how I interpreted it. His mom understood that expression to mean, *Pick me up and rock me.* Clearly there were multiple possible translations for many of Cubby's signals, something that was an occasional source of disagreement between his mom and me. She was seldom willing to concede the priority or the correctness of my interpretations, always believing "mother knows best."

Then there were subtler signals, like the ones for *change my diaper* or *I need a nap.* Those remained totally invisible to me.

It was an aggravating problem, one that gave me trouble every time I took Cubby on an adventure. If I took him on a day-long expedition, he would start out nice, but halfway through the day, he would melt down and have a tantrum. If we were lucky, he would howl a few minutes, get distracted, and become jolly again. But all too often, he would drop to the floor and lie flat on his back, spinning around and around while shrieking at the top of his lungs. That was bad, because the longer he howled, the harder it was to reset him to his usual jolly state. At times, he sank so far into tantrum that he yelled himself unconscious. His meltdowns were terrible to experience.

Most of the time, I couldn't stop him. Petting or comforting him did nothing except get me smacked with little fists. So I tried the opposite approach: yelling, stunning him with sound, or flashing my Maglite at him as he hollered. At best, those distractions did nothing. At worst, they recharged his howl mechanism. Usually I'd carry him outside and let him yell himself to exhaustion away from public view. That was about all I could do.

I figured he was just falling apart for reasons unknown, but I was wrong.

"All he needs is food," Little Bear and other mothers were quick to suggest. They said it as though it was head-smackingly obvious, but it had never even occurred to me. I could go all day without eating, provided I was distracted by something exciting; the idea that a toddler needed more frequent refueling had never entered my mind. I assumed the excitement of a train or bulldozer ride would be all either of us needed, but I was wrong.

And indeed they were right. Stuffing food into his mouth was one of the few things that would actually interrupt a tantrum, to my great wonder and surprise. When it worked, the meltdown just stopped, and he returned to his original bouncing, happy self in short order. It was almost magical, the way his disposition changed with the ingestion of a little food. I marveled at how others could see that he was hungry, while that simple thing remained totally invisible to me.

Where was the Feed Me sign? I could never find it.

Even after I knew failure to feed could trigger a meltdown, I consistently missed the connection. I tried to analyze the problem logically, beginning with my own behavior when hungry. I opened the refrigerator or nosed around the cabinets. My actions were directly and obviously related to the acquisition and ingestion of food. Cubby didn't do that. When he got hungry, he would explode at the suggestion that we should go check out a steam engine exhibit, or howl at the notion of visiting the aquarium. How could I possibly connect those tantrums to a need for food? Any logical person would see Cubby's behavior and conclude he did not want to do what I just suggested. Hearing that he did not want to do something, I said, "Okay. If you don't want to go to the aquarium, what do you want to do?" Many times, that simply elicited more howling and complaining. When I could not get a coherent answer from him, I was stuck. I was trying to solve a perceived activity problem, while totally failing to see the underlying need for feeding.

The way some women can see a child going berserk and simply say, "He's famished, let's get him something to eat!" remains a complete mystery to me. It's as if they see blue and I see red, and each of us believes the evidence of our own eyes. The most frustrating thing was that moms who were not even close relations could see what he needed and I could not. It was humiliating. Sometimes they would look at me accusingly, as if I should have known or as though I was being a neglectful dad.

Why couldn't Cubby tell me what he needed? Why did it fall upon me to remember? I finally realized that he did not know himself. He was too young to know how lack of food affected his mood. At the time, that realization was a shock to me. A few years later, when I learned about Asperger's, my inability to recognize signals like *feed me* made a little more sense. There are many times Asperger's gives me an advantage, but this was most assuredly not one of them.

The fact is, I couldn't see the signals. And I still can't. All I can do is observe what others do, make a behavioral rule, and do my best to remember and follow it. For example, I could make a rule that we would set off on adventures with a timer set for two hours. When it went off, I fed him. Whether he said he wanted food or not, he needed it.

I used that same logic to stay on top of his other needs, too. Instead of waiting for a stench or a yell, I learned to check his diaper before we set out on a journey, and at regular intervals during the trip. Like most dads, I wished there was a way to make him poop on demand, so I could get him changed by Mom before departing, but I never figured that one out. Even without that, though, my system of logic, timing, and inspection proved invaluable in keeping Cubby happy and quiet.

Food, drink, clean diapers, and naps were the keys to Cubby's good mood throughout his infancy. Important as those things were, though, he never learned to ask for them by name. Other children are probably the same, and the strategies I developed will quite likely work with them too. I'll put that notion to the test at some future date, when Cubby produces grandchildren.

Dads like me could learn a lot from successful veterinarians, who learn to read discomfort in animals. Unfortunately, I did not know any vets with whom I could apprentice, and now it doesn't matter because Cubby is finally old enough to speak for himself. However, advancing age, awareness, and verbal skill came with their own problems, as Cubby began articulating his critical need for every toy, candy, and kid treat that passed before his eyes on morning television. I began to suspect what one grizzled old mom had told me was true: "They're cutest when they're tiny."

10

THE AERIAL CHILD

Now that Cubby had surmounted the challenges of walking and running, he figured it was time to learn to fly. I had been an avid aeronaut myself, until a bad crash cured me of the habit at age five. Cubby didn't have a jet pack or wings, but he did have me, and he was quick to seize the opportunity. He even had words for it. "Baby toss," he'd say, raising both stubby paws as high as he could. That was a signal I could easily interpret!

I had never tossed him as a baby, because I took Little Bear's warning about his fragile baby brain seriously. But now that he was a toddler, all bets were off, and I experimented with various tossing techniques, including the rocket launch, the sandbag toss, and the inverted rocket. His favorite was the sandbag toss, where he lay on his back in my arms, and I tossed him up and caught him in the same pose.

I had tossed our cat—Small Animal—in much the same way before Cubby was born. The cat liked to wrestle and play, and thought tossing was fun sometimes, but he bit me on other occasions. Cubby always loved flying. He never bit when tossed.

Rocket toss was where I lifted him under the armpits and

launched him straight upward. He liked that too, but not as much. I worried about it myself, because I always imagined shooting him up into the ceiling and having his head bang right through the Sheetrock. Being male, I probably overestimated my tossing strength.

He would laugh maniacally every time I caught him and zoomed him into the air again. It never occurred to him that I might miss, leaving him to go splat on the floor. I guess kids are trusting about that until the day you drop them. He would go up and down, squealing with delight, until my arms wore out.

"Come on, Dad. Toss me again!" Even with my muscles built up from months of practice, the sandbag toss remained very tiring. I couldn't pause, even for a second. Cubby insisted on constant motion. The moment he hit my arms on the way down, he giggled and yelled, "Again!" and I had to shoot him back up into the air instantly, lest he howl with dissatisfaction. I was beginning to understand why people said parenting was exhausting.

Baby Toss became a regular activity for Cubby and me. We did it until he got too big to toss and catch reliably. "You can do it," Cubby would say, but I wasn't so sure. That was when we discovered the carousel game, where I took both his little hands in mine and whirled him around and around, lifting his feet off the ground.

He loved it, but Little Bear wasn't so enthusiastic. "Don't spin him too fast," she would say. "You'll pull his little arms right out of the sockets." Hearing that, I had visions of myself, holding two arm stumps while my kid sat on the ground howling and wondering where his arms had gone. I don't know why moms are so cautious. She wasn't that way before he was born. Something must have changed with the arrival of the kid.

I've seen some pretty rough play in parks in my day, and I'd survived without any damage. When I was Cubby's age, my Uncle Bob swung me so fast I flew right across the yard to land in a pile of leaves and straw. I never saw anyone's arms come off, back then or since. Of course, it's possible that those earlier armless kids were too ashamed to be seen in public. I always heard there were strange children living in the Prodigialis family's basement down the street when I was a kid.

When Cubby got a little bigger, he became too big to toss and too heavy to swing. Some dads would have given up at that point. Not me! That's when we made the move to machinery. Our local playground had a parent-powered carousel he could ride, and I could spin it fast enough to twirl his head into next week. He liked that a lot. Sometimes we'd see other tykes there, and we discovered that they liked the carousel too. And I mean *really* liked it. They'd see me spinning Cubby and pile on with him. In no time at all, I'd have three or four laughing and screaming kids who kept yelling, "Faster, faster" no matter how fast I moved.

Other dads seemed more cautious around playground hardware. Sure, they pushed their kids on tire swings and encouraged them to crawl through giant pipes. But few tossed their kids in the air, or swung them till they flew across the yard, sliding like a ballplayer for home plate. Maybe the other dads were more sensible, but the kids I entertained truly squealed for joy, and hardly any of them ever lost an arm or head in the process. That just goes to show you: True playground euphoria requires a lot of energy and a dash of danger to achieve. I may have been a loser with the other kids when I was growing up, but I was a hands-down winner as an adult.

11

MONSTERS

One of the signs that Cubby was getting bigger was that he claimed his own space. "My room!" he exclaimed proudly. His mom had spent a lot of time making it perfect, and it showed. The bed had nice soft sheets and a warm, tasty blanket. His toys were in a big box in the corner, except for his favorites, which covered the floor. There were even books and clothes, in drawers and in piles. The only problem was the monsters.

I don't know why kids are scared of monsters, but every one I have ever observed has that fear. It must be genetic. I cannot recall telling Cubby to be scared of monsters even once. Yet he feared them, and I remember feeling the same way as a little boy. *There are things out there that eat kids.* You just know it.

I remembered my own fears of being eaten, and my parents assuring me that monsters were not real. It didn't work. The problem was, my dad was a philosopher, and he relied on logic, which failed us horribly when it came to monsters. He had no answer to the monster paradox, which said: If monsters ate every kid they caught, there would be no survivors to tell us they were real, because the kids who knew the truth would all be in the monsters' stomachs. I concluded that kids who said there were no monsters were either hopeful or ignorant, and I believe Cubby came to a similar conclusion, thirty-some years later.

Most of the time, other activities like eating, sleeping, or making demands on parents distracted him. Those times, monsters were forgotten. Then there would be the moments when he was alone, in a reflective mood, and monster thoughts would come to the fore in his little brain. If he thought about them too long, he'd get scared. When that happened we knew it, because he'd come running. "Mama! Dada! Monsters!" He would leap into his mother's arms, where he was warm, safe, and protected. She would reassure him and pat him gently on the back. After a moment, he would usually settle down and return to his Legos and other amusements.

I watched that happen time and again. Sweet as it was, I thought it would be better if he learned self-defense. Mom agreed. She knew she would not always be there to protect him, and he needed to be able to resolve monster scares on his own.

She filled an empty spray bottle with colored water. "This is monster spray," she said as she handed him the bottle with the greatest of gravity. "Keep it with you, and spray anywhere you think there might be monsters. They hate the stuff, and will always run away."

"But if they don't . . ." She gave him a plastic Wiffle Ball bat. "If you see any monsters, whack them hard with this." Cubby put the bat next to his bed. He went back to his Legos with a newfound sense of security. It was amazing, the way that tyke accepted whatever his mom told him, as if it was The Word.

A few weeks later, I decided to test Cubby's preparedness. Placing a blanket over my head, I crept around the corner from our room to his. Poised in the doorway, a shapeless blue blanket mass, I growled. Softly, but with menace and conviction.

Cubby turned around. "Hey," he yelled, but I didn't answer. I wasn't sure if he recognized me, so I just growled in return. In the blink of an eye, Cubby spun around, grabbed the bat, and began pounding the blanket as hard as he could, all the while yelling at the top of his lungs, "Mama! Monsters!" It was shocking how hard and fast that tyke could swing a bat. I threw the blanket off, stunned, and he whacked me square on the head. Then he did it again, either before or because he recognized me. Quick as a flash, he dropped the bat and ran past me into the living room, yelling, "Mama! Save me!" He leapt into her arms as I rounded the corner to see her laughing.

"Very good, Jack. You defended yourself and the monster just turned out to be Dada."

What could I say to that?

I didn't growl at him very often after that, and he didn't whack me with the bat.

12

CHILD SUPPORT

Cubby continued to get bigger and stayed healthy. That was good, but it also meant a never-ending stream of new expenses as Cubby outgrew one thing and needed another. He was nothing like a dog, which was practically set for life once you got it a food dish and a blanket. Kid ownership is expensive. Before Cubby was born, we had purchased nesting materials, and that was costly enough. After he arrived, there were new bills every day. Little Bear nursed him, but her milk alone wasn't enough. There were baby foods to buy, too. Then there was the Stork Diaper Service and an endless array of clothes. There were objects to stimulate his growing brain—mobiles to hang overhead and chunky rubber things to grab and chew. This list of baby paraphernalia kept growing, with no end in sight.

Seeing all that, I redoubled my efforts to make money, and it began to pay off. Though I wasn't restoring many cars, my ads were bringing in service customers, and the money was enough to support us. The bank account stopped its alarming downward spiral. Now I just needed to reverse the trend. I began to think I might actually pull it off.

Just then, my business partner decided to pounce again. "I've been thinking," he said. I had learned those words always presaged something bad, and this time was no exception. "You're doing pretty well out there in that shop. I think it's time you started paying me some rent. You can give me a few thousand every month, starting next Monday."

I could almost feel my blood pressure rising. I had to earn back the money I had lost and pay rent on top of that. It was becoming clear that the big loser in this arrangement was me, and there was nothing I could do. Nothing except make money for him and keep a little for myself.

So I came up with a plan, which I prayed would get me out of the hole I'd gotten into. It was time to revisit the business of selling cars. That was where the real money could be made. I was making fifty- and hundred-dollar profits on service jobs. If I was smart, I could make ten times that on a single car sale. That became my goal. I used the credibility I was building in my service department to sell cars in a nontraditional way.

"If you want a late-model Mercedes," I told people, "I'll go to the Mercedes-Benz auction and find the one that's perfect for you. You pay me a six-percent commission, just like a real estate agent. I'll buy you a better car than you'd find at any dealer, for a better price. You're hiring me to be your expert."

In those pre-Internet days my idea took off. Soon I was buying five, ten, and even twenty cars a month. I wasn't worried about finding buyers for my inventory, because everything I bought was presold. Customers loved the transparency of my system. If I paid ten thousand for a car, they paid me ten thousand six hundred. There was no fear that they'd paid too much, or that an unscrupulous salesman had taken advantage of them.

I made fifty thousand dollars selling cars that first year. That was when the next problem surfaced. My partner announced that I had to pay back the money I'd lost "after taxes." So making back a hundred grand was not enough. I had to make back two hundred grand. A year before, I'd have been crushed, but now I saw a light at the end of the tunnel. Unfortunately, the better I did, the nastier my so-called partner became. There were days I just cringed going to work, he was so venomous and ugly. He could not stand to see my business take off, as his own company withered and he got older and sicker. He was a mean, bitter old man.

He lurked in his office, looking out over the parking lot. Whenever he saw the chance, he'd charge out and belittle me in front of customers. "Move that car," he'd bark. "Get that oil off the ground." I don't know what he thought he was doing, but my customers came to see him as an arrogant bully, and they wondered why I put up with him. I just kept my mouth shut. I knew I was winning. Slowly but surely, I was building a bank account and planning my escape.

By that time, I had learned to keep my new son as far from my work as I could. I never shared with Little Bear how ugly the situation at work had become. Perhaps I was ashamed, since I blamed myself for getting us into the mess. The worst was when Little Bear would visit, bringing Cubby along. It made me sick, the way my partner acted nice while they were there and they had no idea what a beast he really was.

It was a hard grind, the hardest work I'd ever known, but I knew inside I could win.

13

THE BEST KID IN THE STORE

I've observed a lot of kids, and one thing they all have in common is a strong curiosity about their origins. Once the basic words like *Mama, Dada,* and *car* are out of the way, and the first yelled exclamations *(I'm hungry! Gimme that toy! I don't want a nap!)* have been learned, they move on to calmer and quieter philosophical issues. Sure enough, one day Cubby reached the stage where he asked the Big Question: "Where did I come from?"

Where indeed? There were many possible answers, some more interesting than others. Some people say, "God brought you to us." Unfortunately, that didn't answer anything. *If God brought me, who is he and where did he get me?* A religious person might answer, *God created you,* but I'm a rational guy, and, knowing the sperm-egg thing, I could not in good conscience use the God explanation.

Cubby's mom substituted her own fanciful creature, saying, "The stork brought you." But Cubby didn't seem to find that explanation especially satisfying either. The very idea of a bird carrying him around was troubling, to say the least. He might have been dropped from a great height! In any case, his mother often contra-dicted her explanation a few seconds later by saying, "You came from Mom and Dad." That answer didn't work either, because no tyke can possibly conceive how he might come from Mom and Dad, even though that's true. Even to a three-year-old, Mom and Dad are two distinct individuals, so how could they produce a kid? Was it like baking a cake?

If I had been a more dedicated parent, I might have tried to ex-plain the science of procreation, but I wasn't. Instead, I turned to the familiar. I knew Cubby needed an explanation that made sense, one his thousand-day-old brain could comprehend. That is exactly what I found at the place every middle-class suburban toddler in America comes to know and love: the mall.

Even before Cubby could talk, he accompanied his mom and me to the Holyoke Mall, where we bought goods of various sorts. Cubby saw food taken from grocery store shelves and placed in our refrigerator, only to be eaten a short while later. He saw a crib car-ried home in a box, to be erected for his containment and pleasure. He saw books put in shopping bags, to be read to him on the living room sofa.

Almost every single thing that came into our house came from some kind of store. Cubby reached that conclusion early on. He even figured out that we went to stores in the car, which was fu-eled by gas I bought at filling stations. I know he understood fill-ing stations and gas, because two of the first words he learned to say were *BP* and *Mobil*. And when he learned to read signs a few months later, the first one he read said: *Michelob*. It's always been a mystery to me how he read that sign, which glowed red neon in the window of the gas station we visited every couple of days. I do not drink beer and never buy Michelob, but somehow Cubby picked up that word.

By his third birthday, Cubby was well on his way to read-ing signs, using stuff, and understanding commerce. He did not grasp the finer points of business yet, but he definitely understood that we had to buy an item before eating it or using it at home. That was particularly true at the grocery store, where Cubby had already learned not to get caught eating food directly off the shelves.

Buying toys was something he (and I) understood all too well. Of course, Cubby had no idea how much things cost, where the money to pay for them came from, or how it was exchanged. All he knew was, we went to stores, gathered up stuff, and brought it home.

That made understanding his origin very simple, when I got around to explaining it.

"I bought you at the Kid Store."

"Really?" Cubby digested that answer with puzzlement and wonder. No matter how many times he repeated the question, I answered it the same way. Yet he kept circling back, time and again.

"That's where you came from," I repeated in a tone that didn't brook any argument. I had to be careful to answer firmly and quickly so he would not sense uncertainty, which opened the door to competing explanations, like his mother's stork story or even the "growing inside Mom" fable. "There was a Live Kid Department in one of the stores at the Holyoke Mall, and I kept seeing you up there in the window, and one day when they had a sale, I just went in and bought you.

"You were stuck to the window in a big display basket, looking out at the shoppers as they walked through the mall. Your mom thought you were really cute, and I thought you'd grow up to be a hard worker around the house. They had you out there on display because you were the best-looking kid they had, and stores always put their best stuff out on display. They wanted to give me a wrapped kid from the stock in back, but I knew you were probably the best specimen, so I insisted on the display model, and here you are."

Cubby was not sure what to make of that explanation. He surely compared what I said to what he heard from his mother and grandparents. He realized that buying things in stores was something he observed almost every day. In comparison, he had never seen a stork deliver a baby. And other possibilities occurred to him, too. Just recently, he had taken some sea horses out of a box, put them in water, and seen them come to life. *Maybe the same thing happened with kids,* he might have thought.

The thing that confused him was that he did not know *where* the Kid Store was. If he had seen a Kid Store with tykes for sale he would have accepted my explanation without question. As it was, he was unsure and somewhat troubled. That made me work even harder in hopes that my explanation would prevail. At times I wondered what would happen if he made it to his teens still believing I'd bought him in a store. The possibility was slightly alarming, but I sensed it would never happen.

"Can we go to the Kid Store?" Cubby asked. I never knew if he wanted to buy a brother or sister, or just get validation. Either way, it was too late. All the mall had to offer was different species. "I'm sorry, Cubby. They put a pet store in where it used to be," I said. "But they still use some of the same cages and stuff. Let's go there and maybe you'll recognize where you used to live." However, he never did. Recognize it as home, that is.

Whenever he complained about chores, cleanup, or any other parental request, which was often, I countered by reminding him of all the claims that had been made when I bought him. Cubby had heard salesmen describe products, so he knew it happened. The only question was what they had said about him.

When he thought to ask, I reminded him never to rely on spoken claims for anything. In the car business, they call that talk salesman's bullshit. People will say anything to get a deal. You should only rely on what you see in print, because that isn't as likely to change.

"I wish I still had the papers that came with you," I told him. "They made a lot of promises, more than you got from the average car salesman, and I'm still waiting for some of them to come true."

Guaranteed to grow, they said, and he sure had done that. Cubby had quadrupled in weight, in just three years. My Land Rover, in comparison, weighed pretty much the same as when I got it. "You're good value in the growing department, for sure," I told him. "The Land Rover consumes a hundred pounds of gasoline every week. I'll bet you don't even eat ten pounds."

Eats regular food. That was always important to me. It's bad enough having to put premium gas in the car. I couldn't handle a kid that ate only premium baby food. Cubby was the human equivalent of a military vehicle—one that goes anywhere and eats whatever you feed him.

Obedient. "Cubby," I said, "that was true in the beginning, but the older you get, the more rebellious you become."

Does all chores. That was a tough one. "From the moment you could walk unassisted I said you were born to the yoke. Parents raise kids to help them with work around the house and elsewhere. For a dad like me, more kids equals more opportunity. If I had ten kids, I could open a coal mine. If I had twenty, I could have a clothing factory too." That was what I told him, but it never came true. It was very hard to get useful work from Cubby. He was friendly, and even superficially cooperative, but when it came to hard labor, he was always someplace else.

In fact, when he got older, he became a lot like Tom Sawyer in his ability to get other kids to do his work for him. Since I had been careful never to read him Mark Twain, so as not to give him ideas, that seemed to be a natural-born trait. I was proud to see it in action, except when I wanted him working for me.

Despite all the problems, I made it clear that I was pretty satisfied with my purchase. As well I should be, for what he cost. "You were two hundred dollars," I would say in my most serious voice. "Plus tax. The best kid in the store, and the second most expensive! The most expensive kid was three hundred seventy-five dollars, but he came with a third eye, and I did not see the sense in paying for that extra eye. A two-eyed kid was good enough for me. They use three-eyed kids in mining and industry, but they look funny in a community like this."

Cubby always liked the notion of being the best in the store. It's nice to be the best of something. Only problem was, his mother persisted in offering him alternate origin stories. Eventually, she actually convinced him that he grew inside her, and he ended up believing that and not my own colorful account, which was really a shame.

I think it was the pictures that made the difference. After all my talk about believing what you see in print, as opposed to salesman's bullshit, his mother turned that around on me and won him over with photos from *National Geographic* and the *Encyclopaedia Britannica*. I could not trump that, because there were no Kid Store photos available. If only I'd had the Internet and Photoshop back then! The only thing that could have trumped my story then would have been a pregnant Mom, and Cubby ended up an only child, so I'd have won, hands down.

Without photos, my creative explanation was defeated. The inherent believability of the Kid Store alone was not enough. Realizing I had lost, I felt a bit sad. In fact, that experience led me to question the meaning of "right answers." When you have a kid, and he asks where he came from, what's the correct response? Is it the most entertaining story? Or is it just the dry, boring facts? After much reflection, I decided that the world is what we make it to be, and that the best answer for a little kid is the one that gets him thinking. That was what I tried to do.

There was a time when Cubby derided my imaginative explanations, but now that he is grown I can see that they had an effect;

I made him think, and questioning the conventional wisdom is never a bad thing. Someday, when he has a kid of his own, I would not be surprised if he offers even more imaginative answers when faced with the Origin Question.

The Third Generation will be something to see.

14

WONDROUS DADA

As Cubby grew from babyhood into kidhood, he was like a plant that grows six inches overnight, changing before my very eyes. Talking was probably the biggest milestone, even bigger than learning to walk. As soon as he could talk, it was as if he'd spent the first year and a half of his life in a state of extreme deprivation and had to make up for lost time. Until then, I thought we'd taken pretty good care of him. We certainly felt like we'd catered to his every whim. However, when he started talking, he made it clear how wrong we were.

First came the one-word demands, like *Drink*! Such demands could come at any time with no warning, even when he'd been fed and watered on a regular schedule. Then we progressed to two-word statements, which did not presage anything more appealing. One of his favorites was *Poopy diaper*! Everything was said as an exclamation, and if not satisfied immediately, a meltdown ensued.

At the same time, the stimulating back-and-forth of adult conversation was totally lacking in my exchanges with Cubby. There was really no conversation at all—just a demand from him and compliance from us. If I asked him what kind of tires we should get for the Land Rover, he would just give me a blank stare. And when I asked what he thought of the government or the latest increase in gas prices, he didn't say anything at all. That concerned me. However, when I expressed my worries to his mother, she was quick to leap to his defense. *He's just a little boy!*

I could not remember when I had acquired the ability to discuss politics, religion, and cars, and I didn't have any other kids, so I was at a loss to evaluate my son. However, after some covert listening to other toddlers, I concluded Little Bear was probably right. Cubby seemed to have a good vocabulary for his age, and the other toddlers I saw were just as vacuous when it came to adult conversation. At the same time they were equally rude and aggressive in their efforts to get their own way.

Still, that did not mean I had to accept bad manners. I could do something about it. Indeed, as a parent, I believed I had a duty to civilize my child.

We had arrived at one of those turning points in tyke rearing. Little Bear was still willing to coddle him and be at his beck and call, but I wasn't. I knew what basic manners had meant to me. As a kid who always said and did the wrong thing, a modicum of politeness was all that saved me from extermination on many occasions. With that in mind, I concluded there was no time like the present to get Cubby on the right track. If my kid was going to make more and more demands, he was going to learn to make them politely. I began his training immediately.

"Cubby," I said, "now that you are talking, it's time to learn politeness. You have to say please when you want something. That way it sounds like you are making a gentle request, not an obnoxious demand. People are more likely to help a polite kid than a rude one." He just looked at me, but I could see he got the gist of what I was saying. I gave him an example. "Please give me the milk." I said it slowly and deliberately.

"Please gimme milk," Cubby repeated right away. Then he said it again. I looked at him and wondered if he'd gotten stuck in repeat mode. After another two "please gimme milk" loops I concluded Cubby actually wanted milk and was not just practicing the words. When I gave it to him he slurped it down as though he had not had a drink all day, although there had been no sign of thirst before I started training him, using milk as the example.

Had he been thirsty before I tried teaching him to ask for a drink? Did saying it make it so? I never did find out. It was enough that I had gotten him to add "please" to his request, and I resolved to move on to the next step.

"Okay, that's good. But there's more. If you want to be a good speaker you also need to add what we call a *salutation* when talking to grown-ups. It's a sign of respect."

Cubby stumbled at the word *salutation*. "Hard word," he said. I was encouraged to hear him say that, because it told me that his comprehension exceeded his speaking ability. He was mulling over what I'd said and thinking through the meaning of the words. I could see that Cubby had an idea what *salutation* meant even if he could not pronounce the word. That was a sign of intelligence, a portent of things to come. We all want to think our kids are smart, and parents cherish any evidence of that reality.

"Yes, *salutation* is a hard word. But the actual words you say to show respect are not hard at all. What you are doing is praising someone before you ask them to do something for you. If you say, *you're the best,* and then ask for something, you are a lot more likely to get it than if you say, *you're no good.*" Cubby nodded, and I believe he got the picture. "For example, if you wanted me to get you milk, you could say: 'Please, Wondrous Dada, may I have some milk?' "

"Wondrous Dada?" he asked with a hint of skepticism. He actually wrinkled his nose as he said *wondrous.* Why would he do that? Could a toddler be that cynical? The few child-rearing manuals I had read suggested that small children view their parents as the source of all things wonderful. Clearly, Cubby did not fully embrace that point of view. But he did pay attention. Sort of.

When he wanted an Oreo, he'd say, "I want a cookie." As any adult knows, *I want a cookie* is not a request, it's just a statement. I'd hear that and say, okay, if he wanted a cookie he was welcome to go get one. That produced a momentary pause as he waited for me to give him a cookie, but of course, that was not happening. We reached a standstill where each watched the other and neither said or did anything.

After a pause, the most common result was a clarification from Cubby, where he would repeat his original statement or perhaps convert it to a demand: "Gimme a cookie."

That didn't move me either. I always praised him for making the leap from statement to request, but kids who make rude demands don't get rewarded. When I heard that, I replied with, "What do you say to get a cookie?"

He knew what to say, but he was highly resistant. The process became an elaborate dance, one in which he knew all the steps but chose not to follow through, because he was determined to use the maximum demand and the minimum manners, and I was determined to teach him the opposite.

When "Gimme a cookie" failed, he generally tried the "please" alone first. That usually worked for his mom and the folks at day care. It even worked now and then with me. When it didn't, he knew what to do.

As soon as he heard me say, "What's the magic phrase?" he would wrinkle his nose and spit the words out: "Please, Wondrous Dada." I was never able to get him to articulate that phrase with any kind of enthusiasm, but I did at least get him using some manners right from the beginning.

I wish I could say that he grew up to be a young man who said, "Please, Wondrous Dada," and "Thank you, Wondrous Dada," every single day. But he didn't. The best I ever got was grudging compliance under duress. And even that faded with age. If you asked him today, he'd probably deny the whole thing happened.

I recalled the way my grandmother had taught my cousins Leigh and Little Bob to say yes, ma'am and no, sir. They never did stop talking that way. Of course, I knew they didn't mean it. My cousins snickered and made fun of grown-ups when they weren't looking, but they did learn to show respect and I tried to do the same with Cubby. It didn't work out as well with him, though.

Yet we had a few good years. When he was five, I was pretty consistently wondrous. When he hit seven, I could insist on Wondrous Dada if he really wanted something, but he was highly resistant. By age nine, it was all over. He'd say, "You're not a Wondrous Dada at all!" I was heartbroken.

It's possible that Cubby will recognize me as wondrous now that he is grown, but I doubt it. Still, I can take comfort in the knowledge that I did teach him some modicum of manners. That's something any dad can be proud of.

15

TUCK-IN TIME

From the beginning, Tuck-in Time was a critical juncture in Cubby's day. After all, the process of settling a kid in bed, carefully pulling up the covers, and ensuring that every extremity is covered is known far and wide as the only reliable way to prevent monster attacks in the night. Every child knows this truth: A kid without a tuck-in might just as well be standing in monster alley, wearing a sign that reads Eat Me. Cubby did not want to suffer that fate, which meant he never ever failed to remind me by saying, "Tuck-in time, Dad!"

There were many things I did without question, just because my little boy asked. Tucking him in was not one of them. The tuck-in was indeed an important event, but it had to be preceded by the even more important Bedtime Cleanup. A successful cleanup was required for Cubby to be tuck-in qualified. I may not have taught him many manners (despite a mighty valiant effort), but I surely taught him that.

Big corporations get ISO 9000 certified, and it's a complex and lengthy process. My son became tuck-in qualified by a much simpler series of steps, but to him it was a bigger deal than any achievement of corporate America. Success didn't come easy; he resisted cleanup vigorously, wheedling, cajoling, and distracting me from my goal at every opportunity. All the while, he kept circling back to that tuck-in request in hopes of getting safely tucked in without proper qualification. But I remained steadfast. Finally he gave in, and the house was a better place for it.

First, Cubby had to pick up all the toys from the floor. Food had to be eaten or put away. Clothes had to be in their drawers. His teeth had to be brushed and sharpened. Finally, he had to put on his pajamas. Only then was he eligible for tuck-in. He climbed into bed and I arranged his covers neatly, making sure there were no exposed toes for monsters to grab. Then I sat down to begin a story.

For toddlers, bedtime stories are like crack cocaine—give them a taste and they're hooked. Cubby would get so excited that he'd bounce up and down when we tried to put him to bed, saying, "Story time! Story time! Read me a story!" Even after he could read perfectly fine on his own, Cubby still loved to hear bedtime stories. In fact, I read or told stories to Cubby right up till his sixteenth birthday.

If you asked him how it began, he'd say he was always fond of stories, but of course he wasn't. How could he know he liked stories without adults to tell them to him in the first place? In my experience, toddlers grow up liking most of what grown-ups expose them to. They have very little ability to actually experience the world on their own, independent of their caretakers. So your kid is really what you make him. If you read Shakespeare to your tyke from the beginning, he'll grow up to be an articulate and well-spoken gentleman. If you teach him to squash cockroaches with a mallet and pull the legs off frogs, you'll create an illiterate serial killer.

At first I read stories from children's books—classics like *Green Eggs and Ham* and *Where the Wild Things Are*. I had a preference for tales I'd enjoyed myself when I was his size. His mom tended to like newer compositions like the Thomas the Tank Engine and Berenstain Bears series, but it really didn't matter what we read. Cubby liked them all. In fact, he more than liked them. He was totally in love with stories to the point where we could read the same material over and over and he'd just smile contentedly as he went to sleep.

I know that's true because I tried it. If I read a single page and then went back and read the same page again, Cubby would always notice. "Keep going!" he'd exclaim. That told me one page was below Cubby's repeat threshold. However, if I read the whole book and then restarted at the beginning, he would almost always lie there quietly, failing to notice that the story was repeating. Or maybe he did notice but he was happy to hear it twice.

That was particularly true when I read the wonderful works of Dr. Seuss, whose words rolled like pebbles down a mountainside, making a melody that Cubby could relax to and follow as he nodded off. In the beginning, Cubby fell asleep pretty rapidly, making reading a fairly brief exercise. However, as he got older, he began paying more attention to the words themselves, even asking questions at times. He was obviously making an effort to stay awake.

That presented a small problem, because I got bored rereading the same stories every night. How many times can you recite *One Fish, Two Fish* before going nuts? I began interjecting subtle modifications, being careful to ensure my changes flowed just as smoothly as the Doctor's original material. My fish became aggressive, and the gremlins acquired weapons. I thought the changes lived up to the Seuss standards, but Cubby almost always caught me, and quickly too. "Read it right!" he'd yell.

No matter how nicely it rhymed, the original Dr. Seuss never said things like, "the one in back, he has a gun," or, "black fish, blue fish, I'll eat you, fish."

That led me to search for more variety in storytelling. I tried reading him sophisticated stuff—articles I read for my own enlightenment or entertainment. The results of that experiment were mixed. He liked stories from *Scientific American,* but he became bored with the *Proceedings of the Institute of Electrical and Electronic Engineers.* We both enjoyed *Professional Mariner,* while *People* magazine proved largely incomprehensible.

I also exposed Cubby to the classics. Unfortunately, that was not very successful. He found the tales of Poe scary, and older works by Aristotle or Plato did not flow melodiously enough for his five-year-old mind.

I discovered that what he liked most were clever turns of phrase, alliteration, and topical variety. Things like acrimonious armadillos, pedantic penguins, and goons with guns. He just didn't want them to pop up unexpectedly in the middle of *Green Eggs and Ham,* which he preferred in its virgin state. Since I couldn't get away with incorporating the penguins into the stories and articles I read him, a new plan was needed. I decided to create my own bedtime stories. They would be Wondrous Dada originals.

I had always been a storyteller, even when I didn't have an audience. As a tyke in the sandbox, I constructed elaborate fantasies around blocks and toy trucks. I imagined whole cities with sophisticated machines to run them. All that was missing were people to tell my stories to. Sometimes other kids would join me long enough to enter my worlds; other times when they departed, adults would stay and listen to my tales. They were my first audiences.

When I turned eight, my mother got me a little brother, whom I called Varmint. Varmint followed me everywhere and paid close attention to anything I said or did. He loved my stories, which presented me with daily challenges as I struggled to dream up a never-ending variety of fresh material.

I realized Cubby was much like Varmint; if I thought it up, and it made sense, he would listen and like it. And by then I had twenty-some additional years of life experience. That was a lot of story material.

Cubby's favorite bedtime beastie was Gorko, a flying lizard. Gorko had been born far away, in Flying Lizard Land, which is below and to the right of Australia on certain secret maps of the world. By the time I first told Cubby about him, Gorko was eight years old and had already mastered solo flight and medium-strength fire breathing.

Gorko was my own invention, but I knew how much Cubby liked his routines, so I wove all his childhood favorites into Gorko's stories, distorting them mightily as I went. I had Gorko leading a lizard army into Bear Country and rounding up the Berenstain Bears for the Lizard City Zoo. On the way there, they passed Road Kill Phil and the Cat in the Hat, who was destitute and homeless. Gorko's friends the Cargo Lizards went to the Isle of Sodor, where they picked up Thomas the Tank Engine and carried him south to the Lizard Country Railway. Cubby loved it when I put all his favorite characters together, an approach that had the advantage of reducing the number of creatures, places, and things I had to conjure out of thin air.

Like many good fables, the story of Gorko was inspired by life—in this case, the lives of Zeke and Pete, the fire-breathing lizards that lived next door to Cubby's GrandMargaret in Shelburne Falls. Everyone in town knew them. We didn't actually catch sight of them much, of course, because fire lizards are very shy and because they lived in the basement. But we knew they were down there, and it's comforting to know there's a quarter-ton lizard next door if you need it.

Zeke and Pete worked for George the glassblower, who had a shop down the street from my mother. Townspeople said George walked his lizards to work every morning before dawn and took them home after dark. They worked long hours, those lizards, but they had fun and it kept them busy and away from bullies who might otherwise have tormented them.

Bullies were always a problem for lizards like Zeke and Pete. Anyone who's different attracts bullies at some point growing up, and lizards are *very* different, so they can end up being bully magnets, especially in unenlightened hill towns. Up there, mean kids would throw rocks at them and even jab them with sharp sticks.

Like the rest of their kind, Zeke and Pete were placid, tolerant creatures, but they had their limits. And when they got mad . . . watch out! An angry lizard could turn a mean kid into a pile of cinders in a matter of seconds. A hundred years ago, a lizard might have gotten away with defending itself, but modern lizards didn't stand a chance. Sometimes the lizards ended up in jail; other times they got run out of town on a rail. That's how Zeke and Pete had ended up in Shelburne Falls. They'd been run out of Wappingers Falls, New York, after a scuffle that ended with two toasted lowlifes and one burned police car.

George had taken them in, befriended them, and given them a warm place to sleep next to his furnace. That was very unusual, because most glassblowers grow up alongside their lizards. Very few bond as grown-ups. Zeke and Pete knew that, and repaid George's kindness with faithful service in his shop. Sometimes Cubby and I would go to the art galleries in nearby Northampton, and we'd speculate as to which lizard blew the fire for particular pieces of glass sculpture. Folks said Zeke had the stronger fire, so we figured he blew the biggest ones, whereas Pete was renowned for his small, precise flames and beautiful detail work.

Cubby loved to watch glassblowers at work. He was captivated by the idea that glass could be heated red hot and pulled and twisted into strange shapes. Before seeing a glassblower at work, he had assumed glass was an immutable solid, like rock, unless you dropped it and it shattered. Seeing it flow like taffy was a shock. But he knew ice melted, so he was able to grasp the idea that glass melted too. You just needed a lot more heat. And that was what hit us as soon as we entered the glassblower's shop: heat from the lizards. Even if you couldn't see them, you couldn't help but feel the heat pouring out of their mouths as they blew that glass.

Whenever we opened the door to the glass shop the little bells would tinkle, and if we were quick, we'd see Zeke and Pete's tails swish as they slithered out of sight behind the counter. Some people said it was unfair, the way they had to hide on the floor, but I thought it was for the best. After all they'd been through, it was no wonder they were shy. George always said they were happier keeping to themselves.

Anyway, as long as you stayed by the door, you could glimpse the fire lizards at work, and it was truly a marvel to see. From that vantage point, we watched George shape bowls, vases, and other glassware as Zeke and Pete blew jets of blue fire up through holes in the stone benches. George always worked barefoot, using his toes to press his lizards' tails to signal the precise amount and temperature of fire he needed. Watching the three of them, it was as if they were telepathic. It was an ancient trade, like fortune-telling or the Gypsy arts.

We always knew Zeke and Pete as big, gentle, slow-moving creatures. As I told Cubby, it takes a massive reptile to blow that much fire. Not surprisingly, they ate a lot of food. George always had a pile of meat in his shop, and Zeke and Pete were known far and wide for the way they cooked their own dinners. Some say that's where our caveman ancestors got the idea.

Given his attachment to Zeke and Pete, it didn't surprise me that Cubby wanted to know all about Gorko. He asked how flying lizards differed from fire lizards and whether fire-breathing lizards were the same as dragons. He even wondered why Gorko didn't live in Shelburne Falls too, since it seemed to be a lizard-friendly town.

I did my best to answer his questions. I explained that ancient people called flying lizards that blew fire dragons, and that many books had been written about the age-old struggle between dragons and humans. Gorko, being a young, modern lizard, was a lot mellower than the dragons of old, I told Cubby. He watched TV, played games, and seldom got into fights. Also, he got along with humans. There was a time, long ago, when lizards ruled the world.

All that had changed, I told Cubby, thanks to helicopter gunships and radar-guided missiles. Now humans were in charge of most worlds while the great lizards were relegated to Flying Lizard Land. The lizards that ventured out into human space were the ones that could get along with people without getting arrested or shot down by fighter jets.

They surely had their fun, playing pranks, doing stunts, and being big kids. They did all the things I'd have done if I had wings and a tail. Cubby loved it all, and when bedtime came, he couldn't wait to hear more.

Those were the creatures that Cubby went to sleep with every night.

16

ROLE MODELS

When I was growing up, the adults around me were quick to tell me I'd never amount to anything. As the years passed, and I became commercially successful, people stopped taunting me with words like that. By the time Cubby came along, people were actually telling Little Bear and me what good parents we would be, something that struck me as pretty peculiar, given our family backgrounds.

Neither of us had any idea what to do with a kid. Yet there we were, raising Cubby. We'd read a few books, and visited some zoos and jails, but we remained totally lacking in functional role models. Both our dads had been nasty, mean drunks when we were little. Now that we were all older, their dispositions had mellowed, but it was too late. We were adults; our chance to grow up with wise and wonderful parents had passed. However, Cubby's arrival gave all of us a second chance. To my amazement, our dads actually added real wisdom to the pool of knowledge we deployed in pursuit of that enlightened goal of Perfect Parenthood.

I had never imagined my father as a baby-centric sort of guy. Of course, until Cubby came along, I'd never seen him with a little kid either. Whenever I was present, my father was very thoughtful and reserved, not the sort of person you'd associate with babble and drool. I guess I shouldn't have been surprised, because I am exactly the same way.

My dad taught philosophy at the University of Massachusetts. He took his work very seriously. Actually, he took everything seriously. They voted him department head in the 1980s, and by the time Cubby was born, he had turned UMass Philosophy into one of the top-ranked departments in the country. My dad could discuss Heidegger or Kant all day, but talk of Dr. Seuss or Thomas the Tank Engine brought him to a complete and sudden halt. He'd say, "Yes, Jack, that's nice," and wiggle Cubby's baby paws with one of his own giant fingers. Beyond that maneuver, I didn't think he had any idea what else to do with a baby.

I was wrong.

As soon as Cubby was able to stand on his own, Little Bear began to alternate dropping him off with my mother or my father while she went to school. My father and his wife, Judy, only worked in the office part time by then, and they were surprisingly enthusiastic about watching a tyke. My father even put together a basket of toys that he pulled out whenever Cubby came calling. I don't know where he got the stuff; some of it was older than me! He had a real Lionel train and a big green sack of Lincoln Logs, just for Cubby. Seeing them brought back memories of my own Lincoln Logs and the way they tasted as I chewed them in my sandbox.

My father seemed to share my own philosophy when selecting toys for Cubby. Both of us bought him things we'd loved when we were little. To us, time-tested wood and metal toys were infinitely superior to the modern plastic stuff they advertised on TV.

Little Bear's father was in many ways the opposite of my own. He paved driveways, and people called him the Old Boy, or Easy Ed. Friends from the paving industry, where smoking-hot asphalt is laid down four inches thick, had their own name for him: Half

Inch. My father was distinguished and very well spoken. The Old Boy was a genial thug: three feet wide, five feet tall, with a firm handshake and a ready laugh. My father had stopped drinking years ago, but the Old Boy still loved his whiskey.

The Old Boy and his second wife, Alice, loved to feed the wildlife, and there was plenty of it where they lived. He'd built a house at the base of Mount Norwottock—a few miles from our home—with nothing but woods for miles behind him. Black bear, raccoons, squirrels, foxes, deer, and just about every other creature that lived in those parts came calling on the back patio, all clamoring for treats. Visiting their house was sort of like being in a zoo at feeding time, except that there were no cages and we were in the way.

The Old Boy and Alice presided over their wild kingdom, doling out meat to the carnivores and corncobs and table scraps to the plant eaters. It was a remarkable thing to see. Predators and prey would be side by side on the patio, eating the Old Boy's food. Foxes and turkeys might have been sworn enemies in the forest, but they got along fine at his place. I never saw a fight.

Cubby's grandpa also liked to get the family together for picnic dinners, thinking the same model of harmony through food could be achieved with humans. After attending a few of those dinners, I became a little leery of them. So did Little Bear. After all, anytime you mix twenty people, a lot of liquor, and hungry wild animals there is good potential for trouble. There were moments when it really wasn't clear which of us were the eaters and which were the food. One night I was sitting peaceably at the picnic table when a raccoon walked right up into my lap and took a piece of meat off my plate. When I say raccoon, I'm not talking about some soft, cuddly woodland creature. This was a burly thirty pounder with teeth an inch long and claws to match. Not the sort of thing you want to fight over a scrap of steak, especially when it's already in its mouth. The Old Boy laughed as that fat old coon wandered into the woods with my dinner. I got a new steak off the grill, where the Old Boy stood guard with a big set of tongs. He was the undisputed Duke of the Patio. No beast dared to take food from him.

I realized at that moment that what seemed friendly might not be, and it was possible the animals were all putting on an act just to get food. I know some of the people were that way, though it was the liquor that lured them, not corn on the cob.

Cubby had an even harder time. Not only did he have to watch for aggressive wildlife, he had to keep an eye out for pets, too. The Old Boy had two dogs, Bailey and Beaver, that were just about his size. They were friendly as could be, but if he walked onto the patio with a donut they wouldn't think twice about taking it for themselves. They'd chase him, knock him down, eat his chocolate cream donut, and then lick him good. He was left on his bottom, empty-handed, with sugary chocolate slobber all over his face as two laughing dogs divvied up his dessert.

Cubby didn't like being bullied by hounds. At first he grabbed his mom for protection, but he got bigger fast, and pretty soon he stood up to the dogs himself. When one or the other of them grabbed for his food, he'd swat it on the snout and yell "Bad!" as loud as he could. The dog would tuck its tail down and back off with the most awful hurt expression.

Raccoons were another matter. "Don't swat them on the nose," I warned him. "They're liable to bite your paw off if you do."

The Old Boy and Cubby went fishing together, too. He was an avid sportsman, both at home and at a cabin he built in the Maine woods. He was also active in the preservation of nature, though that idea didn't mean much to Cubby at his age. He had spent many years on his town's conservation commission. In fact, the year before they had named a small body of water in his honor: Easy Ed's Peeper Pond. He took Cubby there to catch bluegill. He loved the name, but it didn't help with their fishing. They would stay there all day with nothing to show for it but sunburn and bug bites. Not even a nibble. Luckily, the Old Boy had a stuffed fish at home, and he showed Cubby what might have been.

Easy Ed wasn't the only grandparent who loved the outdoors. My dad—John senior—spent as much time as he could in the woods, and he owned a whole mountaintop in rural Buckland, Massachusetts. He had a hundred acres up there, with a big tractor and a shed full of machinery to take care of it. Cubby was happy to help.

My father and Cubby spent hours chopping firewood and stacking it under the deck for winter. Cubby helped with the big two-handed saw, working it back and forth to take down a tree and strip off the branches. My father never used his chain saw when Cubby was around. "Too dangerous," he said, "and the old ways work just fine." His own grandpa had been a county agent for the Department of Agriculture, helping farmers in northwest Georgia. They worked slowly and carefully, with the same hand tools his Grandpa Dandy had used back on his farm.

The two of them managed the forest, repaired the old stone walls, and even planted a vegetable garden. They caught toads, watched birds, and picked rocks out of the meadow. My dad taught Cubby the names of all the plants in the yard, which Cubby was proud to repeat to me. Of the vegetables they grew, his favorite was squash. Not for the taste, mind you, but for the shape. He'd pick up big ripe squashes and swing them around his head. Grown-ups may have seen them as food, but he imagined squash as war clubs, rockets, and missiles. They were the best thing going, until the tomatoes started to rot.

Then there was the machinery. Besides the tractor, my father had a Honda four-wheeler that he used to ride around the property. He towed a wagon with his tools and used a chain to drag firewood back to the house. Cubby loved to ride it with him, but after a few trips he wanted to do more.

"Let me drive," he said. That was an audacious suggestion, because he was barely three feet tall. "Okay," his grandpa told him.

"Put your hands on the bars and I'll help you steer." Cubby grinned real wide and squealed with delight as they motored across the meadow. "One day you'll be able to drive it all by yourself," my father told him. Cubby never forgot.

Sometimes my son would climb the trees to survey the countryside. He wasn't very tall yet, so being in the treetops gave him a real advantage. He also liked climbing because it was one of the few places my father couldn't follow him. His arthritis was too bad for that. My dad would stand on the ground, watching closely and making sure Cubby got down safely.

Cubby was almost out of diapers the first time Little Bear left him with my father overnight. I was at the car auctions, she had to be out late, and my dad was eager to keep him. When bedtime came, my father and Judy led him down to the guest room, in a cozy corner of the finished and decorated basement. Nice as it seemed to my father, there was no way Cubby was going to stay down there. Monsters eat kids in basements. Wild "aminals" might come in the windows. Even at two years of age, he was determined to survive the night. Cubby followed them back upstairs, to my father and Judy's warm bedroom in the third-floor loft. He turned to my stepmother. "You stay down there, and I'll stay here with Grandpa." And that's what she did. From then on, Cubby stayed upstairs with his grandfather and Judy stayed in the guest room.

They loved having him there. My father kept that box of toys in a corner for the next ten years, just for Cubby's visits. Cubby outgrew the toys, but they didn't care. When the holidays came, they decorated a spectacular Christmas tree together and made a Christmas village. The only thing missing was the story of Santa, and I provided that.

17

ELVES

Most kids don't know the history of Christmas; they just know it's the day they get lots of presents. I wanted more for my son; I wanted him to know how it came to be and why we celebrate. After all, an informed child is a happy child. Not only that, an informed child will be full of stories to share with his friends. I'd never done too well at childhood story sharing or friend making, but I had high hopes for Cubby's greater social success.

With that in mind, I told Cubby the greatest secret of Christmas: how Santa got his reindeer. The story began with Santa's great-grandfather. He was the one, I told Cubby, who started the Christmas reindeer tradition, back in 1822, after he found himself shipwrecked in the far reaches beyond the Arctic Circle.

Cubby bounced up and down, eager to hear the story. He liked to bounce when my stories got exciting. Here is what I told him:

Captain Santa was whaling in the Northern Ocean, far, far from home. The weather had been unseasonably warm, and he'd ventured up the western coast of Greenland, farther north than he'd ever gone before. By late September, he was beginning to think he might make it all the way to the North Pole.

Most years, the ice would have stopped his northward prog-ress, but in 1822 the oceans were clear. He was in deep water, far offshore, without a single iceberg in sight. Little did he know that the sea and sky were luring him into a trap.

The cool afternoon turned to bone-chilling night. It got so cold that sailors' breath left masks of frost on their faces. The wind roared, and waves shattered the railings. Seawater froze against the rigging faster than the crew could chip it away. By morning, the ship looked like a fairy-tale castle of ice, and the heaving sea had gone silent, frozen solid.

They were trapped. Within a few days the ice around the ship was five feet thick. It looked like they'd never get free, and the men fell into a state of deep despair.

For the first week of their captivity, all they saw was ice. Nothing moved except the wind, and that never stopped. A fro-zen wasteland stretched as far as the eye could see. Santa was afraid they would all perish, but on the morning of the fifteenth day, the ship's lookout spotted movement on the horizon. A series of dots were making their way toward the ship. By midday Cap-tain Santa could see that the specks were a herd of reindeer. He'd heard legends about creatures of the arctic, but he'd never seen any up close.

The reindeer approached with curiosity. Sensing that they might be hungry, Santa offered them bread from his meager stock of provisions, and they gobbled it up hungrily. With that gesture, he made some new friends and saved himself and his crew.

I had taken Cubby to see the reindeer at the Roger Williams Zoo in Providence. They were gentle creatures, very different from the deer that ran wild in our local woods. Cubby even got a chance to pet one. He remembered the feel of its fur as I told him about Santa. Cubby always enjoyed having a personal connection to my stories.

The reindeer settled down near the ship, eating Santa's food and cavorting on the ice. As he watched them, an idea took shape in his mind. The ship was trapped in ice and going nowhere. But perhaps he could build sleds from its wood and harness the reindeer to pull himself and the crew back to civilization.

The men set about making sleighs with enthusiasm, and two days later, three fine sleds were ready. Sailors made harnesses from the ship's rigging so that the reindeer could pull the heavy sleds. Everyone was amazed when the reindeer stepped willingly into the rig the crewmen had made. They loaded a month's supply of food, some clothes, and some weapons. Then Captain Santa blew out the oil lamp in his cabin and left a note on his door for anyone who might someday find the remains of his icebound ship.

It was an epic journey. Captain Santa and his crewmen fought off giant seals and ravenous beasts. Their whaling harpoons came in handy on more than one occasion, when enormous polar bears decided the men might be good to eat. They traveled hundreds of miles, always heading south. Things were looking good, until one morning when they reached open water as far as the eye could see. How would they cross the ocean? They had started in a boat, but now they had only sleds. Santa was not a religious man, but he knew one thing: If there was a time to pray for salvation, this was it. If you're up there, he prayed, and you help us find the way home, I'll retire from the sea and devote my life to helping kids. It sounded corny, and he didn't know if it would work, but they were out of options.

Santa pulled up on the reins as they approached the edge of the sea ice, and something magical happened. Instead of stopping, the lead reindeer flexed her powerful shoulders to reveal wings! As soon as the lead reindeer spread her wings, every other reindeer in the team did the same. With a great blast of air and much flapping, they lifted themselves, the sleigh, and a startled Santa straight up into the air. Looking back, Santa saw the other reindeer beating their own stubby wings and following him into the sky.

Like every explorer, Santa had heard of unicorns and winged beasts. But there's a big difference between just reading about them and actually flying with mythical creatures. He and his crewmen held on tight. It was a long way down, and they were moving fast. It was as if the reindeer knew the way to shore all by themselves.

Soon they came within sight of land and alighted at the boundary of grass and snow. The reindeer seemed tired, so Santa turned them out to pasture. Five minutes later, they were contentedly chewing grass with no sign that they'd just flown across fifty miles of ocean with several sleighs full of sailors in tow.

The next day, the ship's carpenter made wheels for the sleighs, and the reindeer pulled them all the way home to Boston. They arrived just in time for Christmas, and to celebrate his safe return home, Santa and his men spent the holidays delivering presents to the needy children of Boston.

That was how Christmas got started, but it almost ended as quickly as it began. After the first Christmas, most of Santa's former crewmen returned to sailing. He could never gather and hand out all those presents alone, but he was serious about his promise, so he started looking for help.

"Where did he look?" Cubby asked.

I told him that Grandpa Santa had opened a bar on the Boston waterfront called the Sailor's Rest. In fact, it's still there today. Cubby and I visited it on a number of occasions. We sat beneath the famous lighted Budweiser sign and admired Santa's old whaling harpoon that hung in a place of honor above the cash register. He remembered that as I continued my story . . .

Seamen of all sorts frequented the Sailor's Rest. That was where Santa found the answer to his crew problems. They'd arrived by the greatest of good fortune on a cargo ship from Finland: elves. The Finns had been using elves as crew on their ships for years. The elves were small, so they could go places regular sailors couldn't. They didn't eat as much as full-size people either, and that made them less expensive to keep. Santa signed up an elvish crew and off he went!

He sure made a strange sight when he headed out for Christmas: a fat old sea captain on a sleigh pulled by reindeer with a pack of seedy-looking elves following in his wake, handing out presents everywhere they went. The kids loved him, and the grown-ups just stared in wonder and shock.

Santa's fame grew with every passing year. By the turn of the century, he had a team of one hundred elves, and he could barely keep up with all the deliveries. Santa kept his presents in a warehouse right behind Boston's Black Falcon Terminal. It was filled to the brim with toys the elves had liberated from ships that passed through the Port of Boston.

The demand for toys is one of those things that never stop growing. When I was a kid, we played with sticks and rocks, and we were glad to have them. By the time Cubby came along, it took a hundred dollars' worth of the latest toys just to keep a kid in a sandbox.

I don't know where parents would be if not for Santa. We sure are lucky his kids continued the Christmas tradition, even though the reindeer are only a memory. Years passed, and Donner, Blitzen, and the rest of the team got old and died. As they passed on, the memory of flight seemed to die with them. The younger reindeer didn't even have wing buds! By the turn of the century, reindeer didn't fly at all, but the original herd continued to grow, and there were more elves on the job every season.

Today Santa's great-great-grandson handles Christmas. He's no longer in Boston, because he had trouble with the law over all the toys in the Black Falcon warehouse. There were allegations that some might be stolen, and of course there was the matter of customs duty. To avoid those troubles, he moved to Rotterdam, the busiest seaport in the world. There, from his perch atop a container crane, he spends the entire summer unloading ships and picking off the very best toys from the shipping fleets of the world. He calls what he does "liberation for the children," while insurers write checks for theft and pilferage. Meanwhile, the elves stack the containers of toys and spend the whole year getting ready for an orgy of gift giving every December 25.

I wish I could have shown Cubby the reindeer, but they were all gone by the time he was born. Modern elves, I explained to him, deliver presents in plain white vans. We'd see them driving around as holiday season approached. It was nice to see elves at work, but it didn't feel the same. Two dwarves in a cargo van could never match the glory of costumed elves on a sleigh, even if they did have a full load of Pokémon cards or the best Yu-Gi-Oh! deck ever.

Once the season started, Cubby and I made a game of spotting which vehicles were driven by elves and which were just ordinary vans. Cubby could always pick them out, or so he believed. "Maybe we could rob them," he would suggest hopefully, as he imagined us hitting the Christmas jackpot. I always advised against it. Elves were cuddly, but armed dwarves were tough as nails. I warned him about that when we pulled up alongside one of their vans near my grandmother's house in Alabama. You didn't want to confuse jolly elves with vicious dwarves, especially at night.

"Look close," I told Cubby. "Check out the elves in that van. I'll bet they work for Santa. They must be delivering presents."

Cubby looked over and saw the same thing as me: featureless gray glass and plain white sides. Were there elves behind that glass? Who knew? He decided to agree, because after all, Dad always (sometimes) knows more. "Yeah," he said. "Elves. I wonder if they have anything for us."

Christmas was coming and we would soon find out. Grandpa John already had Cubby's stocking out. "Which do you think it will be, Cubby?" I asked him. "Lumps of coal or fun toys?"

Cubby glared at me. "Dad! Fun toys!"

18

THE OXBOW INCIDENT

The winter of Cubby's fifth year didn't come with much snow and ice. Sometimes that happened in New England. We had years when the ground was covered three feet deep, and others where the grass was green on New Year's Day. Cubby was too young to have much experience of winter, but I could already see that he liked clear ground for running and playing. Some kids liked huge snowfalls, but he wasn't one of them. He didn't want to crawl in deep snow or hide in snow castles. He wanted to run! That was something he did quite a lot of. He seemed to have two speeds, standby and full. He had yet to discover what older people call the middle range.

He began running around the moment he woke up, which was my signal to get him out of the house so Mom could rest. She liked going out with us sometimes, but by Sunday morning she was generally pretty tired from taking care of Cubby all week while I was at work. That meant we usually headed out alone. It was a boy and his dad, out for adventure.

I wasn't as much of a runner, and I knew both of us needed food to start our day. That led to a tradition of Sunday brunch, and we usually chose the same place. I am, after all, a creature of routine and habit, and he was too. So we would climb into my old white Rolls-Royce for the fifteen-minute drive to the Depot Restaurant.

I was real proud of that Rolls, and I loved to take Cubby places in it. Cubby liked it too, for the leathery smell and the soft lamb's-wool carpets. I'd bought it the year before, when a bank foreclosed on a real estate speculator and they put his car on the block. I'd won the car in a sealed bid auction and had fixed it in my spare time at work. The ten grand I bid was a lot of money for me at the time, but I borrowed it from a bank, not a loan shark, and I paid it off within a year.

My vintage Rolls was one of the first signs that I was finally making it. After all the money I'd lost, I sure felt I'd earned it. I was careful to keep that car hidden from my "partner" at work, because I knew he'd try to grab it for himself if he thought he could. Luckily, he went to Florida for the winter, so I had six months of relative freedom and I made the most of it.

You could get breakfast plenty of places, but we liked the Depot best. Other places served pancakes and omelets, or strange and exotic things like boar's snout with asparagus, but the Depot was the only place where you could get twenty strips of bacon and a plate of scrambled eggs. And then go back for more.

Anyone with a powerful desire to eat could appreciate a place like that. As soon as we parked, Cubby would start bouncing. I'd release the buckle on his seat and he'd pop up and shoot out the door. In just a matter of seconds he'd be a hundred feet away, running through the parking lot as fast as he could and yelling "Come on, Dad!" I always worried that someone would run him over, but luckily that never happened. A few kids are lost that way every year; I was glad mine was not one of them.

I'd round him up and lead him in the door, where there were enough distractions to keep him still for a little while. We usually started with the lobster tank. Cubby liked to make faces at the lobsters and watch as they snapped their little claws. (Most people just think of lobsters as dinner, but stick your finger in their tank, or mash your face against its side, and you find out pretty quick that they see us the same way—as food!) A few years before, the Depot had been a falling-down ruin, but a developer had restored it to a fine state of faux Victorian glory. There were new "antique" fixtures everywhere and a lot of exposed brick. Best of all, there was a sculpted steam locomotive protruding through the wall into the former lobby, which was now the dining room.

Right near the train they had installed a rope. When you pulled it, the train's steam whistle would sound. I never knew what ran that whistle, because there was no obvious source of steam, but it sounded a wonderful breathy hoot with every tug of the line. Cubby could not enter the restaurant without pulling the rope. Every time he did it, he'd grin and bounce. After two or three pulls, he'd be satisfied and allow the hostess to lead us to our table.

We liked the tables near the fireplace, and the hostesses came to know and accommodate us. We rewarded their treatment of us with regular tips, and by never starting a food fight, no matter how much some of the other diners tempted us.

I always felt like taking a nap after eating a big brunch, but Cubby was the opposite. He became even more energized. When that happened, I had a solution. I called it The Oxbow Run.

We'd head down Route 5 to Island Road, the dead-end street that led to the marina where we kept our old Sea Ray cabin cruiser. Even though there was never much traffic on Island Road, it was paved, so it was an ideal place to run. The road ran half a mile up the center of a horseshoe formed by a cutoff loop of the old Connecticut River. The modern river course ran straight, on the left side of Route 5, with the old Oxbow slowly silting in to the right. There were nine houses on the right and eight on the left. The Oxbow Marina was at the end.

When doing Cubby runs I always stopped in the same place—the little bend in the road alongside the first house. I'd let Cubby out and send him in front of the car. "Go, Cubby, go," I said, and off he went!

After all, I'd tell him, he had a tradition to uphold. I hadn't run in years because I'd hurt my knee, but I'd been pretty fast at his age. My dad had been a star on his high school track team thirty-some years earlier, and Grandpa Jack—for whom Cubby was named—had run against Olympic star Jesse Owens back in the 1930s. We had Jack's medals upstairs at home.

Cubby ran up the center of the road with me following close behind in the Rolls. I had to drive carefully so as not to run him over, but I preferred that to the risk that some other car would flatten him if I were not up close and tight, guarding him. I knew it looked strange, but it worked. The mass of my car protected Cubby from any rearward assault. And anyone driving in the opposite direction was a lot more likely to see us because my car was so much bigger and more visible than a kid alone.

Another benefit of following close in the car was speed measurement. The Rolls had a good speedometer marked with one-mile-per-hour graduations, so I could tell the difference between six, seven, or fifteen miles an hour. "Go, Cubby," I would yell. "You're only running eight miles an hour. A good horse can go almost fifty." Hearing that, Cubby would speed up. The more I ran him, the faster he got. He never attained the speed of a quarter horse or even a quick dachshund, but he still got to where he ran at a good clip, compared to most humans.

Most of our runs were uneventful, but one day we ran into trouble. Right before the marina there's a big meadow where kids gather on weekends for soccer tournaments. The moms lurk at the edges, shouting exhortations at their kids and egging them on. They are an aggressive bunch, often fighting with the coaches, and sometimes with each other. It was one of those female warriors who gave us trouble. She saw us and stormed into the road, blocking our further progress.

"What do you think you're doing, chasing that child with a car? You should be locked up!" Cubby looked at the renegade mom with curiosity and puzzlement. He didn't say anything—he was too shocked for words. I was pretty annoyed too. That wasn't the first time I'd been upbraided by some sanctimonious adult over my seemingly marginal parenting skills. People like that irritated me because they had no sense of sport, adventure, or rational risk assessment. And frankly, it was none of their damn business.

"I'm not chasing him. He's running, and I'm following."

"You're going to run him over," she said accusingly.

"You're nuts," I said patiently, "I'm protecting him with the car. Protecting him from crazies like you! Let's go, Cubby." With that, we swung ourselves and our car around her and ran the rest of the way to the marina.

The mom remained in the road, glaring, obstructing whatever traffic might come after us. She was about five feet tall, solid, belligerent, with short curly hair, big round glasses, and a self-righteous expression. She looked like the kind of person who sat on sharpened fence posts to stiffen her spine, and she remained in sight till we turned the corner at the marina building. I wondered briefly if she'd call the cops or cause us more trouble, but nothing else happened, and she was nowhere in sight by the time we left.

Cubby and I talked about the situation afterward, and we agreed, Little Bear would never have behaved like that. True, she wasn't crazy about Cubby running in the road, but she had a totally different solution to his excess energy: She enrolled him in a weekly gymnastics class.

That turned out to be a great idea. Our son was really wiry and strong, so many of the sport's moves came naturally to him. Cubby often resisted trying new things, but he had such a good time in the gym that he wanted more. We began taking him twice a week, and I even stuck around to watch him.

I was really proud of Cubby. I'd always been a clumsy kid, so seeing him on the balance beam, the rings, and the parallel bars was particularly impressive to me. He could balance perfectly on a beam, high above the floor, like a circus acrobat on the high wire. He could hang upside down from the rings and spin in a complete circle on the bars. "I could never do stuff like that," I told him, and he smiled happily. He was thrilled to be "better than Dad." His surprising prowess almost made me question my conviction that he learned just about all his skills by watching me.

In fact, Cubby did so well that the coach invited him to join his team and compete against other schools. That was a big deal, because the Hampshire team was one of the best in the region, and one of its founders had competed on the U.S. Olympic Team. Joining also meant he had to practice three days a week, and we wondered if he'd be up to that commitment. He was. Cubby attended every practice and got better and better. The team was led by Cal Booker, a great young coach who really liked my son. Cal spent a lot of time showing Cubby how to do the various moves, and his attention paid off. Cubby might not have been a superstar, but he became a solid member of the team and he traveled with them to competitions all over New England. Looking back, I have to agree with his mom. Compared to running down the road, gymnastics was a much better way to burn off his excess energy.

Best of all, the moms in attendance never yelled at me. They yelled at their kids instead.

19

THE OLD BOY

Cubby liked the people in his life, but he wanted more. There was a gerbil at day care, and he'd met a number of kids with pets. A few had cats, some had dogs, and one had a snake. He decided the answer for our family was a puppy, and he began agitating for one as soon as he turned five. Before agreeing to get one, I tested his intentions.

"Would we feed him fattening food and eat him when he got big?" I asked.

"No," Cubby squealed. "He would be a pet. You don't eat pets!"

I was encouraged that he understood that concept. He was actually downright indignant that I would suggest eating the dog, even though he had never had a pet of his own. I didn't want to eat our pet either, but I had to be sure he felt the same way. Pet care and protection must have been innate to his nature, because I was quite sure we'd never had a conversation about pet consumption before.

"What would you do with a dog?" I asked.

To my surprise, Cubby's answer was immediate. "He would be my friend! He would play with me." I wasn't sure if that was really true, but his thoughts were in the right place, so I continued.

What about feeding the pup? Cubby was very adamant. "I'll feed him and take care of him!" I doubted the truth of that, but Little Bear was gradually getting on board with the idea, and I knew that being a mom, she would do most of the work.

For his sixth birthday, Cubby's mom resolved to make it happen. I have asthma and I'm allergic to many pets, so we needed a hypoallergenic dog. I wasn't exactly sure how we would find such a thing, but Little Bear did some research and decided a poodle was the dog to get. I would have gone for a free critter from the local pound, but we found a kennel in Pennsylvania that had some purebreds for sale. "Dogs from a professional breeder are always better," she assured me, though neither of us had ever bought a dog before.

I knew about poodles because I had had one of my own as a toddler. My feelings about them were mixed. I'd liked mine well enough, but he'd bitten me more than once, and he'd once chewed a hole through my bedroom door. I knew poodles had sharp teeth, and I hoped whatever Little Bear brought back would be nicer than the dog I remembered.

After a two-day, four-state odyssey, Little Bear arrived home in time for Cubby's birthday. Our newest family member revealed himself to be a nasty cur that growled for no reason at all and bit at the slightest provocation. I would have demanded my money back, but Cubby was instantly delighted. Since he'd never had any experience with pets, he thought the pup was great. He named him Shenzi, after a character in *The Lion King*. Shenzi was white, with thick curly hair, a short straight tail, and a bad temper. He was occasionally friendly, but if you grabbed him too quickly or teased him, he bit hard. God help you if you approached too close with a stick or a vacuum cleaner.

Still, he became part of the family. Shenzi was like a bad-tempered uncle who snarled and spit when he was drunk, and tore up the place every now and then. We figured he was with us to stay, and we made the best of the situation. We kept at a safe distance when he was eating and learned to avoid the other things that set him off. He began accompanying us on walks and even traveling in the car at times. In fact, with the passage of time, he proved downright companionable, at least now and then. Cubby relished those moments, and we came to love him as one of our own.

One day, as Cubby was watching Shenzi wag his tail, I said, "You had a fine tail too, but we cut it off when you were little."

Cubby looked at me, unsure as to whether I was serious. He was often skeptical of what I said.

"I did not have a tail!" He usually responded to unappealing news with denial.

I decided to tell him the story. When he was born, I began, he had sported a very fine tail, half the length of his leg, covered in fine blond hair. He wagged it almost immediately. Cute as it was, I knew the tail would be trouble. Some kids have small tails, which they hide in their pants. A tail like his, though, was too big to be hidden. In olden days a great big tail had been a badge of honor, but in modern America kids with long tails ended up exiled to the safety of their parents' basements. If he appeared at school swishing a tail it would lead to teasing, and I didn't want that to happen.

So we had it taken off, I told him. It's a common operation; doctors do it all the time. The only problem was, his tail grew back. We had to take it off three times before it stopped regenerating.

With some kids, you can cut stuff off and it stays off. With other kids, it doesn't. I was glad it was just a tail and not a third ear. I didn't want Cubby to end up as a freak, or the subject of some B-grade documentary. When I was growing up, there had been a boy down the street with three eyes, and he'd spent his whole life in his uncle's attic, sorting old coins and making incredibly detailed drawings of the termites and carpenter ants that lived with him in the rafters. I'll bet he's still up there now, I told Cubby.

Cubby looked a little alarmed at that, but I continued my story because every child needs lessons on diversity. I didn't have a tail, and neither did Cubby's mom, I informed him, but his Grandpa Ed did. Tails were like that. Red hair was the same. They skipped generations. Cubby's grandpa had grown up during the Depression, so his parents didn't have much money. When his tail had grown back they'd just left it on, and he'd tucked it in his pants leg his whole life.

I explained to Cubby that there were other grown-ups with tails around us even at that moment. They were the people who never wore shorts, even in summer. Having a tail was embarrassing—a sign of poor upbringing. After all, even very poor people could take a sharp knife and trim their newborn babies' tails. So what kind of parent left a kid to grow up with a tail and get teased and harassed?

Most people never knew Cubby's grandpa had a tail. But we'd sometime stop by his house at night, and he'd be sitting there in his underwear, and the tail was plain to see. It stuck out just above the waistband of his underwear—thick, leathery, and covered with black tarry spots at the end because of his work as a paving contractor. Even when it was tucked into his pants, the tail would get tarry whenever he walked on fresh blacktop and his boots sank in. And you couldn't miss the tail when he'd been drinking, because he'd swish it from side to side when he got tipsy. If he got really drunk, he could even break furniture with the thing. Luckily, that didn't happen too often.

Cubby nodded in quiet agreement. The whole thing made a strange kind of sense. He wondered who else he knew with a tail. He liked the Old Boy, but he was never quite sure what to make of him.

When Cubby was little he would crawl over and try to pick tar off the tail the way you'd pick a scab. I reminded him of that, but he claimed he didn't remember. Usually the Old Boy didn't even notice, but sometimes he'd feel something and slap his tail on the floor, shaking the house and rattling the furniture. He seemed to do it unconsciously. He'd be talking and all of a sudden the tail would smack the floor. At first I thought the tail had a mind of its own, but then I realized it was like a fellow swatting a mosquito on his arm while he was talking to you. Whatever the reason, it scared Cubby, and he learned to snatch his fingers away fast if the Old Boy swished the tail.

The Old Boy never let his tail out in public, but sometimes at home he'd do things like hold the door with his tail, and if he tripped he'd quickly swish the tail to regain his balance. It was useful enough that I never understood why kids teased each other over such a useful appendage. It seemed kind of sad and wasteful that the rest of us had to have our tails cut off. I guess it was just one of the things grown-ups do. They cut the tails off Doberman pinschers too. Stuff like that sounded nutty to me as a kid, and some still doesn't make sense today.

Unfortunately, our good times with the Old Boy came to a sad end when Cubby was six. Grandpa Ed got sick while he was at his cabin in the Maine woods, miles from anywhere. Something started hurting inside him, he became weak, and he developed a scary 105-degree fever. When his wife finally got him to a hospital, his body was dangerously overheated and his heart was erratic. The doctors discovered he had a burst appendix, and they had to operate right away.

It's shocking how suddenly something like that can come on. The last time we'd seen him, he'd been in fine fettle, but in the space of only two days, he moved from fishing in his backyard to fighting for his life in intensive care. Alice couldn't even bring him home, because he was too sick to move. Little Bear raced to visit him in the hospital as we stayed home, waiting for news. The operation might have saved his intestines, but we'll never know, because his heart stopped for a few fateful minutes. They got the heart going again, but his brain wave was a flat line. He never awoke.

He died a few hours after Little Bear arrived. She didn't think he even recognized her. His eyes were wide open, but there was not even a flicker of recognition. "It was like gazing into the eyes of a cow; there was no sign of my father in there," she told me afterward.

The funeral was a few days later, in Granby. It was the first time someone close to Cubby had died. I don't know if he fully understood what had happened, but he knew his grandpa wasn't there anymore, and it made him sad. His mom was even sadder, though we tried our best to comfort her.

With the Old Boy gone, Little Bear did not have any close relatives in the area. Her mom lived in Florida, so we saw her once a year at most. She had divorced the Old Boy when we were teenagers and married a retired Canadian Mountie. They had moved south long before Cubby was born, so he never had the chance to know her the way he did her dad. She came to visit every summer, but she didn't really play a starring role in the raising of Cubby. And my brother had moved to San Francisco.

It was just Little Bear, me, and my mom and dad.

20

THE POWER OF WIZARDS

One Sunday morning as we drove through Amherst, Cubby made an unexpected and disturbing discovery. "Look, Dad, a stone kid!" He was bouncing up and down and pointing. I looked at the object across the road. There was indeed a stone kid standing at the end of a driveway, right there on Red Gate Lane. He was light gray, frozen in position, with a lantern in his outstretched hand.

I slowed down so we could get a good look at him as we passed. Like many kids his age, Cubby was familiar with Transformer toys. He knew superhero action figures could change into rocket cars or even bizarre animals, so the idea that a kid could turn into something else was not totally alien to him. Even so, it was unsettling. How had such a thing happened? To my adult eye, the answer was obvious.

"There must be wizards in that house," I said. "And I'm sure the kid did something very bad."

"Yeah," Cubby said, with a worried edge in his voice. What other explanation could there be? I remember wondering the very same thing myself. When I was his age, I saw the dinosaur skeletons in Philadelphia's Franklin Institute, and heard how they had once been alive, millions of years in the past. Then they had died and turned into stone. They were scary, because you could see right through them and they looked fierce and unnatural. I had bad dreams about dinosaurs for a long time.

Then I saw stone people, and stone animals guarding the entrances to the museum. I wondered how long it had been since they were alive too. I wondered why they still looked like kids and animals, while the dinosaurs inside were just skeletons. I concluded they must be newer, and possibly friendlier too. I never had bad dreams about stone kids. But I sure did wonder about how they came to be the way they were. It wasn't until years later, when I read about magic, that I learned the answer.

"I wonder what that kid did to aggravate the wizards? Do you think they will turn him back into a kid or just leave him stone forever?" Cubby looked concerned, but I was quick to reassure him. "We're in a car, and there are no stone cars in sight. So I'm sure we're safe as long as we don't go any closer to the house."

I could see that the idea of being turned to stone was troubling to Cubby, so I comforted him with a story from my own life. "When I was your age a wizard turned me into a dog for two weeks. I ate a squirrel and it was tasty, but mouse made me gag. Being a dog was kind of fun because I could run really fast and even bite strangers!" Cubby grinned at that, even though the idea of eating raw squirrel was sort of repugnant.

"If I was a dog, I'd bite *you*!" he exclaimed. Cubby was nothing if not spunky. He asked why the wizard had turned me into a dog, and I admitted I'd thrown rocks at his house. Cubby was glad he had not done anything to provoke the wizards on Red Gate Lane.

The idea of Dad as a dog lasted until we got home. Cubby trotted over to his mom and asked, "Did my dad really turn into a dog when he was a kid?" Little Bear was used to Cubby's strange questions. She knew that our reality sometimes differed from hers.

"I don't think your dad was ever a dog," she said slowly.

That was the problem with Little Bear. I would tell Cubby something, and she would contradict me. For some reason, Cubby would believe her. That really bothered me. Cubby had no way to know which of us was right. I told him a nice story about my life as a dog. I filled it with fun tidbits like eating the squirrel, playing outside, and chasing children. My story was well thought through and eminently believable. In contrast, all his mother said was, "Your dad was never a dog," and he chose her over me. Just like that, my careful creation went up in smoke.

But no matter what his mother said about me as a dog, the stone kid remained. You could say what you wanted about me, but the stone kid stood there, mute testament to the power of sorcery. Cubby believed in the stone kid because he was tangible and real, and he had to have come from somewhere. An older kid might have assumed that an object like the stone kid had emerged from a concrete mold, but to a five-year-old, sorcery is an easier explanation to grasp than the operation of a factory.

"It's a shame we live in a different school district. If that kid had been in your school, we'd probably know who he was. I wonder why his parents don't try and change him back. Maybe he's a stray, without any parents. Or maybe the wizard made them into frogs."

"Yeah," Cubby said slowly. He always watched that house closely whenever we passed by. I could see he was thinking about the Stone Kid and what he might have been and done.

A few months later, Cubby changed schools and we didn't pass the stone kid too often anymore. With time, he faded from both of our memories, but the idea never really left us. After all, the world was a big place. There must have been other sorcerers out there, turning kids into rock. And what about pets? Dogs and cats could be even more annoying than children. Surely there were fields full of solidified animals out there somewhere. Cubby and I talked about the possibility whenever we saw evidence of sorcery in someone else's yard. We decided it was one of those mysteries best left unsolved.

I found some of the stone kid's cousins when Cubby was eight. They were just two hours from our home, in Rhode Island.

Every Father's Day, I go to the Newport Car Show. It's a very pretty event, set on the grounds of Portsmouth Abbey, with a few hundred classic cars parked on the grass overlooking Narragansett Bay. Most years, Cubby went with me. But every now and then, he was disagreeable and objected, and I ended up in Newport without him, free to graze and explore. It was one of those years.

The car show had ended, so I headed for the waterfront. There were always interesting things to see down there, especially at the ship chandler's and the nautical bookstore. I was walking the alleys off Thames Street when I turned a corner and stopped short. There in front of me, behind a low iron fence, stood a herd of alligators, bears, and other fierce creatures. Stone children stood among them, little herdsmen frozen in time.

I approached slowly and encountered a sign. Aardvark Art, it said. I looked down, and as far as I could see, I was surrounded by reptiles and beasts with mouths agape, ready to devour me or at least tear off large chunks of me for their eating pleasure. I reached down to pet the nearest beast. Its skin was cool and a bit rough. Some were metal, others were stone. I looked for the wizard; I had to have one for Cubby and me.

After a brief negotiation and a small scuffle with a merchant who was busy turning a large pot of frogs into bronze paperweights, a four-foot alligator was purchased and loaded into the back of my Range Rover. The snout was concealed beneath the load space cover, but the tail curled upward and was plainly visible just inside the rear window. I headed home, beast in back, to pick up Cubby. When I arrived, Cubby climbed into the Rover without noticing the tail sticking up in back.

I quickly apprised him of the new situation. "Cubby, I got us a pet alligator. I found a wizard in Rhode Island who turns animals to metal. They said he will stay metalized, but you never know with these wizards and demons. He might come back to life, so don't go grabbing him. And let me know if you see the tail moving, because that means he's waking up." Cubby turned around and caught sight of the tail. His eyes got a bit wider, but I was quick to reassure him. "As long as he's metal, he's no more likely to bite than any of your other metal toys." That must not have been reassuring enough, because his gaze remained locked on the tail all the way to our house.

When we got home, I opened the tailgate and prepared to lift out the alligator. Even in its metallic state, it was heavy. "He probably ate something big just before the wizards caught him." Cubby seemed to accept my explanation, but he remained wary.

"Dad! Watch the teeth!" Cubby warned me whenever I got close to the snout, which was frozen into what alligators probably think of as a welcoming toothy smile, ready to snap my arm off if he should wake unexpectedly. We got the gator settled in alongside the house. Cubby would not tolerate having it inside, but he gradually came to accept it among the rocks and bushes outdoors. The longer it stayed in one place, the more confident Cubby became about the metalization spell.

Within a few months, he began taking friends out back to see the alligator. They developed a ritual. He called it Pet the Teeth. He was very proud of himself for being brave enough to stick his little paws right up by the metal beast's mouth without getting them snapped off. Other children weren't so sure, but he reassured them, just as I had.

"It's usually okay," he told them. "He hardly ever eats kids."

21

BECOMING OWNERS

I was glad to have taught Cubby a healthy respect for wizards, but it was equally important that he learn to respect heavy machinery. Either one had the power to squash him like a bug if he made a wrong move. One way to teach him that lesson was by going railroading. There is no mistaking the power and grandeur of a string of heavy diesel freight engines as they thunder ahead of a hundred loaded freight cars.

My relationship with railroads began when I was four. That's when my dad took me to see the giant Baldwin locomotive in the basement of the Franklin Museum. The sight of that huge black engine would have terrified many kids, but I was entranced. There it sat, dominating everything else in the room. Seven hundred thousand pounds of steel. Thirteen feet high and eighty-eight feet long. It was the most impressive sight I had ever seen.

My dad lifted me up into the cab, where I grabbed hold of the controls and imagined the big steam engine moving under my command. I worked the levers and watched the boiler gauge as I rolled the engine out of the station, huffing and puffing and blowing the whistle at every crossing. It's been fifty years, but I can still remember the feel of the big throttles and the sound of the engineer—really a museum worker—as he told me, "Watch the water gauge! If it drops too low, you'll have a boiler explosion!" That was the beginning of a lifelong love of trains, and a wariness of high-pressure boilers and indeed anything under pressure in a big steel vessel.

Could I find some trains for Cubby? I wondered . . .

Steam locomotives were long gone by the time he was born, but Conrail ran its big GE diesels right through Springfield every day. In fact, they had a terminal less than twenty miles from our house.

"Cubby," I said one day, "would you like to go see some trains?" "Yeah," he said, bouncing a good six inches off the floor with excitement. So we climbed into the car and headed south for Springfield. All the way, Cubby asked me about trains. What did they do? What did they look like? Could he drive one? Could he take one home to keep? I realized Cubby did not have a good grasp of what we were about to see. Some things are just beyond imagining, especially for a toddler.

Rolling down Memorial Avenue, we could see the train yard to our right, running for half a mile alongside the road, filled with hundreds of boxcars, tank cars, gondolas, and even rail cars loaded with new automobiles. They call those auto-racks.

Unfortunately, seeing was not the same as entering. Try as we might, I could not find an entrance to drive an automobile into the yard. Yet I knew there must be a way in, because I could see workmen walking around, working on the trains. We finally spotted the entrance, across from the Big E Fairgrounds. We drove into the yard, bounced over some unused tracks, and parked next to a dirty gray shed.

We had found our train yard. Right in front of us, two engines rumbled at idle. "Those are smaller switchers they use to move cars here in the yard," I explained. Beyond them, on the long track out of the yard, five enormous GE mainline locomotives sat waiting. "Those engines have over three thousand horsepower apiece.

They'll need five of them to get a heavy westbound train over the Berkshire Mountains." Cubby was impressed.

Over the next few years, we visited the West Springfield yard more times than I can remember. We made friends with the train boss, who presided over the yard from his perch in the shed. Engineers and workmen would come and go as Cubby watched close and said little. In time, he became something of a mascot to the guys in the yard, and they let him have the run of the place. Cubby was very safety conscious, never once losing a leg or even the tip of a finger. He knew trains could flatten quarters like pieces of paper. That was enough to keep him well clear of the wheels and tracks and do his watching from a safe distance.

One day we were watching the men move cars around the yard when the engineer stopped his big diesel right next to Cubby and climbed down. "Would you like to drive the engine?" he asked. Cubby grinned and leaped straight up the ladder and into the cab. The engineer explained the engine's controls. Cubby listened closely, and in a moment he was ready. Cubby and the engineer moved the reverser lever forward, released the air brake with a hiss, and pushed the throttle forward a step. With a rumble and a clank, the locomotive began to move. Cubby wiggled his ears and looked out the window. He was driving a train!

With me as a passenger, Cubby and the engineer moved freight cars between the main yard and a siding in East Springfield. Our trip took us back and forth across the Connecticut River and through the Amtrak commuter terminal. We waved at the passengers and Cubby blew the horn. It was quite an adventure.

Now our appetites were stoked for even grander adventures in locomotion. We began to wonder: Were there more train yards out there that we could see? Maybe bigger or better ones? We had driven past some huge rail terminals during our journeys to Boston and New York, but they were surrounded by fences and guarded by police. They weren't open, like West Springfield yard. We needed a way in.

In fact, we needed a way into more than just train yards. We needed an entrée into all the facilities where good things happened: quarries, nuclear power plants, and even the Boston seaport. All those places were full of machinery and fascinating things happened inside, but ordinary people could not get in to watch. Somehow we had to become something other than ordinary.

The answer hit me out of the blue one day: We would become owners. Owners cannot be refused admission or thrown out. Owners are not trespassers and they are certainly not ordinary. They are a class unto themselves. I explained it all to Cubby. "You have the general public," I said, "and then you have the owners. Owners get to go inside and see all the neat stuff, because they own it."

Cubby understood my solution immediately, and together we conceived a plan. We would buy stock, beginning with railroads. People who own stock are called stockholders, and *stockholder* is just another word for . . . owner. I had a few stockbrokers as customers at work, so I called one and asked what shares of our local railroad might cost. The answer shocked me. I could buy a piece of Conrail for less than one hundred dollars! Being a big spender, I immediately bought ten shares in Cubby's name. The certificates arrived a few weeks later, along with a whole bunch of printed material expostulating on the performance of the railroad. Our railroad. Cubby couldn't read any of it, but he certainly admired the pictures. He immediately spotted some key differences between the images in the brochure and observed reality in the West Springfield yard.

"Those trains are cleaner than ours!" Even at that age, he recognized advertising spin.

"Yes," I explained, "they photographed specially cleaned and detailed engines for the reports. Our West Springfield yard is filled with dirty workingmen's engines."

Cubby thought about that a minute, and said, "I'll bet they have cleaner engines in the big-city yards. Let's go see them!"

That Sunday, we set out to test our new status. Armed with our investor package, we headed for Boston. Our destination was Conrail's Allston container yard, a location we had previously been turned away from by gruff railroad policemen. "Things will be different this time," I told Cubby. "Now we're owners. Watch what happens." Cubby studied the annual report as we rolled down the turnpike toward Boston.

Having previously been refused admission in an ordinary car, we were returning in style, in our white Rolls-Royce. I was very proud of that car, and it showed. The dash was done in fine burl walnut and the upholstery was soft black leather. No mere carpets for our car—the woolen carpets were covered in fine sheepskin overlays, softer than any blanket. The engine was smooth and silent, moving the car with unmistakable grandeur. My Silver Shadow was thirty years old; a grand dame of automobiles. I was especially proud that I'd gotten her at auction for less than most people spend on a Kia.

You get a lot more respect in a Rolls-Royce than you do in a regular car, no matter who you are. You may look the same, but when you step into that car, the world sees you differently. The car says you belong, that you're not a trespasser. I was counting on that to get us by the guards at the gate.

Just as I suspected, my idea worked like a charm. We rolled smoothly and silently right past the stunned gate guard, giving him a polite wave of acknowledgment as we passed, motored serenely into the yard, and parked next to the operations center. I unfastened Cubby from his car seat and we climbed out of our vehicle. The gate guard had followed us in, at a polite distance. I turned to him and said, "My son is a stockholder. Could you perhaps find someone to show him the facilities?"

With those words, all the bluster and authority evaporated from the lawman. Instead of challenging our presence in the yard, he became what you might call cautiously deferential. He led us to the office, then he went to find someone with greater authority.

In most places, the police work for the government. Not there. The railroad is one of the few places where you'll find gun-toting cops who work for the company, which in this case was the Consolidated Railway Company—Conrail. And since we were owners (stockholders) of the company, that meant the railroad police worked for us. More specifically, they worked for Cubby, as he actually owned the stock.

If you are a wise employee, you do not threaten the boss, even if he drives up unannounced and asks for a tour. If the boss looks a little weird, like maybe he's just three feet tall, you do not make jokes or snicker. Not if you want to keep your job. This fellow knew what to do.

He returned a moment later with the general manager of the yard, who knelt down very seriously and ceremoniously and shook Cubby's hand. He shook my hand too. He asked Cubby how much stock he owned, and Cubby smiled enigmatically. Was it ten shares or a million? He wasn't telling. The manager commented politely on the finish of my Rolls-Royce, which sat next to a row of Conrail pickup trucks and an old Mazda sedan. I thanked him for complimenting my paint and refrained from explaining that I'd done it all myself. As my grandfather had taught me, it's sometimes better to look dumb and rich than poor and resourceful. I also refrained from suggesting that I had probably bought my car for less than our railroad had paid for the Chevy pickup parked next to it. Such are the benefits of being a skilled mechanic with friends in banking.

"This yard has an excellent safety record. It's one of the best run in New England." The manager was clearly proud of his operation, and as an owner, Cubby was naturally happy to hear that. "We'd be honored to see the place for ourselves," I told him. He gave us hard hats and we embarked on our tour. But first our guide ducked into the office for a moment.

In a display of prudence and wisdom, the manager hedged his bets by handing Cubby a Reese's Cup, which my son accepted with the slightest of nods and all the dignity of a potentate. As Cubby chewed, he followed us on a memorable and detailed tour of the trains, tracks, and supporting machinery. We particularly enjoyed seeing the loading and unloading facilities, especially the container cranes in action. Those articulated monsters took containers from the backs of trucks and set them onto special railcars. "We're very proud of our new intermodal terminal," he said, as we both nodded in agreement.

Cubby enjoyed seeing the newest GE locomotives parked on a siding. As he observed, they were the same model as the ones in the annual report, but a little dirtier. Big engines like those passed through Springfield without stopping most days. These are neat, he said, with wonder and admiration. And best of all, they were his, thanks to ten shares of stock. Knowing that, I was glad the engines were so large. Otherwise, he would have asked to take one home and I don't know where we would have put it.

Cubby was impressed by that day, on many levels. First of all, he enjoyed seeing new things, and the Boston rail terminal was full of new and exciting stuff. But more than that, he was impressed by the idea that we could gain control of it all with a simple phone call to a stockbroker. Luckily for me, he had not yet mastered the telephone, so I retained some measure of control.

Once we were home, I investigated other places we might go, and how to buy their stocks too. Before long, we owned Northeast Utilities and all the power plants and power lines of New England. We also acquired Mobil Oil, American President Lines, and by extension, many big buildings and most of the cool ships in Boston Harbor. We even purchased United Airlines. For a few thousand dollars, we were on top of the world, and we made the most of it.

Many doors were opened for us. It may be hard to imagine in today's world of terror threats and hypersecurity, but in those days trains, trucks, ships, and planes were mostly out in the open, and anyone could walk up and check them out. So that's what we did.

We toured the Port of Boston, where Santa's father had worked a container crane. Across the harbor, we visited the big Boston Edison coal-fired power plant. We saw the mountains of coal, some of which would be burned for power and some of which would be given to children for Christmas. We went into mines, quarries, and all sorts of places we didn't belong. But thanks to our stock ownership and our antique Rolls-Royce, we remained safe. Never once was Cubby greeted with anything other than the greatest politeness.

Sometimes we'd go west, to watch the trains cross the Berkshires on their way to New York and beyond. It was exhilarating to stand by the tracks as five or even six huge locomotives thundered past us at full throttle, pulling heavy trains over the mountains. After the trains had gone, we often stopped off to see Grandpa John and GrandMargaret. They lived about five miles apart, just ten miles from the famous Hoosac Tunnel. Each of them kept toys and treats on hand for Cubby, and they were always glad to see him.

When Cubby got a little older, Conrail was bought by CSX, an even bigger railroad. The locomotives changed color, and the railroad got a more corporate feel. Many of the old-timers we knew at West Springfield retired or moved on. By then, though, we didn't care. Cubby had also moved on, to new friends and hobbies. We still have the memories, and the money we made from the stock came in handy years later when Cubby developed more expensive interests.

CUBBY VERSUS THE SCHOOL

Cubby always dreaded going back to school after our adventures. When I tried to unravel the reason, I came up short. Finally I asked him if the problem was the other kids, and he said, "Dad, I show them things and they make fun of me." That was such a sad answer. He was never bullied or beat up, but he was isolated. Hearing him made me remember how I'd been teased for knowing the answers when I was his age.

Kids shouldn't hate school, especially kindergarten and first grade.

I recalled a day he was at the museum, looking at dinosaurs. A mom and her son walked by Cubby as he gazed up at a large fossilized creature. Directing her own child's attention to the skeleton, the mom said, "Look, a triceratops!" Cubby's eyes moved from the dinosaur to her and then to the little boy. He looked back at the mom and said, "It's not a triceratops. It's a protoceratops. See, it's much smaller and it only has one horn. Triceratops has three."

He was right, of course. But when you're a kid, being right doesn't make you a superstar. Sometimes it just earns you a reputation as a know-it-all. I learned that the hard way. I wondered if that was one of his problems now. What do you say to a smart kid? Act ignorant? Be quiet? It didn't seem fair.

Firing off too many right answers or not fitting in weren't the issues we heard about from Cubby's teachers, though. "Jack doesn't do his assignments," they said. "He plays, and gets distracted, and when he does do the work, his answers are mostly wrong. He's just not trying." His mom and I saw him flounder and get things wrong, but we also saw his pain at failing, and we knew he was trying his best. We just didn't know how to help him focus and succeed.

Cubby's challenges stood in sharp contrast to his gifts. For example, he had an extraordinary memory; he could watch a movie once and parrot it back to us word for word. My brother, Augusten, has that same ability, and it had helped him to establish a very successful career in advertising. (Today everyone knows my brother as the author of *Running with Scissors,* but back then he was just a guy in an ad agency, his first book still a few years in the future.)

"He'll be fine," my brother reassured me. "You dropped out of school in tenth grade and I quit school before that. We ended up okay. He will too." As much as I appreciated my little brother's reassurance, I sometimes confused his carefree attitude with irresponsibility. After all, I was the one with the kid, and I wanted Cubby to do his schoolwork, get good grades, and graduate with honors. Those were three things my brother and I had never accomplished.

There was no mistaking the way certain things we took for granted totally passed our Cubby by. Reading was the most obvious example. We didn't know why, but he just didn't get it. Both his mom and I had been exceptional readers from a very early age, so our son's difficulty was a real mystery to us. He just didn't seem to be connecting with the words on the page, and from first grade to third grade it only went downhill.

His first-grade teacher wasn't much help. After watching our son struggle to read for the first half of the school year, she looked at him and said, "I guess you just can't read." And that was that. He didn't read in school for the next two years.

Writing was even worse. He had terrible difficulty forming letters and shaping them into words. His handwriting was jagged, rough, and barely legible. That, too, was a sharp contrast to my own remembered childhood. When I was his age, I spent hours at my desk writing out page after page of exercises in flowing cursive script. When I wrote block letters they were as carefully formed as if they'd been typeset. Cubby, in contrast, could barely print his own name and he couldn't write script at all.

Was the school failing him? There is always a temptation to blame your kid's failure on his teachers, or even on the school system. We weren't sure. There was also the possibility that his performance was not really that bad; maybe our own memories of reading and writing were distorted. Perhaps we just weren't as great as we liked to remember.

Cubby's teachers scuttled that idea for us. They didn't know anything about either of us, but they did see how our son performed relative to his peers, and that was not encouraging. Neither his reading nor his writing was at grade level. The worst part was, they didn't know what to do either. They just reported what they saw.

Meanwhile, other educators saw our son differently. Cubby often accompanied his mom to the university, and her professors got to know him pretty well. "He's got a rare intellect," her adviser told her when Cubby was just seven. Indeed, he could solve shape puzzles as quickly as her professors. Why couldn't his elementary school see that?

Things got worse as the school year unfolded. The teachers wrote out assignments on the blackboard and he ignored them, or copied an incomprehensible jumble on his page. Little Bear and I could see what he was doing wrong, but neither of us knew why. His teachers believed he was deliberately uncooperative, because he understood many complex concepts with no trouble at all. He was way ahead of the other kids in math. And his vocabulary was nothing short of extraordinary. When he failed to do simpler things, what could they think except that he was obstinate? Smoke curled from my ears when they expressed that sentiment. I recalled all too well my own teachers saying the same things about me. They hadn't been true, and Little Bear and I suspected they weren't true about our kid either. We were sure of only one thing: Cubby was not deliberately refusing to do his work. He wanted to do well. Luckily, he had Mom on his side, because I was too frustrated to be effective. She was a tireless advocate for our son, insisting the teachers find out why he was struggling. Finally, the school agreed to test him in an effort to determine exactly what was going on.

We started with the school psychologist. By a strange twist of fate, she'd taught Little Bear many years before and was now charged with evaluating our son. She said it was plain that Cubby had a reading problem, but she did not believe Cubby was "slow." Cubby was able to solve complex problems, and everyone who heard him speak agreed that his command of language was extraordinary for his age. The psychologist seemed stumped about the cause of the problem. All she could recommend was more testing.

That was the last thing the school wanted to hear, because they had to pay for the evaluations. As far as we could tell, they preferred to simply label Cubby stupid or obstinate. But since the psychologist told them Cubby had a reading problem, they were stuck. Public schools have a legal obligation to make education accessible to kids who are impaired or have learning disabilities. The two things they don't have an obligation to remediate are "dumb" and "stubborn," so that's what they wanted him to be.

To us, it was the school administrators who seemed stubborn and obstinate. Getting them to pay for a first-rate evaluation of our son, as the law required them to do, proved very difficult. In fact, it was one of Little Bear's greatest challenges as a parent. As they dragged their feet, the school year passed and his grades got worse and worse. Richer parents might have paid out of pocket for the testing, which was quite expensive, but we were barely making ends meet, so we were forced to wait for the school district to live up to its obligation. Some parents in our situation take the school district to court. Others give up on public education and homeschool their kids. It's a shabby state of affairs that's come about because our society hasn't given schools the money to do what needs to be done.

Finally, as Little Bear got ready to take them to court, the district agreed to pay for testing. But by then we had lost faith in the capacity of our local school to educate Cubby. We held the school district to its obligation to pay for tests, but we withdrew Cubby from public school. Little Bear had been looking into alternatives for several months and had settled on a Montessori school in Amherst. She was very impressed by the staff and its teaching method. Even better, the school had a sliding scale of fees, which made it affordable for us.

Cubby embraced the relaxed environment right away. The South Hadley school was huge, and filled with unfriendly people with formal-sounding names: Mr. Parker, Miss Williams, Dr. Halpern. At Amherst Montessori, his new teacher knelt down, took his hand, and said, "Hi, I'm Julie, and this is my assistant, Karen," and he smiled at her right away. We knew that we'd found a place our little boy would feel happy and safe. Finally, our son liked going to school.

The first step, though, was to take Cubby to the Yale Child Study Center in New Haven for his evaluation. It took a number of visits over a three-month period for the doctors there to make their assessment, but in the end they painted the first clear picture of what Cubby could and could not do. No one had done that for us before, at least not in a comprehensive way. They showed us how he differed from other kids his age, and where his strengths and weaknesses lay. They didn't give a name to Cubby's differences, and they didn't call him disabled. They just identified his difficulties and suggested strategies to help him improve.

That was a real eye-opener. For me, the biggest surprise was the difference between how Cubby processed what he saw versus what he heard. To demonstrate, the psychologist drew a tic-tac-toe board on a blackboard and asked Cubby to copy what she was doing. To my surprise, Cubby couldn't do it. He looked back and forth from the blackboard to his paper, struggled visibly, and finally got it wrong. I didn't understand how that could happen. It was a simple grid.

And it didn't end there. When the psychologist filled in the Xs and Os and asked him to follow her lead, Cubby did that wrong too! With nine boxes to fill in, Cubby was seeing top left on the blackboard yet marking a totally different box on paper.

His mom wondered if Cubby's difficulty with this task was a sign of dyslexia, but the psychologist's answers just confused me. "Dyslexia is a very broad term," she said. "It can mean many different things, like reading words backward, recognizing shapes as letters, or not being able to make sense of the words. We want to be more specific about where your son has trouble."

Cubby could follow spoken instructions with no problem. The psychologist could hand him a sheet of paper and say, "Draw a tic-tac-toe board," and he'd do it correctly. She could say, "Put an X in the top right box," and he'd get that right every time too. What went wrong in Cubby's head when she drew on the blackboard instead of talking to him?

My mind kept circling back to another of the Yale evaluator's comments: He said Cubby had "near-normal" intelligence, which I took as a euphemism for "not very smart." Good as Cubby was with puzzles, language, and math, I could not help worrying that maybe the evaluator was right. He was, after all, the professional, and I imagined every parent was sure their kid was a genius even though logic tells us most are not. How does a parent distinguish marginal intelligence from a learning disability? I'm sure the answer would be obvious today, especially to a special education professional, but it was not at all evident to me.

Cubby was such a study in contrasts. He could barely read, and he couldn't write. Yet he solved math riddles intuitively, with nothing more than a brief introduction to the problem. That was obvious when Julie handed him a trinomial cube. The cube is one of the puzzles Montessori uses to help children master the skills of solving algebraic and numerical equations. It can be very difficult and frustrating for children to put together, so they're introduced to it very slowly.

Not Cubby. Julie introduced him to the puzzle one morning soon after he started at Montessori. His eyes never left the cube when she took it apart and told him to put it together. She looked away for a few minutes, not expecting anything much to happen. When she looked back a few minutes later, it was sitting solved on the table.

Seeing his interest, she showed him the second step of the process. He figured that out in a matter of minutes too. Finally, she began making random algebraic equations with the cube, and he solved them all, as if it were an entertaining game. In the space of twenty minutes, he mastered a puzzle that takes most kids an entire year to learn.

But he couldn't read or write. Yet. That was looking like a major problem.

There were times when I wondered whether Cubby was like the Peter Sellers character in the movie *Being There*—a fellow who was totally illiterate and uneducated, but still gets tapped to run for president of the United States because he's sweet, polite, and nods sagely at the right moments.

As I worried that my son might be on the borderline of intellectual disability in some areas, another evaluator revealed how Cubby concealed his comprehension problems. "He's very good at changing the subject away from something he has trouble with or doesn't want to do. He's also very stubborn," he said. This cheered me greatly; Cubby's skill at distracting us sounded like another sign of intelligence. I had described him as a future barrister on more than one occasion.

Before Yale, I had assumed Cubby was just strong willed. It was extremely difficult to make him do chores like cleaning his room or cleaning up his dishes. Larger-scale tasks like raking the yard were well-nigh impossible. Those weren't things that appealed to a kid, but they had to be done. We were never surprised when he resisted and tried to divert us; we knew we just had to persist and make him do the work.

When he showed the same kind of resistance to reading a book for school, I assumed the reason was the same—that he just wanted to play and do what he wanted. Now I understood that he resisted reading because it was hard for him and he didn't want us to know. Until that day, his behavior around books hadn't made sense. He said he liked books, but when I set one in front of him, he'd put it aside as if he wasn't interested. Yet he loved hearing us read to him. I had never understood how he could love the stories yet show no interest in reading them himself. It had never occurred to me that he was being obstreperous or acting indifferent to hide weaknesses.

I still didn't know how he came to be that way, since I read encyclopedias at his age and his mom was a better reader than me. Was it genetics, dropping him on his head, or something he ate? That was one of those questions that just never got answered. Eventually, I concluded that knowing he had the problem was enough. The why didn't really matter.

With all the testing the Yale people did, no one looked at his social skills. If they had, I am sure the psychologists would have diagnosed him with Asperger's syndrome. Looking back, his social ineptitude, his rigidity, and his unusual special interests make it pretty obvious. Yet at the time the word *Asperger's* was barely in the medical lexicon and no one thought to test for it in the context of his school problems. My own diagnosis was still a few years in the future, and Cubby's diagnosis would not come till some years after my own. But it didn't matter. The name wasn't what would help us to help him. What we needed was insight into where he was struggling and how we could support him in those areas. The Yale specialists did a fine job with that, and his mom and I will always be grateful.

Little Bear took the Yale results to the Montessori school and reviewed them carefully with his teachers. The Montessori staff nodded in agreement at some things in the report, while other findings came as a surprise. It had only been a month, but already our son was happy in school and doing well. For the first time, he was excited about going to class. He made friends with the younger kids at school, and they all looked up to him. Inspired by my example, he told them stories about Gorko, Zeke, Pete, adding his own twist: penguins. I'd made up Gorko, and now he invented Fishy, the King of the Penguins. He might have struggled with school, but he was already learning to entertain his classmates.

Once we knew a little more about Cubby's difficulties we saw him in a whole new light. I was relieved; I'd been afraid they would find some kind of major cognitive impairment. To me, a mere reading challenge was nothing. Of course, Cubby still had to solve the problem. We could help, but he was the one who had to overcome the visual problems and learn to read. That was essential if he wanted to get ahead in this society.

Julie and the others at Amherst Montessori worked very hard to bring his skills up to where they needed to be. To her credit, she did get him reading, but there was one thing she could not do, and that was to make him like it. She taught him the mechanics of reading, and how to sound out and say words. He learned what they meant, too. But it didn't catch fire in his mind. He didn't want to do it, didn't like to do it, and didn't do it unless he had to.

As it turned out, the thing that changed all that, at once and for-ever more, was the power of Harry Potter. That was the one thing that finally made our son want to read.

23

READING

As much as Cubby loved my tales of Gorko and his lizard pals, I have to concede that his all-time favorite story was Harry Potter. He was enraptured with the characters, the magic, and all the fantastic places. The only problem was, the books themselves were daunting. They were thick, heavy, and bereft of illustration. For a third grader who struggled to read picture books, they were overwhelming.

I didn't know what to make of that, because I was reading at a high school level when I was in third grade. By that time, I had gone from Dick and Jane straight into *Encyclopaedia Britannica*. I could not understand why my son hadn't done the same. "He's not like you," his mom would say defensively.

Meanwhile, he could not get enough of the stories. "Read Harry Potter," he would say, as he handed us a book from his collection. "You read it," I would answer, and he'd look annoyed and hand the book back to me as if I were an uncooperative dummy.

He had better luck with his mom. She was much more likely to read on demand, and he'd sit there for hours, watching the pages turn as words flowed from her mouth. He'd look at her, and look at the book, but he struggled with the next step. Sometimes she'd put her fingers on the page to highlight the words as she read. She always hoped Cubby would chime in and read aloud with her, but he never did. Listening seemed to be enough. Even after three years of class, the testing at Yale, and the first steps with a tutor, reading remained very hard.

That spring Cubby's mom completed her master's degree. To celebrate her graduation, my brother bought the two of them round-trip tickets to Mexico, and they rented a house in San Cristóbal, Chiapas, for six weeks. They planned to head south just as soon as Cubby was out of school. I didn't like the idea of Cubby being away for so long, but I knew it was a great opportunity for them. It turned out to be one of the best experiences of their lives.

They took a circuitous path to Mexico, driving our old Mercedes station wagon to her mother's place in Florida, and then flying from there. Little Bear brought the first three Harry Potter books on tape, and Cubby listened to them on the way down. The books were so long that it took a journey of that length to hear them all. We hoped hearing the books might get him reading them, but it didn't. He listened happily and held the books in his hands, but the pages didn't turn.

The fourth Harry Potter came out while Cubby and his mom were in Mexico, and I bought it so Cubby would have it when he came home. This time, we didn't give him the audio version. We handed him the printed book, and he carried it everywhere. He still wanted us to read to him, but something was changing. He sat there alone, struggling with the words himself.

Later in the summer, he brought Harry Potter with him to Chesterfield Scout Camp. The scouts camped in tents, and when bedtime came, the kids lay on their bedrolls, reading by flashlight. Cubby followed their lead, as hard as it was, because other scouts were talking about Harry Potter and he had to keep up if he didn't want to be left out. The peer pressure must have provided a push we grown-ups couldn't, because the results were visible as soon as he returned from camp.

Now he held books and actually read. He read at lunch. He read in bed. I'm sure he was struggling mightily at first, but something clicked in him on that book, because he got faster and faster, almost before our eyes.

Looking back, I think that the process of Cubby learning to read was similar to how I learned digital engineering when I was in my early twenties. I knew analog audio engineering, but I had to master its digital counterpart for a potential job. To do that, I picked up several textbooks and read through a few years of focused classroom curriculum in a two-week marathon, soaking up the knowledge. The process of reading the text, examining the examples, and looking at the result of my own experiments somehow did the trick.

Some people call that kind of sudden self-directed learning a savant ability. People with autism often have an unusual ability to concentrate. Sometimes we get fixated as a result, and that's a disability. Other times, we lock in on something that captures our interest, and then our concentration can be an extraordinarily powerful advantage.

No one knew how that kind of learning could be possible when Cubby and I were young, but neuroscientists are getting a glimpse of the answer now. Advances in functional magnetic resonance imaging allow us to see the activation of tiny chunks of brain matter as we think and perform tasks. Recent studies have shown that one hundred hours of concentrated study and practice can change brain activation patterns enough that researchers can pick up the differences using fMRI. Even better, they are correlating changes in brain imagery with tangible improvements in skills. Other studies have shown that the brains of people with autism are more plastic, or changeable, than those of ordinary people, so some of us may have a unique advantage when it comes to acquiring skills.

If only we knew more about how to harness this ability! Even so, as the experiences of my son and I show, we autistic folks may be able to reconfigure ourselves in ways others find incredible.

That's surely what happened for Cubby. When the school year finished he was several years behind his classmates in reading. By the time that summer ended, he'd passed them all and moved close to college level. And it didn't stop—he was improving every day. It was almost as though someone from Hogwarts had waved a wand.

It wasn't just Hogwarts, though. Cubby's progress at the Montessori school was almost miraculous. To this day I don't know if it was the method, the people, or both. I do know that Cubby has stayed in touch with Julie to this very day. She's one of those teachers who's made lifelong connections with a small army of kids, one at a time.

In an ironic twist of fate, her assistant, Karen, would be called for jury duty years later when Cubby was on trial. She was actually interviewed as a potential juror, but excused when she revealed their Montessori connection.

24

AN OFFICIAL GEEK

Cubby's reading breakthrough wasn't the only momentous thing that happened that spring. While Cubby and Little Bear were in Mexico, my "partner" came back from Florida, looked at the books, and said, "I can't believe it. You paid me back fair and square." I almost choked at his seemingly casual comment, but the meaning was clear. I was done with my obligation to him. I had already been looking for a new home for my business, but now my search kicked into high gear. With my servitude done, I wanted out of that place as fast as possible. I found a promising building less than two miles away and signed a lease for fifteen hundred dollars a month. I had twice the space of my old shop, in a nicer building, for less money. I was psyched.

I rented the new building, hired workmen to get it ready, and went there every day after work. Each day for a month, I brought over more parts and tools. When the last weekend of the month arrived, I moved everything else and swept the floor clean. I called the customers who had cars at my shop and told them where I was going. That weekend, I called everyone with appointments for the following week and told them the same.

I never went back to the old shop. At first I worried that my former partner would try and muscle in on my new business, but he left me alone.

My new landlord could not have been more different from my old one. He was cheerful, accommodating, and did not interfere in my business. Freed of my former partner's negative energy, my business boomed. Soon I was hiring more technicians and adding more space. For the first time in my life, I felt like a success.

Best of all, I was the ruler of my own domain. Customers came to visit and stuck around. Some even became my friends. I'd had a lot of trouble making friends when I was younger, but that seemed to be changing. Was it maturity, commercial success, or the way I looked? Whatever the reason, in the past year I'd started receiving invitations to lunch, and even the occasional dinner. People were treating me more like a friend and less like a workman or servant. Things felt pretty good.

One of my new friends was a therapist who worked with troubled teens at a local private school. He was a great big bear of a fellow, always cheerful and full of interesting insights. He had taken to stopping by near lunchtime, sometimes alone and other times with his wife. She worked with kids too, as a special ed teacher in a local school system. We'd go to a restaurant and talk while the guys fixed his car. I had hired a receptionist, which freed me to spend time with customers, something that was becoming a bigger and bigger part of my job.

One day the three of us went to lunch at a place in downtown Springfield that was owned by a couple of our customers. We sat down at a booth, with me on one side and my friend and his wife on the other. "There's something important I want to tell you," he said. "Therapists learn not to diagnose their friends, or else they don't have any friends. So I thought about whether to tell you this for a long time. This is a condition people are talking about more and more. It fits you to a tee. In fact, you could be the poster boy for it. It's called Asperger's syndrome."

With that, he handed me a small blue book. The title was, not surprisingly, *Asperger's Syndrome*. It was written by a psychologist named Tony Attwood.

My initial response wasn't very favorable. I set the book on the table and looked at it, then looked at him. "What the hell is this?" Over the years, I'd had plenty of experience with so-called friends and teachers and counselors sitting me down and telling me what was wrong with me. They always said the same thing, "I'm telling you this for your own good." I knew there were people who said things that sounded critical but were truly meant to help me, but they were in the minority. Over the years, different "well-wishers" had assured me that I was a sociopath, a potential serial killer, or at least a career criminal in the making. None of those predictions had come true yet, but as the predictors would say, there is still time.

When I was a kid, I believed those ugly suggestions and concluded I was defective. As an adult, I became wiser and more cynical. I realized some people built themselves up by knocking others down. I also learned that people criticized me for having traits they had themselves. They might say, "You are tricky and dishonest," because they were tricky and dishonest. If I called them on that, they'd feign anger or say something like, "It takes one to know one."

Attacks like that often came when it was time for customers to pay their bills. Some thought they could make me feel bad about myself in order to get our work for free. It took a while for me to catch on about that, but once I did, I stood my ground, to my critics' surprise and dismay.

All those thoughts swirled through my head as I considered what I'd just heard. I realized there was an important difference. There was no bad event or forbidden action precipitating this unexpected and startling diagnosis. That set it apart from the critiques I had received as a kid. Back then, I would hear something like, "You broke into the closet because you are a bad kid." Not only that, my friend was not seeking anything from me at all, and when I looked at him, he seemed serious and earnest, as opposed to mocking and nasty.

"Look," he said, taking the book and opening it to a section he'd highlighted in the middle, "the book talks about how people with Asperger's develop special interests in things and are driven to learn everything they can about them. That's how you are, with cars."

I had to agree with him. I could not see a bad side to that. Later, after I'd had a chance to think about it, I realized other people might call those special interests "obsessions" or something else even less complimentary, and they were not always good. But I still took his point. In the context of what I did for work, being obsessed with every small detail of Land Rover cars gave me a big competitive advantage over less focused service managers.

He then turned the page and showed me other traits of Asperger's: difficulty reading nonverbal cues from other people, the tendency to say inappropriate things at inopportune moments, difficulty in making and keeping friends. The more I read, the more I agreed he was probably correct. By nightfall, I had read the whole book and I was certain. He was right. I'd been given a wonderful gift of insight. This had never happened to me before. Even so, it was a big shock. I knew I'd need some time to process what I had just learned.

I had, and still have, mixed feelings about my Asperger's. On the one hand, it's a relief to have an innocent, neurological explanation for some of the behaviors that got me into trouble as a kid. It was proof that I wasn't just a "bad kid." Now I understood that it was my Asperger's that caused me to look at the ground or into space when I answered a question. I wasn't being tricky or evasive or deliberately disrespecting the other person by refusing to look at him or her. Until I read Attwood's book I had not really understood what was going on.

That was the good part—the insights into why I was the way I was, and the knowledge that those differences were not my fault. The bad part is, those differences were part of me. If I was just "acting bad," I could presumably choose to "act good" and change what I was doing. But if I were wired differently, I might just be stuck in an undesirable way of being. That made me a bit sad. That's especially how I felt when I read the words *there is no cure for autism.*

My mother and brother were quick to embrace the concept of Asperger's, though the idea that it was a form of autism was rather startling. To my surprise, my brother Augusten said he'd always wondered why I acted strangely. I'd had no idea he was thinking those thoughts. My mother had lived with unspoken shame over my lack of "normal" responses as a baby, always wondering if my logical and unemotional demeanor was a result of bad mothering on her part. The Asperger diagnosis put much of her guilt and worry to rest.

When I told Little Bear about Asperger's, she said, "There's no way you have anything like that!" To her, Asperger's was nothing more than a figment of the imagination. At the time, it didn't occur to me that her quick denial might have been because the diagnosis hit a little too close to home for comfort. The discovery that she, too, has Asperger's was still some years in the future.

Then there was Cubby. As much as my Asperger diagnosis meant to me, it made no difference at all to my son. He and I still interacted the same way. But I had read that there was a genetic component to Asperger's, and I wondered if Cubby might be touched by it too. At that time, I still saw Asperger's as "what was wrong with me," and I was none too eager to envision my only son carrying the same burden.

Consequently, I made mental lists of Aspergian traits and convinced myself that they didn't fit Cubby. For example, I told myself that he didn't have Asperger's because he had friends. He didn't share my all-consuming interest in electronics either. In addition, we had taken Cubby to several evaluations and the psychologists had never mentioned Asperger's. They had told us of his problems reading, paying attention, or translating what he saw on the blackboard. Nothing they told us really had a name; they just illustrated the issues.

Some were subtle, but others were obvious, even to me. Like compulsive grooming. Cubby had taken to brushing his hair for fifteen minutes when he got dressed in the morning, until he brushed it right out of his head. I didn't know why, but the thought of a bald-headed grade schooler was unsettling. I'd never done anything like that as a kid. Or if I did, I'd long since forgotten.

Yet there was no escaping some parallels to my own life experiences. He was struggling in school, just as I had. His teachers said many of the same things about him that mine had said about me. There were the squabbles with other children over sharing, and the way he showed them the "correct" ways to play. I recalled his fixation on Beanie Babies, and his intense desire to know every single bit of minutiae about them. The only thing that could distract him from Beanies was the arrival of Pokémon and Yu-Gi-Oh! cards, which replaced Beanies in his mind.

In the end, I wrote his behavioral aberrations off to geekiness. *The doctors must know best,* I thought. *He's just eccentric. He's not Aspergian like me.*

The alternative was too unpleasant to contemplate. At that time, I still saw Asperger's as a disability. I had yet to embrace it or connect it to my successes, and it certainly was not a source of pride. I was still trapped in that "defective child" shell. Admitting Cubby had Asperger's would put him in there with me, and that was something I could not do.

25

DIVORCE

By this time my marriage was on a steep downward trajectory. Actually, it had been headed that way quite a while, though both of us had tried to deny it. It felt like we couldn't agree on anything anymore, even simple stuff like how best to clean the floor. I'd want to mop the thing and be finished, and Little Bear would be fixated on cleaning the cracks and crevices. Perhaps that was her version of Cubby's compulsive hair brushing; the crevices would be spotless while the house as a whole was a disaster. However, I didn't make that connection at the time. Instead, in my Aspergian way, I assumed it was about me. I figured she was angry with me and the mess was a form of punishment. Meanwhile, we'd argue and nothing would get done. As the household spiraled out of control we grew in totally different directions, drifting further apart with every passing year. Both of us were unhappy, resentful, and withdrawn.

Conditions at home had deteriorated to the point where I spent several nights a week in an old cabin cruiser I'd bought and fixed up. I also spent as much time at work as I could. I'd been down so long I was probably clinically depressed, and Little Bear was angry.

Finally, Cubby's mom and I made the decision to separate. As hard as it was to admit that our marriage had foundered, it was also a relief. I was ready to move on with my life, whatever that might mean. My biggest worry was what would happen to Cubby. He'd had an awful time in the South Hadley public school and was finally settling in happily at Amherst Montessori. Would our divorce blow that up too?

We agreed to use a mediator rather than fight it out with lawyers. That proved to be one of the smartest things we ever did. Our mediator helped us talk through what to say to Cubby, and how to move forward in the least hurtful way possible. One of the things we agreed on right from the beginning was the idea that we'd continue to parent him together, and that we'd share him fifty-fifty. I'd been reading up on divorce, as I am wont to do for anything important. To my distress, most of what I read was discouraging when it came to dad-kid relationships. According to the books I found, dads tended to fade out of their kids' lives once they left home. I was determined not to do that. Cubby was the only kid I had. I was proud of him, and I wanted to keep him. The only problem was, his mom had the same notion. So we needed a plan. We worked out our kid-sharing arrangement at the mediator's office before saying anything to Cubby.

The plan we devised gave us both pretty much equal kid time. According to our agreement, I would pick Cubby up from his mom after lunch on Saturday, keep him through the weekend, and take him to school on Monday and Tuesday. At the end of that school day his mom would retrieve him, and she would keep him until I picked him up again on Saturday.

The mediator called it a "joint parenting plan." Neither one of us had sole custody. Each of us would be able to deal with doctors, schools, or anyone else we might encounter in the raising of our child. Each of us had the same rights we had when married; we trusted that we could continue to work things out with our son even though we had not been able to work things out with our marriage.

I was happy about that, because I had already talked to other dads who did not have custody of their kids. They were humiliated when their ex-wives—the parents with custody—had to approve every decision about their children. It was as if they became second-class parents overnight. That didn't happen to me.

After the first meeting with the mediator we decided I would move out. But I would not just pack up and disappear. One of the things that frightens kids most is uncertainty, so we agreed that I'd find a place to live before saying anything to Cubby. We also agreed that Little Bear would stay in the South Hadley house, which we hoped would provide a comforting sense of stability for him.

I was lucky enough to find a nice three-bedroom house to rent just eight miles away, and I set about getting it ready. The place had sat empty for almost a year, and there was a lot of cleaning and painting to be done, as well as furniture to be bought. I did everything I could to make my new place look familiar and homelike. First, armed with a pickup truck and a wad of cash, I bought a nice full-size bed and matching dresser for Cubby's room.

I chose a captain's bed—the kind that sits atop two drawers, which in turn sit on the floor. With that kind of bed, there's no place for monsters to hide. Beds like that are essential for kids who've had trouble with monster infestation, and they're comforting for anyone else. When you hear a low growl late at night it's nice to know it's not coming from right beneath you!

Next I went to the storage facility in Northampton where I'd been keeping a bunch of old furniture my grandmother had left me when she closed up her house in Georgia. I picked out two more beds, a dresser, and some odds and ends—enough to fill the guest room. I hoped Cubby would recognize that old furniture and feel comforted by its familiarity. I even managed to gather a few sacks full of Cubby's toys and spirit them from the old house to the new one. Once they were scattered around his room it looked just as if he'd left them himself.

Then it was time for that awful, hard conversation. Divorce is one of the toughest things a third-grader can go through, and I hated having to tell him that our dream had foundered. His mom and I sat Cubby down on the sofa and told him what was going on. He let out a long hurting howl of *Noooooooooo!* I felt as if I had been stabbed. We both reassured him that he was still our Cubby, and that we both loved him. We told him he would split his time between us and that we'd do the same things we'd done before. Then I said, "Would you like to see my new place?" To my surprise, he bounced up and said, "Let's go!" I don't know if his enthusiasm was based on excitement over a new place, or just a desire to get out of an upsetting spot, but I didn't question him. Off we went.

We turned right at the end of our street, and Cubby said, "Are we going to Amherst?" I realized he associated right turns with his mom's school and Amherst, while lefts meant my work and Springfield. This place was somewhere totally new. "We're going to Chicopee," and I let him ponder that as we reached Five Corners and turned onto an unfamiliar road.

Partway to my new place, we came to a trailer park. All the trailers were pretty run-down, but one stood out from all the others. It was a chalky blue mobile home with a fine vintage Mercedes rotting peacefully alongside the collapsing remains of the porch awning. It was the kind of place you could imagine country bumpkins named Earl and Elmer relaxing, spitting tobacco in the tall shaggy grass and tossing their empties into the back of the car. Cubby was very attuned to motor vehicles, and I knew he'd recognize an old Mercedes when he saw it. I slowed down as if to turn in. "Look on your left, Cubby, and see if you can spot our new place." Cubby gazed skeptically at the mobile homes, but when he saw the Mercedes, his skepticism turned to shock and alarm. Old car parts lay all around.

"Is that it?"

Cubby's horrified expression proved once and for all that kids do not just like any place their parents call home. He looked at me, and I could not hide a grin, to which he said, "Dad! Where are we really going?" It was just a mile more to our new place, and he was annoyed the whole way. I parked in the driveway, and we got out. After the Mercedes in the trailer park, he was still skeptical. "Is this it?" I unlocked the door, and we walked into our new home together for the very first time.

My toy-importation scheme turned out to be a good one. Two of the first things Cubby noticed were the toys in his room and the bike in the garage. And of course there was my secret weapon, which I had kept mum about: the swimming pool out back. After he saw that he immediately gave his approval. It was almost enough to make him forget the divorce. Or so I hoped.

Our first night in the new place was sort of like an urban camping expedition. Feeding ourselves was easy: I'd filled the fridge with frozen dinners, Hamburger Helper, bottled water, fruit drinks, and even some desserts, and we whipped up a bachelor feast. There was more food than we could possibly eat. After that it was time to inspect the house for monsters. I presented Cubby with his own bright flashlight with fresh batteries, and together we patrolled our domain before bed. I had made a special point of unwrapping the new sheets and pillows and making up the beds ahead of time, so when it came time for sleep, Cubby settled right in. The light switches all worked and the toilets flushed. And our flashlights were right beside our beds. What more could two guys need?

I'd had the most terrible fears that Cubby would hate our new home or find one thing after another missing, but none of those worries came to pass. We did all right.

26

DREAMING CUBBY

Now that Cubby and I were alone in the house, we had to learn a new dynamic. For one thing, I quickly realized his mom had been right all along: She had done most of the work of keeping the house and managing, feeding, and watering the kid. Now it was time to do my share.

I might have complained about dirty dishes or piles of laundry before, but there was no one to complain to anymore. Like all parents, I hoped Cubby would grow up to do most of the chores, but for now, I had to do them myself. Housework proved surprisingly tiring until I figured out how to minimize waste. For example, we made it a habit to eat food in the wrapper, saving plates. We drank our liquids from the can, saving glasses. We even used our socks two days in a row, generating less laundry. With those techniques, we reduced the housework to a level even I could handle.

Now that Cubby could read, we became a team in the kitchen. "How long do we heat this?" I'd ask. He'd read the label and tell me, and most of the time, he was right. In that fashion we mastered microwave cookery and quickly moved on to greater culinary challenges. We soon excelled at heating multiple courses of our dinner for precisely the right amount of time. We might heat a pot of soup, a bag of vegetables, and a casserole all at once. We also learned to heat things in a pan, on top of the stove, and complete a preparation by adding a second or even a third ingredient after a certain amount of time had passed. Together, Cubby and I became just like chefs.

Meanwhile, I prepared Cubby to do additional housework and looked forward to the day he would deliver me to a state of domestic bliss by doing all the household chores, and cooking too. Sadly, that never happened, though I did get him to wash the dishes.

He was reluctant at first, regarding dirty plates as too toxic to handle, but our new home was only a quarter mile from an old landfill, and I warned Cubby that rats came out of the landfill at night, looking for food scraps. If they found food in this house—out in the sink or on countertops—we would be in the gravest danger. I reminded him of the television shows that showed rats chewing through walls and looked pointedly at his bare feet. After that, getting Cubby to wash dishes was never a problem.

When he balked at additional labor, I reminded him of the promises that were made when I bought him. "Does all chores happily," I told him, but he remained parked in the living room. I could get another kid, one who'd act better, I'd tell him, but he didn't move. I even invoked friends and family. "Uncle Neil had a kid once," I told him. Uncle Neil was a crusty old buddy of mine who didn't even have a dog, so that got Cubby's attention. Seeing the chance, I said, "He got a kid just like you, but he got so frustrated when the kid wouldn't do chores that he sold him to a Sumatran reptile trader, and the kid ended up cleaning cages in a circus."

Cubby didn't even blink at that. "You can't sell me," Cubby replied. "It's against the law to sell kids today."

Housework was not the only thing I had to manage. There was the kid himself. Sometimes he would just get out of hand. He'd refuse to do what I wanted, all the while advancing his own bizarre suggestions for what we should do. His ideas were generally things no normal adult would do. For example, when faced with a sink full of dishes, he said, "Okay, Dad. Let me show you these killer cards that came in my latest Pokémon deck. You can admire them here on the table. Just don't touch." Furthermore, his notions frequently involved considerable expense and often travel to distant locales. "Dad," he would exclaim. "You are confused! We are not broke. You have plenty of money to take me to Disney World!" Something had to be done. After all, I was the parent and ostensibly in charge. Unfortunately, my position as leader who must be obeyed was not always clear, especially to him.

I was bigger and stronger than his mom, but for some reason, he ignored me while obeying her. That even proved true in our new house. "Mom always lets me do that," became a frequent refrain. I had no way of knowing if his claims were true or not, and it aggravated me that she was the main parent in his mind even when she wasn't there.

I had heard of jailhouse lawyers before, but as Cubby became more verbal I realized I had a new life-form on my hands: a playroom lawyer. When I threatened him he responded by telling me that whatever I proposed was illegal, and citing his own interpretation of the law in his favor. To hear him tell it, parents had no rights at all, other than the right to buy their kids games and bring them food. The older he got, the harder it was to defeat him with logic. Threats and arbitrary rules didn't work either. I needed something new to motivate him.

If being alone together was a huge adjustment, introducing a new third party was potentially an even bigger one. I had read every book I could find on the subject of stepparents in an attempt to maximize my chance of success the second time around. One book I read suggested it took one year for every year of a child's life before they would accept a stepparent. According to that theory, it would take eight years for Cubby to accept someone new in my life.

I had met someone new, and I was hoping I would not have to wait that long. Martha was a shy, introverted graphic artist who was as different from Cubby's mom as anyone could be. We shared many interests: computers, graphic design, cars, and quiet time alone. Equally important, we didn't fight over every decision—a very welcome change from my marriage. I've heard that some people go from one extreme to the other in their relationships, and I guess I was such a person. The differences were unmistakable. Cubby's mom was totally disorganized, whereas Martha never had a single piece of paper out of place in her apartment. They even looked like opposites. Little Bear was short and round; Martha was tall and thin. I wondered what Cubby would make of her.

The two of them hit it off right away. Martha didn't have any children of her own. She had gone through a cancer scare some years before and could not have kids as a result. However, she liked Cubby, and he liked her. In fact, Cubby actually invited her to join us in our new home in Chicopee.

"You can stay in the basement," he said brightly. "I would come down and play with you, and we could all do things together." I am sure Cubby could not imagine a more attractive invitation, and he smiled happily when she said, "That sounds like lots of fun!" She smiled back, but never did take up residence by the furnace.

When Martha moved in that first winter, life became more comfortable. I've never done well alone and I didn't have much confidence I could make it on my own, despite the evidence to the contrary, so I was much happier. Martha believed in me and shared my values when it came to running a house. Soon we began working together in the business, and that went well too. And everything stayed neat and orderly.

Also, I found it amazing what a difference two adults made when it came to managing a kid. Cubby was very happy, because he had a new playmate, as well as someone else to do his bidding.

He proved that on one of our first outings together—to the zoo.

As we walked through the entrance Cubby spotted some wheel-chairs sitting to the side in case they were needed. "My ankle hurts," he said, and plopped into the nearest chair. We looked at each other and pondered. *Should we go home? Did we need a doctor?* "Come on," he said. "Push me and I'll be okay." Martha dutifully rolled him all through the zoo, a trip that took several hours and gave her an excellent workout. He admired one animal after an-other from the comfort of his perch.

When we passed two draft horses I decided to test his knowl-edge. "Can you tell which one is nuclear powered, and which is a farm-raised horse?" When he admitted he couldn't, I gave him a tip: "The nuclear ones have hollow hooves, and they move their legs exactly the same way every step, because they're robots." Cubby nodded as if he'd known that all along.

When it came time to leave, she rolled the chair back to the en-trance. I prepared to drive the car around so we could load our injured child aboard with a minimum of walking.

Just as I approached, he popped straight up out of the chair, two feet into the air, and landed on his feet with the biggest of grins, saying, "Ha! Fooled you both!" We laughed so hard, it was impos-sible to be mad.

Tricky as he could be, one thing did not change: He still relied on me for tuck-ins and protection from monsters. He never tried to fool me then. Monster protection was, after all, serious stuff.

I felt like we had the beginnings of a family again.

27

CHILD PROTECTION

One new thing Cubby and I did together was take up hiking.
The house I'd moved to bordered on the Chicopee State Forest, and we immediately began hiking under the pine trees. I hadn't realized how I missed having a place to walk till I found one again, now that I'd grown up. As a kid I'd walked for miles in the Shutesbury woods, and I spent all my time outdoors at my grandparents' in Georgia. I'd lost sight of that as I'd gotten older and tied down to workplaces.

Cubby liked the outdoors too, though he had no experience locomoting himself for miles at a time or carrying a backpack with a lunch or tools. He was clumsy at first, but he took to it like a pro and he became coordinated in no time. The only problem was endurance. Cubby would run out of steam, and I'd have to carry him. Luckily, that ended when he got a little older. By age eight, he had more energy than me and he'd just go and go and go. He was up for hiking anywhere I took him, but I think his favorite area remained the familiar complex of trails behind my house. One main trail at the end of our street led to a network of woods roads that went for miles around the old Westover Air Force Base. One of the old roads went right past the end of the main runway, and you could watch the giant cargo planes fly fifty feet overhead from the safety of the woods. We saw B-1 bombers on occasion too, and when we did, we figured some faraway dictatorship was about to go up in smoke. You could tell the B-1s were special because they took off at night and flew almost straight up into the sky. They roared something fierce and looked like the prehistoric birds I'd told Cubby about as a tyke.

I'd take Cubby with me as often as he'd go. Once Martha joined us, she came along too. Cubby always ran ahead. "Come on," he'd say, trying to get me to go faster.

"You run ahead," I told him. "You're the bait."

Bait? That stopped him dead.

"Sure. What if there's a bear, or even a pack of weasels? They grab you, and I know they're there. Otherwise, if they grabbed me, you'd be stuck. I might be able to rescue you, but you're too little to rescue me."

My argument made perfect sense, but Cubby seemed troubled. Cubby had never imagined himself as a bear might see him: as lunch. He did not like the idea one bit.

After a moment, he responded just like many adults—with denial.

"There are no bears out here, and no such thing as a pack of weasels." He said that with great certainty. Even so, he knew it wasn't true. There are definitely bears in the New England woods. And weasels? Who knows . . .

It's one of those puzzles of childhood. As a kid, you tell yourself there are no bears. But everyone knows there are bears out there. Yet you've never seen a bear. Does that mean they don't exist? Maybe, but perhaps there's another explanation. Maybe the kids who saw a bear got eaten, and the remaining kids in the neighborhood have not seen a bear. Yet. Perhaps that is why the number of children on my street seems to diminish, slowly and almost imperceptibly.

Some say the neighborhood is aging and the kids are moving away, but I suspect something different: They have become food.

Storybook bears like Winnie-the-Pooh are nice. That's because some writer made them up to make nasty child-eating monsters seem cuddly and kind. Real-life bears may look cuddly and kind too, but they're not. That's why I run them off when they enter our yard, even today. On three occasions, bears have come out of the woods while I was working outside. Each time, I spoke to the bear, firmly and positively, and he acknowledged that I was Absolute Ruler of the Yard. I am, after all, quite large and backed up by both a bear bell and a Winchester rifle. Seeing that, the bears retreated into the woods, without the need for sterner measures.

"Go to some other house," I told them, "and eat the pets and children there. These pets and kids are off-limits." I repeated those words to all the woodland creatures that came calling, and Cubby and the dog lived in peace as a result. He still rings the bear bell from time to time, just for reassurance. We haven't needed the Winchester yet.

Some kids would have left it at that. Not Cubby. He knew they were still out there, lurking in the woods. Beyond the reach of the bell. And he wasn't sure what they were doing. That was when animal knowledge failed him and he turned to the law. "You couldn't let a bear eat me. You'd go to jail. I'm a kid. You have to protect me."

That sounded good, but it wasn't true. "The law just says I can't feed you to a bear. It doesn't say anything about a bear coming and grabbing you, all on his own." Cubby considered that and dismissed it all with simple child logic. "You still have to protect me. You're the dad."

That was something I could agree with. "I do protect you, Cubby." My protection must have worked, because we're both here all these years later. Soon, I will be old, and he will be there to protect me.

28

BULLDOZING OFF

As much as Cubby loved bedtime stories, there were nights when they didn't work. Maybe Cubby was sick or scared or excited. There were any number of reasons he might fail to go to sleep, most of which were inscrutable to me. Other parents might lock their kids in the dark and let them cry it out, but I was never a fan of that method.

Before we divorced, Little Bear could always make him go to sleep, often by singing. It was a long, grueling process at times, but it worked. Then I moved out, and I had to get him to sleep on my own. Ninety-nine percent of the time, my stories put him to sleep, but there were exceptions, and I needed a strategy for those occasions. I had read in a child-rearing book that tiring monologues were effective, but that was easier said than done. My first problem was determining what subjects would be "tiring" to a little kid. I had been in plenty of business meetings where presenters stood at a podium and recited endless statistics with bullet points from charts, putting us grown-ups to sleep, so I tried reading him stock prices from the *Wall Street Journal*. My hope was that it would not only put him to sleep but increase his financial prowess. However, he got bored after ten minutes or so and began complaining non-stop. "Read me a different story, Dad," brought the stock report to an end.

I was saddened and disappointed by his lack of interest. Not only was the stock report not putting him to sleep, he wasn't learning anything about finance either! I had read so much about subliminal advertising and how we learn without knowing. I read Cubby hundreds if not thousands of stock prices, and I never heard one single peep of stock market insight from him when he was awake. That plan was a failure, and it explains why he has no money in the bank today.

I tried civil engineering thrillers, like the history of Hoover Dam and the building of the interstate highways, but they had the opposite effect from what I intended: They woke him up. He wiggled his ears and asked questions! Then I tried talking, but conversation woke him up too. I realized the problem was the need for responses. If he had to think of an answer, he had to stay alert to do it, and going to sleep became impossible.

Finally, I remembered a trick my own grandmother had used on me many years before. She called it counting sheep. I updated it to "counting bulldozers."

I had counted bulldozers myself as a child in Georgia. We had two at the edge of our property, a D4 and a big D9. They lived behind the Georgia Forestry Service station, out by the state highway. Rangers used them to bulldoze firebreaks whenever there was a forest fire. That was the kind of thing I could embrace, and it was easy to multiply them in my mind until I had imagined an endless line of D4 and D9 dozers. My grandmother didn't understand that, but she was never a bulldozer sort of girl. Her roots were more farm-animalish. She preferred sheep or pigs, neither of which held much interest for me.

There were lots of ants to count, but I could never embrace that either. Ant farms were popular in those days, with advertisements for them in every major magazine. I never had an ant farm myself. My Uncle Bob told me they were mostly used to pick up girls, but I was too young for girls and I could never see how you could pick up a girl with an ant farm anyway. Also, they might escape and get all over my room and even bite me. I always liked machinery better, and I figured Cubby might too. And he did.

"Just pretend we're at a construction site, and a long line of bulldozers is pushing dirt past our bed. There goes one now—a big Caterpillar. Here comes another one, a littler Cat. Here's a Komatsu. Now I see a John Deere." Sometimes I would even work in older or the less common brands, like Allis Chalmers or Case. I enjoyed variety in my imaginary construction machinery and, equally important, I had to keep changing brands and styles to stay awake myself. The trouble was, Cubby stayed awake too, because he kept asking about the different machines.

"What color is the Deere? Is it green? And if Deere and Caterpillar are named after animals, what is Komatsu named after?" They were good questions, deserving of answers, but the goal was getting him to sleep, not expanding his knowledge of machines.

He would also get distracted by details. When I told him that a Caterpillar with a ripper was going by, he asked what it was. Kids with less curiosity might have let the ripper slide by undetected. Not Cubby. I was forever explaining.

"A ripper is a claw that sticks into the dirt behind the bulldozer. It tears a line in the soil that makes it easier for the next bulldozer in line to dig in. That's why they call it a ripper. It rips the ground. You can do the same thing in your sandbox with your finger behind a toy bulldozer."

My explanation proved to be a mistake, because Cubby suddenly became fully awake and eager to verify what I had just said. Eventually we reached a balance, where the bulldozer stream was monotonous enough for him to go to sleep but varied enough to keep me awake. We'd count one Caterpillar after another, with the oc-

casional Komatsu thrown in for variety. I'd lean against the head-
board, patiently listening as those bulldozers crawled by. "Pet me,"
Cubby would say, and I'd gently stroke the top of his head as we lay
there. Sometimes I fell asleep too, which was fine, until I fell off the
corner of his little kid bed. If he stayed asleep, that was my signal
to head to my room. If he woke up, we started the petting and the
bulldozers all over again.

29

THE STROLLING OF THE HEIFERS

I don't know how it happened, but somehow, when Cubby was ten, he got wind of an event called the running of the bulls in Pamplona, Spain. He was fascinated by the televised images of beasts running wild in the streets alongside strangely dressed humans. We had never lived among livestock, and Cubby had no prior experience as a bull runner, so I could not understand what he saw in either the beasts or the event. But he was stubborn, and his enthusiasm grew in inverse proportion to mine.

"Can we go can we go can we go?" He bounced in time to the words, as if he were on one of those amusement park kangaroos that sit on big springs. Kids have no concept of distance. He begged for a five-thousand-mile trip to Spain just like he'd beg for a trip downtown for ice cream. Cubby had learned early on that the persistent bird gets the worm and the persistent kid gets the treat. I usually gave in, though there was often a verbal tussle.

I might tell him the persistent kid gets chained up in the basement, or eaten for dinner, but he no longer believed in my threats, and he went with the odds in hopes of getting whatever he wanted at that moment. Even a trip to Europe.

Some dads would have balked at the idea of crossing the Atlantic to mix children and large animals in an uncontrolled environment. Not me. I am just fine among beasts. Bull running actually sounded kind of cool. The only part I had a problem with was the distance and the cost. Luckily, I had an answer.

"We don't need to go all the way to Spain. We have a local event, a strolling of cows, right here in Vermont." If Cubby picked up the distinction between cows and bulls, he didn't let on. "Not only that," I continued, "the cows in Vermont are kid cows, heifers, so they are a lot closer to your size." And the best part was that Vermont's run happens a month earlier than the one in Spain. That meant the stroll was coming up the very next weekend. I promised Cubby we'd go. Every time he thought of it, I repeated my promise. Ten or twenty times, some days.

When the fateful Sunday morning dawned, we got up bright and early and piled into the car. Brattleboro is about an hour north, and Cubby chattered excitedly about cows all the way. When he was locked onto something, it did not do much good to introduce alternate conversational subjects. He didn't hear them.

"Dad! The average speed of a bull run is fifteen miles an hour. How fast is that? Can we run fifteen miles an hour?" I wondered where he found the average speed of a bull run and whether it was right. More often than not, Cubby did prove to be correct about things like that. For a kid who didn't read until third grade, he had turned out to be a remarkably good researcher.

There was no traffic behind us, so I slowed the car from sixty to fifteen miles an hour. It felt like we had stopped as I turned to Cubby. "This is fifteen miles an hour." Cubby was sure he could run considerably faster, but I sensed a bit of apprehension as we got closer. Cubby had read about people getting trampled or gored, and I'm sure he did not want his name added to that list. "It won't matter, Cubby, because this particular event is a stroll, not a run. That means they go slower. We won't be in any danger."

As vivid as my descriptions had been, Cubby still wasn't absolutely sure if he believed in the Brattleboro Cow Stroll. He knew the one in Spain was real, but he wasn't so sure about the one in Vermont. Maybe the whole thing was a giant deception of mine. When we got off at the exit, he knew immediately something was up. The road was totally jammed. We'd never seen anything like it on any previous visit to Brattleboro. Parked cars lined both sides of the street, with late arrivals disgorging adults and kids, who flowed together into an amorphous mass, headed for town. It was clear that cow strolling—or whatever we were headed for—drew a big crowd. We had a mile to walk, and Cubby talked bulls every step of the way.

His excitement increased when we passed signs announcing the stroll, and he knew for sure it was real. "Maybe they have iguanas and weasels, too," I suggested, but he wasn't losing sight of the cows. He continued to chatter as we made our way along.

By the time we reached Main Street, I knew where bull runs were held, how many people had died in them, how the bulls were herded, the number of bulls in a run, and a thousand other bits of bull trivia. Cubby's ability to gather facts about topics of interest was always impressive. I remembered being that way myself. Actually, to a large extent, I am still that way now. I just mask my enthusiasm a little bit as an adult, because not everyone is as keenly interested in the finer details of life as me. I've always gotten a certain satisfaction from knowing I can recognize all the farm tractors in the parade and explain the features of every single one. That is the joy of a true machine aficionado; something less mechanical people can never understand.

Surprisingly, Cubby had not collected any trivia about this event in Brattleboro, though his mind was filled to excess about bull runs in general. I was pleased to present him something new, because things I knew and he didn't made it hard for him to dismiss me as a total idiot. He was already becoming certain that I was the fool, and he the only one with any worthwhile knowledge. "All kids get that way," my friends told me, but the words did not make his incipient teenage superiority any less aggravating.

Martial music began as we started down the little hill into town. "Hurry," Cubby said. "They're about to start." We picked up the pace and soon a marching band came into view. "This is like the St. Patrick's Day parade," I said.

"No, it's not," he answered. "This is a bull run."

At that point, the first of the bulls came into view. They were huge creatures, far bigger than a fat guy on a Harley, with little gold balls on the tips of their horns. They were led by stern-looking farmers who didn't look left or right, only straight ahead, as they led their bulls at the head of the procession. They looked like the kind of farmers you read about in Stephen King novels, doing unspeakable things in small-town granges. I could imagine them with those same stern expressions, holding torches and advancing on some poor victim on a moonless Maine night.

Behind them we saw young farmers, some Cubby's age, leading smaller versions of the beasts past us. They smiled and waved, a reassuring contrast to their somber-looking elders. "They're not running at all. This is a cow parade!" Of course, I had already told him that this was a stroll, not a run, but my words didn't count. In any case, I didn't want to disappoint Cubby. "Maybe they will take off in a minute. Perhaps someone will jab a cow with a stick, and he will be off like a rocket, trampling spectators and crushing small cars." Cubby looked hopeful. He also looked for a stick.

He was having a good time, which was all that really mattered. We followed the cows all the way through town and down another hill to the Brattleboro Retreat. I told Cubby the retreat was a famous institution for the depressed and insane; his own grandmother had been there once. He had heard stories of her craziness, but she was just a nice old grandmother to him, so I never knew what he made of them. I guess our parents are very different for our kids.

"Will they eat the cows?" Cubby's focus had shifted a little bit from bull running, but he was not ready to make the topical leap from bulls to insanity. A shift from bull running to bull eating must have seemed more acceptable.

As we descended the hill onto the lawn of the retreat, sounds and smells wafted up to greet us. Cubby's attention was grabbed by two things: the Ben & Jerry's ice cream stand and the guy cooking burgers right beside it. "Those burgers might have strolled past us a few minutes ago." Cubby looked at me and then at the cows, and was momentarily speechless.

I don't think he had ever really considered the mechanics of converting cows to hamburgers before. He had a general idea that it happened, but there was no evidence of a factory or a machine to bring it about. Yet there it was. Behind us were hundreds of cows, filling the street. In front of us were hundreds of burgers, sizzling on a grill. The process remained a mystery, but the result was unmistakable.

We ate the ice cream instead.

FROM STOCKHOLDER TO CHAIRMAN

Cubby loved our adventures, but one particular Sunday in June was always special: Father's Day. That was the day we went to Newport for the big car show.

The year of the Heifer Stroll marked another turning point in our lives: My car company received Chairman Mao's Mercedes-Benz for restoration. We've seen some unusual and sweet cars during my quarter century in business, but that was one of the finest. I had bought the car for a client, and we were just finishing an extensive mechanical overhaul that had lasted six months, through the winter and spring. I was proud of the work we'd done, and I liked the idea that we'd restored a piece of automotive history.

The chairman's car was just short of thirty years old—one of the last automobiles the Chinese leader ordered before his death in 1976. It was a massive 600 limousine complete with Chinese diplomatic plates and flagstaffs adorned with Chinese embassy flags on both front fenders. The car was four tons of polished black metal, with an interior of hand-stitched red leather, Macassar ebony, and French walnut veneers. With its blacked-out windows and official banners snapping in the breeze, it made a powerful impression.

Even in a crosswalk, cars like that have the right-of-way. That is the wonder of diplomatic immunity. They can run you over, and all the local cops can do is protest to the State Department. Most times, that goes nowhere. What are one or two flat Americans to the ruler of China, with a billion subjects under his thumb?

Of course, we were not diplomats, and the car was no longer an official diplomatic vehicle. We didn't look the least bit Chinese either. But with darkened side windows and sufficient speed, no one could tell.

Approaching an intersection, the car was sort of like an oncoming train. When you see the locomotive coming, you do not step out onto the tracks, hold up your hand, and ask the engineer for his qualifications. Right-of-way matters little when you face immediate annihilation. They'll be wrong, but you'll be dead. So you jump out of the way, quickly. And salute as they roll by, just in case.

That was exactly what the Springfield Police did the first time I took the massive beast for a road test. Inspired by that show of respect, I decided to take the car for a longer run. The Newport Car Show was coming up, and Cubby and I needed a ride.

It's about a hundred miles from our house to Portsmouth Abbey, where the show is held. We set out at eight in the morning, with a cooler full of drinks and a bag of toys and games. I invited Cubby to ride up front, but the cavernous rear compartment proved irresistible, as I had thought it would. The first part of the journey passed uneventfully, as we rolled down the Mass Pike and Interstate 95. We went through the drive-through at the Sturbridge McDonald's, but the cashier was so jaded she did not even notice Cubby. The fun really started when we pulled off the interstate onto Route 24 for the final ten miles into Newport.

We approached our first stoplight at a brisk rate of speed. The light turned yellow, but cars like that do not just stop at the whim of traffic lights. I applied the brakes and our speed moderated, but we continued sailing forward at a pretty good clip. Some drivers might

panic in a situation like that. Not me. I reached across the dash
and flipped the switch for the annunciator, which began shrieking
like an ambulance siren in an old foreign film. No one in his right
mind would get in our way, including the police car we passed on
our way through the red light. Not surprisingly, the cops pulled in
behind us.

"Watch out, Cubby, we might be getting stopped," I warned him,
but he remained unperturbed. All he did was shut the rear shade,
so any pesky blue lights would not disturb his video game. I wondered what would happen next.

A second police car appeared from a side street, to join the first.
When that happens, you know you are in trouble. One cop car
means a ticket. Two cop cars means you're getting arrested. I wasn't
sure what we'd done to justify such action, but I warned Cubby
and he was ready. Unlike me, he'd never been in jail, and the idea
seemed kind of cool.

But nothing happened. There were no flashing blue lights, and
no one shouting through a loudspeaker, "Pull over and remain in
the vehicle!" We continued sailing along, with all the lights green
before us, and nothing standing in our way. Suddenly, it hit me.
The cops had not pulled out to arrest us. They were there to escort
us. I realized we had best not stop or step out of the vehicle, lest we
spoil their image of Chinese royalty. I accelerated slightly as the annunciator roared briefly at an errant pedestrian. The police could
arrest him later.

We made it to the show in record time, only to find the entrance
blocked. Two hundred cars stretched out in a line as harried volun-
teers admitted people one by one. There was always the challenge
from the keepers of the gates: *Are you parking or exhibiting?* Cars
that were deemed worthy of exhibition were allowed onto the show
grounds. All others were consigned to the meadow down below.

We did not have any doubt as to our car's destination, and with
two police cars to protect us, we saw no reason to linger. Chairman

Mao certainly would not have waited. In fact, in his day, outriders would have cleared the riffraff from the road before he even appeared. In the sixties, the guards at the gate might well have been executed or at least imprisoned for their impertinence. We didn't have armed outriders, but we had the next best thing.

With a brief chirp from the annunciator, we drove into the oncoming lane, around the offending automobiles, and past the startled attendants. Our flags snapped crisply in the oncoming ocean breeze. The people at the gate turned to follow us as we motored by. Then they turned to our escorts. I don't know what happened back there. Either they didn't let the police cars pass, or else the cops decided their job was done. I wished I could thank them, but I didn't want to be arrested for doing so. In the end, we simply watched them recede into the distance as we motored serenely across the grounds.

We found two shady parking spaces and settled the car in with its littler brothers. The chairman's Benz looked big enough to put any two of those smaller Mercedes in its trunk, with room to spare. I opened the door and stepped out into the sun. Cubby opened his door and emerged blinking, Game Boy in hand.

Many eyes had followed Chairman Mao's car in its stately progression across the show field. Nothing like it had ever appeared at the car show before. The crowd may not have known who was inside, but they knew he was important. The way that car looked, they probably expected someone like Oddjob from the James Bond movies to step out the driver's door. Being aware of that, I waved as I got out. I think they expected someone else. Someone perhaps a little more Asian looking. And a passenger in the back with something more in his hand than a Game Boy.

Later that day we learned we'd won a prize: Best in Class for Mercedes. Cubby took the award—a large silver platter—and loaded it with cookies for the ride home.

GYMNASTICS

By this time, Cubby had been doing gymnastics for several years, and he was really quite good at it. He could stand on his head on parallel bars and sit perfectly straight while hanging from a ring in midair. His cartwheels and tumbling put my own teenage efforts totally to shame.

To get to that point, he'd spent countless hours practicing with Coach Cal and his teammates. Together they had made the transition from gawky kids to poised young athletes. As an added bonus, Cubby had made several new friends on the team. He spent all his free time talking to them and hanging out.

The only problem was, the team went on vacation when school let out for the summer. At the same time, Mom decided to go to Mexico for her doctoral research. That meant it was up to me to manage our kid seven days a week and burn off his energy. Even though I'd never faced full-time kid management before, I was undaunted. I had a plan. I would send Cubby to gymnastics camp.

At that time, the University of Massachusetts had a topflight gymnastics team that recruited athletes from all over the country. Cubby and I watched them whenever we got the chance. In fact, they won the ECAC championship that year, and my son and I were there to capture the moment in pictures. On a few occasions, his teammates from Hampshire Gymnastics got to work out with the college team, and when UMass competed in a big meet at West Point, the Hampshire Gymnastics team performed at halftime. The kids were awfully proud of that. Their parents were in the stands hollering louder than the families of the college gymnasts who were actually competing.

When Cubby heard the men's coach was offering a two-week summer camp, he was eager to sign up. Off we went.

Everything went smoothly right up to the end. Coach Roy Johnson told me how much my son had improved on cartwheels, rings, and parallel bars as Cubby nodded his head in excited agreement. Hearing that, I decided to attend the last day of camp and photograph the kids. Armed with two cameras, I followed them through the pool, the bars, tumbling, and even outside for free-form moves on the grass.

As I trailed them around, I could not help noticing that Cubby had made fast friends with several of the college gymnasts who helped Roy with the coaching. I remembered doing the same thing myself, when I connected with the grad students at my father's school even as I failed to make friends my own age. The college students had the mental agility to follow the weird things a geeky kid like me would say, and I had no doubt the same thing was true for my own son. I also saw the way he took the time to help the younger kids and share what he had learned, and how the younger kids looked up to him. I was proud of that.

At the end of the camp day, the coach had a surprise. "We're going to Riverside Park," he announced. Riverside was a large amusement park located half an hour away in Agawam. The kids were bouncing up and down at the thought of roller coasters and other scary rides. The coach had lined up transportation and I wasn't too keen to spend a few hours in a crowded amusement park, so I wished them well and sent them on their way. "I'll see you this evening," I said as I watched them drive off.

Two hours later, I got a call. "Dad, you have to come here. Something happened. Right away!" Cubby sounded very worried. I called back but didn't get an answer. I called the coach, and his line was busy. Frightened, I got into the car and headed for the park.

When I pulled into the parking lot, I could see flashing lights everywhere. It was obvious that something bad had happened. Pushing my way past the gate attendants, I rushed into the park in search of my kid. That was one of those times that it's good to be six foot three and two-hundred-some pounds. I can see over most people and move through them pretty fast.

My eyes were drawn to the mob around one of the roller coasters. The first thing I saw was the uniforms. Then I saw the kids from Cubby's camp. *What had happened to them? Was my son hurt?* I parted the crowd like a snowplow and covered the hundred yards to the coaster in a matter of seconds. As I was making my way onto the platform, I caught sight of Cubby. He looked all right, but scared. "What happened?"

"I don't know," he said. "Something happened to Joel," and he pointed to a circle of EMTs who huddled around a small form, motionless on the ground. As we watched, they lifted the stretcher and headed for the park gate at a trot. As they ran, an ambulance backed through the entrance to meet them. We watched the medics load Joel inside and shut the door. With a chirp of the siren, the ambulance pulled past the gate and accelerated out of the parking lot. As they raced toward Baystate Hospital, I turned to find a parent, to see what happened.

Being kids, the gymnasts had gravitated toward the fastest and scariest rides in the park. The big roller coaster was an irresistible attraction. Most of the kids were eager to ride it, but a few were scared. "Come on," their campmates said, "we'll all ride it." They got on. The gymnastics kid pack made it through every scary and dangerous-looking ride at the park. There was the Cyclone, Mind Eraser, and even more aggressive rides that just about ripped your head right off. Then they arrived at the Twisted Train.

The park brochure said, "This is a great coaster for the little ones. Not too fast, not too rough, but still enjoyable for adults and children alike!" Finally, they'd come to a coaster that even the parents would ride. They all piled aboard.

About halfway around the ride, something went wrong. Joel panicked, threw up, and began choking. With all the noise and excitement, no one noticed. The ride circled the track, over and over while Joel struggled to breathe. As the ride coasted into the station, the kids around him realized something was horribly wrong and started screaming. The ride operators sounded the alarm as worried gym camp chaperones gathered up the kids.

It was too late. Joel died. He was twelve, just a year and a half older than my son. The pictures we took at camp that afternoon showed a smiling, happy kid. I thought I'd be giving my pictures to his parents as souvenirs. Instead I sent them to the coach, who delivered them at the funeral.

Cubby never said much about his experience at the park, but I noticed that he became more cautious. I often wondered what he felt about the events that day, and I tried to understand by relating what happened to earlier experiences of my own. More than one person had suggested that autism insulated me from the emotional ups and downs of life. That certainly seemed to be the case here. There was no question Cubby understood logically what had happened, and of course he was sad that his campmate died. Yet he did not seem terribly sad himself. However, he became very agitated by the very mention of Riverside Park. From that day on, the park remained the one topic that was conversationally off-limits for my son.

Now, when I think back on that time, I realize our son was holding quite a lot in, probably because his Asperger's prevented him from fully understanding what had transpired that day and expressing the feelings. It's regrettable that we didn't know any of that at the time; we did the best we could with the knowledge we had.

Cubby never went on a roller coaster again, and he never returned to Riverside Park. A short while later, Six Flags bought the place and spent millions to update and remodel the park, and still he stayed away. Me too. That was the last coaster ride for both of us.

The following year UMass canceled its gymnastics program in the midst of a budget crisis. Coach Roy was laid off and the athletes scattered to the winds. Shortly afterward, Hampshire Gymnastics replaced Coach Cal with someone new. Cal had always worked with my son one-on-one, and the new fellow didn't do that. Cal explained everything carefully for Cubby and helped him through every new move, one step at a time. The new coach was almost non-verbal in comparison. He'd say, "Watch me and imitate" and expect the kids to follow his demonstration on their own. Cubby couldn't do that, and when he floundered the new coach barked out instructions too fast for my son to follow. Cubby fell behind, and within a few months he was out of gymnastics.

Cubby took up fencing instead.

GEOLOGISTS

After what happened at Riverside Park, it was a relief to spend the last few weeks of that summer walking around and exploring our new neighborhood. It was the sort of place that lent itself to pedestrian activity. All the streets had sidewalks, there was very little traffic, and most of the dogs did not bite. The main road was quite busy, but our house was a quarter mile back in a little warren of looping streets to nowhere.

I'd gotten Cubby a new two-wheeler when we moved, and he still liked to ride it back and forth as I walked alongside him. We cruised the streets on our side of the highway, all of which were named for various spices. There was Sesame Drive, Honey Lane, Nutmeg Street, and Savory Court. There were Cinnamon, Citron, and Ginger Drives. Finally, there was Basil Road, the street we lived on.

If you entered from the main road, our new home was the fourteenth house on the left, which did not have any particular significance in and of itself, but was certainly better than being house fifteen. I assumed everyone knew fourteen was a better number than fifteen, but Cubby evinced both surprise and indifference when I reported that fact to him. From a practical perspective, being fourteen houses back from the main road placed us at a comfortable remove from noise and traffic. Fifteen houses back would be better in that respect, but fifteenth was otherwise a less desirable thing to be, since it was an odd number based on five and three, two more odd and unappealing numbers.

On more than one occasion, I explained arithmetical trivia to Cubby, but he never showed much interest. Numerical facts and co-incidences seldom elicited more than the slightest of nods. Striking out on mathematical curiosities, I decided to highlight other characteristics of our neighborhood. I could never tell what might strike Cubby's fancy. One of the first examples I saw was the street names. Our neighborhood was one of spices; his mom lived on a street named for a college. The streets around her were Cornell, Yale, Dartmouth, and Harvard. After explaining the meaning of those names to my son, and getting no response whatsoever, I realized he was too young to appreciate the relationships between street names and real places and things. He didn't know much about condiments and he knew even less about colleges. His experience with spice was limited to salt and pepper, and the only college he knew was the University of Massachusetts, where his mom went to school.

He was more interested in differences we could see. One of our new neighborhood's most visible features was the profusion of swimming pools. We had never been anywhere else with such an infestation of pools. There were wading pools in front yards, aboveground pools in backyards, and in-ground pools alongside yards. All were new to Cubby, for there was not a single swimming pool to be seen around our old house in South Hadley. There were no pools where I grew up, either. "This part of Chicopee must be unique," I told him. On one occasion, Cubby and I actually walked the streets and conducted a count. An amazing 64 percent of the houses around us had swimming pools. They were as common as garages or barbecue grills in other neighborhoods. Of course, our neighborhood wasn't short on garages either. More than 90 percent of the homes had garages. I know, because we counted them as well. We couldn't be as sure about barbecue grills, because people often kept them out of sight when they weren't being used.

Some say Chicopee is Native American for "plenty," and that may be true. I know it is in the case of pools and garages. I don't know how we came to talk of those two household features in one sentence, but there are important differences between them. Garages serve more purposes than pools, and garages need far less maintenance. You could see that on any quick walk. The pools that received care were clear and blue. Those that did not were deep rich shades of green—biology experiments in process. Some had dark misshapen objects floating atop the green. "What are those?" Cubby asked, and I pointed quietly to the pets, small children, and toys that were all around us. "They are the bounty of the neighborhood, returned to the swamp." Cubby nodded.

"Maybe they grow the spices the neighborhood is named for in those pools," I suggested. Cubby liked that notion. He always liked ideas that explained mysteries, and the naming of our streets was one riddle we never solved.

When we walked around it was fun to speculate about what our neighbors did or what they were like. Seeing a green swimming pool, it was easy to see what they did not do. Seeing what they did do took closer scrutiny. As I told Cubby, you can deduce a lot from the cars, toys, and machinery in people's yards. The guy with a van marked Collins Electric was most likely an electrician, though it's possible he was a spy masquerading as a harmless tradesman. His neighbor, with a Massachusetts State Police car in the driveway, could have been a cop. Either that or he'd stolen the cruiser and was headed for serious trouble with the law himself.

Then there was the house with the gravestone in the front yard. "Does he have his own cemetery?" Cubby asked. I didn't know, but the ground out back was certainly soft enough. Cubby had accepted all the other houses and occupations we'd seen with equanimity, but that one troubled him. One day we met our neighbor, a jolly fellow named Kenny, who explained that it wasn't a gravestone at all. "It's a monument," he said. "I don't even know who's buried beneath it. I have a business making monuments here in Chicopee. Some are gravestones, but others are just nameplates for homes and buildings. If you die, we can make a monument for you." I thanked him for his offer; it's always good to have a monument in reserve, just in case. When I was a kid in Georgia, they sold caskets that way, and farmers kept them in the barn, paid for and ready for use.

My son never did figure out if Kenny had something buried under that stone in his yard, or if it was merely a piece of lawn ornamentation. Kenny sure wasn't saying.

Then there were Kenny's other eccentricities. On hot summer days we'd see him at the edge of his yard, shrieking as he plunged a bayonet into the ground. One spearing episode might have been an aberration, but Kenny did it repeatedly and purposefully, walking around his backyard with his eyes focused on the ground. I asked what he was doing, and he told me about his woodchuck problem. "I'm gonna spear the beasts in their lair," he said with pride and determination. Cubby was puzzled by that, but I explained that Kenny had been to Vietnam to fight in a war and had come back kind of different.

Two homes at the end of our road had tricycles in front. "Those houses have kids living in them," Cubby announced. Indeed, that was a likely conclusion, but not the only one, I was quick to point out. "The people might not have any kids yet. They may have put the toys outside as bait, the way people dangle shiny lures in front of fish. Maybe they are trying to catch kids of their own, using trikes to entice stray children."

Unfortunately, as I said the words, two tykes emerged from the house we were passing, climbed on the trikes, and rode them around the house. "Dad! Those are not stray kids!" Cubby crowed.

There were a few places where the grass grew a foot tall and everything was falling apart. We looked closely at those houses, and sometimes stringy-haired, wild people looked back from darkened windows. "Listen close, Cubby, you can hear them rattling their chains inside there." We speculated about what went on inside. Cubby had not yet seen many horror movies, so his ideas were limited.

"Witches and demons," I said. "Yeah," Cubby agreed. "They are probably ready for Halloween every day." He remembered Stone Kid Road, and the child the wizards had turned to rock a few years before. We agreed it was probably best to stay clear of houses like that, even though there were no stone kids in evidence here. "Maybe this wizard turns them into toads instead." There was no denying the large toad population in our backyard, and one of the nearby homes had a stone toad a foot tall.

Then there was the house on Sesame Drive that had rocks for a front yard. Not big rocks, mind you. Smaller stones, one to two inches in diameter. The kind of rocks that might once have been cats or beagles, if wizards were in the area. They lay in a nice, well-manicured layer. A stone lawn. They were the size you might pick up and throw, or chew on if you were in the desert. Then there were bigger rocks making little walls around bushes and other ornamentation. Even the front steps were rock; big slabs turned on their sides in place of concrete stairs. That house certainly stood out from all the others.

"Those people must be geologists!" Cubby declared the first time we saw it. That was an immeasurably better, and less threatening, explanation than wizardry. I was sure he was right, and very proud of his deduction. All we wanted was a chance to find out if he was right. Yet as many times as we walked by that house, we never saw anyone outside. We lived in that neighborhood five years, and all that time Cubby never got the chance to discuss rocks and science with the people who created the most unique yard on the street.

Still, it piqued his interest enough that he never forgot. One of his friends at school had a mom who taught geology at the university. One day he asked Karl's mom about the geologist's yard.

"If you take a shovel and dig, you'll find that whole area where you live is beach sand and stone. That's because it was the original shoreline of glacial Lake Hitchcock, a huge lake that covered this whole area when the glaciers melted, fifteen thousand years ago."

Cubby was very impressed and curious. It turned out that his own mother knew about Lake Hitchcock, and she told him even more. She told him that when the glaciers began to melt, at the end of the last ice age, they left behind a lot of gravel and rock. Some of that sediment formed a dam forty miles south of us, in Rocky Hill, Connecticut. The Connecticut River backed up behind the dam to form a huge lake. The area where our house stood was at one time submerged under twenty feet of water. Lake Hitchcock lasted three thousand years until the dam broke and the lake drained in a huge flood into the Atlantic Ocean.

"All the sand and stone underground here is actually old lake and river bottom. It's like the stuff you wade on, when we go out in our boat." Cubby had been boating with me on the river all his life, so he knew about river sand, but he had not imagined it would be under our house.

Still, that did not explain why that one house had a yard of stone while every other house had a lawn of grass. All the yards might be built atop a layer of sand and stone, but why were all the others covered up by lawn?

One day I got the courage to knock on the door and ask. "Us? Geologists?" The occupant of the house was taken aback. "Hell, no! We work for the postal service. And we keep those rocks nice with Roundup. Good old-fashioned poison."

I was glad my water didn't come from a well.

33

LEARNING TO DRIVE

My mother tells me that my first word was *car*. I'd start repeating it over and over, and Mom would pop me in the backseat and drive me around until I fell asleep. After a while, she'd park and quietly carry me in and tuck me in bed. In time, I learned to say the words *Mom* and *Dad*, but talking really started with *car*.

I've sometimes wondered if autistic kids are more comforted by a machine than by a human. My friend Temple Grandin certainly feels that way. She famously made a "squeeze machine" at college to rock and hold her tight. I did something similar as a child when I piled pillows all over me. In fact, I still do that! As an adult, I prefer the company of humans to a car ride, but if my mother's memory is right, the opposite was true when I was one. I've always loved the gentle roll of a train, and nothing can beat a ride through the country in an old convertible Jaguar.

When Cubby was born, I figured I should start him out the way my mother started me. When he got upset, if Mom wasn't there to jolly him, we'd often go for a ride in the car. Just as they had worked for me, car rides calmed Cubby. He was usually a great passenger. He loved looking out the windows and pointing out the sights.

When I worked on cars, I brought him along and showed him everything I knew. When my Uncle Bill did that with me, I became a little mechanic. Cubby didn't take after me, though. He just watched. But although he never showed much interest in fixing cars, when he got a little bigger he expressed lots of interest in driving. I couldn't let him drive on roads with traffic, but I often let him steer around the yard at the marina, and on woods roads where there were no other vehicles. We had an old Land Rover that I drove in the woods, and he liked that because he could steer, we went slow, and there were no cars or pedestrians to run into.

He just loved turning the wheel and feeling the car move from side to side. He'd twist that wheel with the biggest grin! His enthusiasm for such a simple thing reminded me of a B. Kliban cartoon I'd seen long ago, with a little girl smiling at the instrument she holds in her hand. The caption read, "Just give Alice some pencils and she will stay busy for hours."

By age seven, he was actually pretty proficient at steering. He could drive for miles on backcountry roads and hit hardly anything at all. His only limitation was his size; he could not reach the brake and gas pedals, so he had to sit on my lap. That was okay with me, though, because I was comforted by the knowledge that I could take over should Cubby suddenly aim us for a tree or a cliff.

When he turned twelve, I decided he was finally big enough to control a vehicle on his own. After all, I had learned to drive the farm tractor at that age in Georgia. The closest thing I had to a tractor was the Land Rover, so I decided to start him on one of them.

Cubby had always been a small kid; whenever we had him weighed and measured he was always at the bottom of the charts for his age. That meant my own Land Rover was still kind of big for him even though he had pretty well mastered steering. He remained too little to handle the whole range of controls. A smaller-scale vehicle was needed, and I knew just where to find it.

A few years earlier, Land Rover had opened a driving school at a resort in Vermont that was less than two hours from our home. The school had just opened its doors to kids, and Cubby was one of the first students. He was very excited. Most weekends, I struggled to wake him up, but the day of his lesson he was moving under his own power at dawn. We were out the door and arrived in Manchester by eight o'clock, when the place opened.

We met Cubby's instructor, a friendly fellow in Land Rover expedition garb. He introduced himself as Mike and reached down to shake Cubby's hand. Cubby wasn't used to that treatment, and he was impressed. He turned to me and said, "He looks like the big-game hunter in *Jurassic Park*. Does he have a gun? Will we see dinosaurs in the woods?" As we walked out to the course, Mike told Cubby about his time with Land Rover. He'd been with the company twenty years, and they'd sent him all over the world. Mike had driven the custom Land Rover Defenders that supported the race vehicles on Camel Trophy rallies in Mongolia, South America, and Indonesia. At that time, the Camel Trophy was a legendary off-road event. We had Trophy videos at home, so meeting someone who'd actually driven one was a real treat.

We saw the school's fleet of Land Rovers. They had all the different models, each of which was painted white with off-road tires, winches, and Land Rover Driving School logos on the sides. Mike explained that those weren't the ones for Cubby. They had smaller Rovers just for kids, he told us. He then led us to another garage, where the school had assembled a fleet of one-third-scale electric Land Rovers, decaled and equipped just like their full-scale brethren, except these were green instead of white. Cubby chose a spiffy two-door with no roof. He climbed in and gave a big grin as he bounced on the seat. Martha waved at him and I took their picture.

The controls on the one-third-scale Rovers were very similar to those on our full-size truck back home. The main difference was the motor. The school had electric vehicles that didn't need to be started and ran silently. Ours was a diesel, which clattered and smoked. Given his diminutive size and lack of motoring experience, Cubby was naturally more comfortable in the school vehicle.

After a quick lesson in how to drive, Mike walked ahead and Cubby followed. "This isn't about speed," he told him. "It's about precision. When you go fast off road, things break. Slow and steady wins the race." Cubby grinned and nodded.

The first obstacle was a hill. Now there are gentle hills, and there are steep hills. You walk up the former and climb up the latter. This particular hill rose several times Cubby's height with about the same slope as our refrigerator door back home. He was about to climb it in a Land Rover.

"Not so fast," Mike said. "We have to talk about what you do if you get stuck halfway up." Turning the wheel and rolling backward could cause Cubby's Land Rover to flip over. If he got stuck, he had to keep the steering wheel straight and motor right back down to try again. Cubby was eyeing the hill with a new look of respect. He hadn't thought about rolling his Rover.

"Steep hill," Cubby said. "It sure is," Mike agreed. "Better get out and check out the ground before you try and drive it. We always do that with rough terrain. Walk it first, and there won't be any surprises later." Mike knelt at the front of the Land Rover and pointed from the bottom of the front bumper to the ground in front of the tire. "See this angle?" he said. "It's called the approach angle. It's the steepest slope you can drive up without digging the nose into the ground." Cubby got out and knelt in front to see if he could make the climb. Then he and Mike walked to the top and looked at the road he was about to drive. To Cubby's surprise, the hill sloped back down just as steeply on the other side.

He had gone up and over hills like that with me many times in our full-scale Rover. He never seemed to hesitate when I was driving, but he looked a little nervous at the prospect of attacking little mountains on his own. After walking up and down the trail and looking carefully at both sides of the incline, he returned to his vehicle. He backed up carefully, looked straight ahead, and accelerated forward. The wheel spun a little as he neared the top, but he stayed steady on the pedal and he made it over.

We all applauded, and he was very proud. I took his picture.

They spent the rest of the day learning how to cross ditches, how to climb and descend slopes, and even how to winch a stuck Land Rover out of the mud. It was a great day for Cubby. I knew he was learning skills that would stay with him the rest of his life, or at least until the onset of senility, when they would become irrelevant anyway.

Cubby continued to grow after his driving lesson. Kids his age tend to do that, especially when fed. By the following spring, he was big enough to reach the pedals in a full-size Land Rover. I taught him how to work the winch, and how to rig lines and straps to pull stuck vehicles out safely. He was a quick study, and was thrilled when he pulled three kids from his school out of a swamp near our home. "If you were driving a Land Rover," he told them, "you would not have gotten stuck." They looked at their Jeep and kept quiet. If it weren't for him, they'd still have been two feet deep in swamp water. Cubby was never strong on either tact or modesty.

He told my father and stepmother about his adventures, and they were properly impressed. Seeing my pictures of Cubby at the wheel gave my father an idea. A few weeks later, Cubby got a call from his Grandpa John. "I have a surprise for you," his grandfather said. "See if your dad can bring you up next weekend."

We drove up to Buckland to find the Honda ATV he had admired all polished up and ready to ride, sitting in front of their house. "I've decided to give it to you," my dad told him. Cubby didn't know what to say. We loaded the Honda onto our trailer and brought it home. Cubby rode it through the woods and even out to the power lines, a mile or more away. That old Honda had never seen such use. My father was very impressed by that.

With all that practice under his belt, we returned to Vermont for an event called Rovers De Mayo, on a wooded course outside the town of Woodstock. Cubby had just turned fifteen. A dozen Land Rovers and their owners gathered at the base of an old road that ascended the side of a mountain. I drove from home to the event, but as soon as we pulled off the main road, Cubby took over. I never let him drive on the road without a license, but off the road was another matter. No one cared on the trail. Traffic laws are the least of your concerns on a mountainside, as you pick your way over three-foot boulders and across roaring streams. Cubby was the youngest driver by far, but he was more capable than many people twice his age.

When Rovers got stuck he was right up front rigging the winch lines and pulling people to safety. When his turn came to cross the obstacles he remembered what the Land Rover instructor had told him—*slow and cautious*—and he made it through undamaged every time.

The Rover drive he's most proud of today happened at a Land Rover club outing near Woodstock. At that event, Cubby took our red Discovery up several steep and difficult hills just fine before handing the controls over to Martha. Shortly after she started driving, the group encountered a particularly rough passage. She got the truck twisted sideways, flipped it over, and ended up upside down in the ditch at the bottom. When Martha and the dog made their way out of the overturned Land Rover, Cubby bounced clear off the ground, saying, "You flipped it over and I didn't."

We didn't realize it then, but that was one of those classic Asperger moments. Instead of expressing relief that they were all okay, he was delighted that she had wrecked the car and he hadn't, which meant his skills were better than hers.

"Maybe so," one of the other drivers told him. "But now she's an official member of the Rolled Rover Club, and you're not!" Cubby was momentarily chagrined.

As the other people from the event gathered around, Cubby led the effort to rig the cables, pulleys, and straps, and winch our Discovery back onto its feet. Rolling a vehicle was an exciting moment at any off-road event, and everyone was eager to help. In a matter of minutes the guys had it back on the trail, on all four wheels, with most of its pieces intact. It was quite an impressive performance.

I was pretty happy to see the way his newfound skills were shaping up. From that point on, Cubby would be the driver and I'd just watch!

34

POWER GENERATION

W hat's that?" Cubby asked. Our car sat on a deserted road in Zoar, Massachusetts, otherwise known as the Gateway to Nowhere. The pavement ahead of us took a right turn and then disappeared into the mountainside. Cubby had seen tunnels before, but this one was different. It was more like an oversize mouse hole—a bare borehole into the rough granite of the Berkshires. He wondered where it went. There was no traffic going in or out.

I explained that engineers had hollowed out the mountain. They had dug tunnels from the Deerfield River, below us on the left, to the top of the mountain, eight hundred feet up to the right. Then the engineers bulldozed out an artificial lake on the summit, with a dam to hold the water in. When there was surplus electricity in the power grid, they used it to pump water from the river to the reservoir. When demand for electricity exceeded the supply, operators released water from the reservoir. The turbines that had pumped water to the top a few hours before now spun backward, generating power as the stored water dropped back to the river. In that way, the mountaintop reservoir acted like a giant storage battery. At full capacity, the Zoar plant generated six hundred megawatts of electricity, enough to power thousands of homes and factories.

Cubby had seen hydroelectric dams before—they were all around us. We had even ridden the fast water beneath the Deerfield hydro dam in our orange Zodiac inflatable boat. Water only flowed one way through a dam. The dam could be open or shut, but the water never ran backward. An installation that pumped water uphill in the morning and returned it to the river that night was something new for both of us. "Why does it do that?" he asked. I explained that demand for electricity falls when people go to work in the morning since their houses are empty. When they return home, lights and air conditioners come on, and the demand for power skyrockets. "It happens like this every summer," I said, "especially when it's hot and humid."

"How does it do that?" If you ever doubted the value of general education, try explaining pumped storage to a curious child. But Cubby was always curious, especially when it came to great works of engineering. With that in mind, I explained how the Francis Turbines at Bear Mountain worked. He had seen water wheels, of course, but turbines were a big jump in sophistication. Still, I always believed that any child who hopes for a future in engineering should understand the basics of turbines. I wasn't sure Cubby had engineering in mind for his life work, but it was the best thing I could imagine for him to do, so I felt it was my duty to try and facilitate it, the same way other parents groom their kids for careers in the Senate or investment banking.

I'd been showing him gargantuan, complex stuff like this since before he could walk, and I was confident he took in enough to understand what he saw a little better with every outing. Some people might doubt the ability of a kid to understand technical concepts, but I knew Cubby was different. He grasped engineering principles instinctively, though terms like *hydroelectric* and *cogeneration* still gave him pause for thought.

To get to Bear Mountain, we had motored confidently around the gates and past the power company's No Trespassing signs. Ignoring the signs—which were obviously not meant for us—we'd crossed over the river and traveled a causeway along the water. The trip was worth it: The inside of the mountain was like a Hardy Boys book come to life. I remembered scenes from the *Secret of the Lost Tunnel* and the *Mystery of the Spiral Bridge* as I steered our old Rolls-Royce into the dark. In a few moments, my eyes adjusted to the tunnel and I saw that it was not dark at all. Our path was lit by gas discharge lights and the passageway was finished to a high standard. The road wound its way in, and we proceeded along.

When we arrived at the end, the differences between this tunnel and the ones in the Hardy Boys stories were unmistakable. Most obviously, there were no criminals in sight—only power company workers. A good-size parking area held a number of pickup trucks and a few company cars. The workmen were pretty surprised to see Cubby and me in an antique car, but we knew our rights. We were stockholders, there to inspect our property. By that time, we had long experience exploring, and on that day the foreman was friendly and happy to oblige. He explained the concept of the New England power grid. He showed us the turbine area, the transformer farm, and the rooms where they control the plant. We even saw where the water was finally released into a section of river they call the dryway. "We can dump a thousand cubic feet of water every second," the foreman said reverently.

"That's a slug of water about the size of our car," I explained to Cubby. "So if it was cars getting dumped into the river, at one every second, the junkyard would fill up pretty fast. But it's not cars, it's water, so it just flows downstream toward the Connecticut River at Deerfield." Sometimes Cubby accepted my explanations. Other times he seemed annoyed by my analogies. It's hard teaching engineering principles to a kid, so I just took whatever success I got.

Over the years, thanks to the access our stock ownership provided, we saw most of the great engineering works of New England. Cubby didn't say much about the places we went, but I knew the nuclear power plants, navy ships, rail yards, and dams made an impression. You could tell just by watching him on our tours. The little cogs were almost visible, revolving in his head.

I always hoped our adventures made Cubby a little smarter. Some people said intelligence was innate and you couldn't change it, but I knew a foundation of experience would have a powerfully beneficial effect on whatever reasoning ability he was born with. Experience was what made common sense possible, and as my grandfather always said, common sense isn't common at all.

I also hoped he'd see something that caught his interest. The only way I found electronics and cars—my two great loves—was when grown-ups showed them to me and helped me to unravel their secrets. Right from the beginning, I resolved to do that for Cubby.

I knew he'd have a great advantage in life if he found his interests early. The trajectory of my own life had shown me the value of acquiring skills in my teen years. Those years were fast approaching for Cubby. If I could help him find things he wanted to pursue and encourage him to study and go to college, I knew he'd be on a good path, with excellent odds of success.

I learned the value of college the hard way—by not going. Instead, I left home at sixteen and made my own way, without any legitimate credentials. Sure, I'm educated today, but I had to do it myself, a difficult and arduous process. Growing up was a rough ride, with times when I had nowhere to live and and foraged in Dumpsters, and I wanted to protect my son from that same fate. The best way I knew to do that was to teach him as much as I could, thereby giving him a head start on a real education—one that would make people want to hire him when he grew up. People complimented me for making my own way, as if it were admirable. If only they knew how much I'd rather have taken the easy and normal road!

For Cubby to take that gentler road, though, he had to find an interest and chase it. I could not make him want something just because I thought it was neat; he was manifestly different from me. The realization that he was not simply a newer version of me came to me over and over, and it was a surprise every time. His interest in trains waned, yet he never acquired my love of electronics and music. I was worried and troubled. *Was it possible that he simply wasn't smart enough to fully appreciate the things I'd loved when I was his age?* He didn't show a passion for civil engineering or electronics. He rode in cars but didn't show an urge to take them apart. He used computers but didn't try to modify them or make them better. For a dad who loved machines, it was surprising and unsettling.

There was, however, one thing he loved: a card game called Yu-Gi-Oh! Cubby became a walking encyclopedia and statistical index to that game. He went to tournaments at the local mall, where he challenged freakish pimply twenty-five-year-olds and even stranger eight-year-olds. More often than not, he won.

The question was, what did those victories mean? I had played cards too as a kid, but I played poker with ordinary playing cards. Poker is a game of chance and skill, where a good player can calculate the odds and gain an advantage over less skilled opponents. The deck itself is always the same, not a tool manipulated by the other player.

The trading card games Cubby played were quite different. There was no such thing as a standard deck. People assembled their own decks, and some cards were better than others. Those cards cost more, and they had to be purchased or won. So you had a situation where a sharp player could work with anything, but he might get beaten by a little kid with rich parents who bought him an unbeatable deck.

At first I was disgusted, but then I realized real life was exactly the same. The deck of life is stacked in favor of rich, entitled people;

kids who played Yu-Gi-Oh! and Pokémon were just experiencing that early.

When I won at poker, I took my money and bought dinner in town. That gave winning a purpose outside of the game. When Cubby won, he expected me to buy him rare and exotic trading game cards that would make him a more powerful player next time. His reward came from my pocket! There was always a better card to buy. Yu-Gi-Oh! was what I called a closed loop. One played it in order to play more. Some people would call that addiction, and I wouldn't disagree. The degree to which Cubby and the other kids immersed themselves in the game was almost scary.

I began to wonder if Yu-Gi-Oh! was a game of skill or a game of resources. If it was the latter, what did Cubby's winning mean? I could not tell if he was a smart player, or if he was simply good at talking me into buying expensive winning cards. I spent some time learning about the game, but my question remained unanswered. One thing became clear: Whoever invented Yu-Gi-Oh! had created a real cash machine. In that game, the inventor was the genius, and all the rest of us were just marks, like suckers at a county fair. But when I expressed that opinion to Cubby, he got mad. I realized he could not even conceive of a simple game of skill or chance, like blackjack or poker. All he knew was trading card games, where acquiring (usually buying) rare cards was the key strategy, as opposed to skill.

Naturally, he disagreed with me on the topic of ability. He claimed his success with the games was due to his cleverness and his skill; according to him, I just bought him the basic equipment that allowed him to deploy those skills. He even went so far as to suggest that the games of my childhood were simplistic compared to what he did. With a start I realized I'd been worrying whether he was as smart as me, yet all the while Cubby had assumed the opposite. He figured he was Robison 2.0 and I was little more than a dumb brute from the cave compared to him. I wasn't convinced, but his chutzpah was admirable.

I did have to concede that he applied a lot of brainpower to the game. Other players saw that too. That was obvious by the way he was greeted when I took him to the tournaments. He got a remarkable amount of respect for a kid who wasn't as old as many of the cars in the parking lot. However, I still wished he'd apply himself to something with potential commercial value.

I watched and waited, and finally I was rewarded when he discovered chemistry. Even though I had taken him on countless explorations of technology, it was his mother who introduced him to chemistry through her interest in rockets. She had been a rocketeer as long as I'd known her. When we were twenty-two, she assembled Estes rocket kits on the kitchen table and flew them on weekends. She even fitted one of her rockets with a camera and shot pictures of us gazing up as the thing took off. In fact, one of her friends made her a wedding rocket, and we launched it when we got married. By the time Cubby came along, the wedding rocket was long lost, but she kept making more rockets and launched them with him.

I should have known that would turn out to be his passion. From the moment he was born, I don't think he missed a single launch. When Cubby saw her getting ready, he latched on and didn't let go until they recovered the pieces from some downrange field. He even brought the idea to school. He got together with an adventurous teacher and three other kids, and they founded a rocket club. The objective: put a rock into orbit by the time he turned sixteen.

Finally, Cubby became so interested in rocketeering that he put his trading cards aside. The change was remarkable to watch. I first thought his interest was similar to my own fascination with model car kits, where the challenge lay in gluing the rocket together in the manner of a skilled artisan. However, I quickly realized that I was just projecting myself into my Cubby-view, and that was wrong. He was interested in the physics of the thing and the chemical reactions. That was far more sophisticated than simple model making.

The rocket fascination had an interesting side effect. It sucked up so much of Cubby's attention that he didn't have time for his "little compulsions," none of which he was even aware of. I'd been watching, and I noticed that the more he got wrapped up in rockets, the less he brushed, washed, and obsessed.

As I thought about it, I realized my dad had been the same way, in reverse. When I was younger I can't remember him having any compulsive behaviors, but he was busy then. Now that he was older, and mostly retired, he had to check the house five times before he could leave. He checked the stove twice after turning it off once. He washed his hands a lot, too. Sometimes he and Cubby did it together. It was funny to watch, until I put it together. Then I wondered, *What are my obsessive behaviors? Am I blind to them, or are they hidden because I'm busy? Or did obsessiveness skip a generation?* I never talked to Cubby about those things, but I wondered a lot.

Meanwhile, the Pokémon and Yu-Gi-Oh! cards sat in his room, abandoned. I wondered if I could recover some of my investment by selling them on eBay. He must have divined my intentions, because he growled like a guard dog whenever I went near them and began closing the door to his room. I didn't complain, though, because I saw chemistry as a special interest with a future, and I was delighted to see him studying. The cards could be gotten out and sold later, when he was launching a rocket or off at school.

He got a periodic table and the *Handbook of Chemistry*. He started reading, and telling me what rocket engines were made of and how they worked. He even asked about my experience with rockets, fireworks, and explosives. The changes had started, and Robison 2.0 was in beta!

35

BOOM!

Rockets, rocket fuel, and explosives make some kids dream of being astronauts. Not Cubby. He dreamed of becoming an organic chemist.

I wasn't surprised that Cubby found explosives fascinating. Ever since my dad first showed me how to make rockets from baking soda, vinegar, and a pop-top bottle, I've felt the same way. It's possible we are unusual, but I suspect every boy loves fireworks, deep down.

That's especially true of boys who love chemistry. There are many uses for chemists in the adult world, but every teen chemist I have ever met thinks about one of two things: explosives or drugs. Given that choice, as a dad, I preferred the former.

There's something irresistible about rockets powerful enough to light the sky and shake the ground. The bigger the blast, the more you feel it. I loved watching fireworks displays as a kid, so when I worked rock and roll as a young adult, I jumped at the chance to use them in our shows. That was where I discovered the real power of thunder. I already thought metaphorical thunder was cool. I loved it when the drummer rolled the heavy tom-toms or a timpani to make a point in a musical performance. Inspired by that, I created amplifiers that could deliver rock-and-roll thunder without self-destructing and punch the audience smack in the chest. I was proud of what I'd accomplished, and I thought I knew the state of the art, until the first time I saw KISS play a big civic center.

I knew KISS used a lot of pyro (pyro stands for pyrotechnics, another word for fireworks), but I had yet to see the band in action. Their show started like many others, as I stood at the control area with the crew. There were five of us on a little fenced island among a sea of fans. The producer hollered commands into the intercom as guitarist Paul Stanley leaned forward over the front of the stage to scream out his intro. "Do you people want a little bit of rock and roll? Shout it out loud!" With that, he lit into his guitar and the meters on the sound system swung all the way into the red. The band was playing the only way they knew: full throttle. That was the moment that pyro master Hank Schmel pushed the button, off to stage right, and the first of his bombs went off.

Before that moment I might have described the roll of the big drums as thunderous, but after, I knew the truth: Real thunder comes from the sky or out of the barrel of a cannon. That's what Hank had, sunk into the stage on both sides. Four-inchers, stubby versions of the guns on old navy destroyers. When they fired, it was as if time stopped. The flash lit the room, and the power of it rocked us back on our feet

That's how KISS started every show. It left me with a profound appreciation of the power of explosives, and a good sense of comfort using them. When I returned home, I brought knowledge of flash powder, rockets, smoke bombs, and all sorts of other loud, bright, and powerful special effects. My KISS experiences helped me to transform the shows of many other bands and even a few discos. They also helped me liven up several Halloweens.

There's nothing like a sack of explosives to brighten up your day.

People my age who work in special effects, or mining, or demolition have a lifetime of blowing things up, but my connection to fireworks faded as I got older and stopped producing music. And Cubby's only exposure to fireworks was watching them on the Fourth of July. He liked the displays, but they hadn't yet affected him in the visceral way KISS pyrotechnics got to me, many years before. In retrospect, I see that's probably because I didn't let him close enough to really feel the magic. It wasn't for lack of his trying. Cubby asked me to buy him bottle rockets, sparklers, and bangers, but I was wary and kept them at a safe distance. Some dads hand their kids M-80s as soon as they learn to walk. Not me. I'd seen my share of accidents and injuries, and there was no way I'd let my tyke get burned or get a finger blown off.

My agricultural grandparents had raised me with a real fear of losing body parts. Farmers know that risk all too well. Hooking implements to the tractor, if you weren't careful, could cost you a finger. And pyro was even more dangerous. With fireworks, if you made a mistake, you lost a whole arm, or more.

"Yep," they'd say, "Billy Joe ain't with us no more. Blew hisself up with dynamite while digging a fish pond." The old men always told me stories like that, whenever I went to the hardware store to get supplies for my grandpa. They kept the dynamite in back, stacked up in cases by the Moxie and Dr Pepper soda.

Now I was older, and times have changed. You need a federal license to buy dynamite, and stores have to keep it separate from the soft drinks. Lesser explosives like fireworks are actually illegal in Massachusetts. Not that that mattered much to an outlaw like me, but it was one more reason to tell Cubby no when he wanted his own rockets after seeing a July 4 celebration.

Cubby finally managed to circumvent my caution when he turned ten and his mom once again took him to Mexico. She was finishing her doctorate in modern-day Mayan culture, and she and Cubby spent most of that summer in the mountains of Chiapas. Chiapas is no fancy tourist resort. It's beautiful and wild high country, full of drugs, lawlessness, Zapatista rebels, and the Mexican army. You are on the border of Central America, but the country is so high that you need a sweater at night. A hundred miles away, on the coast, people bask in hundred-degree heat, but the mornings up there are fifty degrees and foggy. The countryside is broken up into little plots of land that are cultivated by innumerable subsistence farmers. Some of the fields are on slopes so steep you struggle to walk them, yet they produce crops. The roads are interrupted by vicious speed bumps they call *topes*. If you race over them, they'll break your suspension, but if you stop and crawl over them, you may get robbed by predators lurking in the bushes. Every Sunday, the villagers get drunk and pass out like corpses, right in the middle of the highway. The native people—most of the population—are descendants of the Maya, who worship the old gods in mountaintop temples accessible only on foot or by mule.

The villa Cubby's mom rented was in San Cristóbal, a town where American academics had formed a sort of expatriate community. Little Bear got acquainted with the other adults and Cubby made friends with their kids. His favorites were two brothers, Ben and Jordan. Ben was three years older than Cubby. Jordan was his same age. The kids hit it off immediately. They quickly discovered a shared love of video games, toy guns, and explosives—even pretend ones—and all those things were readily available in Mexico.

Cubby's mom gave him a ten-dollar allowance every week. Ben had some money, too. One afternoon, when Cubby's mom and Jordan's dad were distracted, the two kids went shopping. The market in San Cristóbal was unlike anything Cubby had ever seen. Vendors sold counterfeit sneakers, fake Gucci handbags, the latest movies, and all the hot video games. And in the back . . . fireworks, smoke bombs, and rockets. Best of all were the prices. Ten bucks got them a whopping sackful. The kids embarked on an orgy of fireworks buying.

Meanwhile, I was back in Massachusetts, Cubby's mom was studying, and Ben and Jordan's dad was engrossed in his own research. With no one to keep a close eye on them, the kids ran wild. They loved it.

They began experimenting right away. They launched objects into the sky and attacked targets on the ground. They did what any boys would do, given explosives, summer days, and minimal adult supervision. It was a formula for disaster, but they were all basically gentle kids, with no desire to hurt people or animals, or to blow the doors off houses. And they were not desperate enough for money to try blowing up safes or a bank vault. They just wanted to make some noise and have some fun.

Some kids would have become bored after a few days, or run out of things to detonate, but Cubby and Ben were clever and resourceful. They never ran out of new things to blast. Ben had a new dog, and his dad expected him to clean up after it. Thanks to their newfound arsenal, Ben was able to vaporize the dog poop rather than pick it up, to the delight of all the children except those unfortunate enough to get splattered by high-velocity feces.

The kids had definitely gotten the pyrotechnics bug. Once they mastered the basics of usage, they moved on to the next step: research and development. Even as a ten-year-old, Cubby was certain of his ability to improve things, especially those that caught his fancy. So Ben and Cubby took their fireworks apart and reconstituted them in different and more aggressive forms. They even staged an exhibition, to show the adults their mastery of the craft. It was clear that they were learning, and I hoped they were safe when I heard the news on the phone. They were certainly exuberant.

Unfortunately, their exuberance and noise attracted the attention of a pack of unfriendly indigenous children. The urchins began shelling them with rotten fruit and calling them names. Cubby and Ben's position in the street quickly became untenable. Realizing that, they scampered to safety behind the walls of their house (most houses in San Cristóbal sit behind high walls). Unfortunately, their attackers continued the assault by climbing trees on the adjacent property and tossing epithets and projectiles over the wall.

The kids were at a loss for a minute, but then they had an inspiration. Seizing a handful of smoke bombs, they began lobbing them at the rock-throwing urchins. They could not see over the wall, but the noises suggested their smoke was having the desired effect. Sensing they had the upper hand, Cubby, Ben, and Jordan then opened the door to the sidewalk and emerged with a handful of bottle rockets and a lighter. Grinning demonically, the three boys launched a fusillade of rockets at the bullies. With missiles whizzing everywhere, the attackers ran for the hills, the wind in their faces and their asses on fire. Technology and pyrotechnics carried the day. Cubby and Jordan were very proud of themselves.

There was only one problem. A stray rocket flew into the neighbor's garage and lodged in a car, and its owner complained to Ben and Jordan's father. In the United States things might have escalated into a lawsuit, and in the Sierra Madre someone might have been shot, but in San Cristóbal, Chiapas, everyone ultimately concluded that boys will be boys, and the matter ended with a chuckle and a drink.

That night, Cubby's mom reminded him about my interest in pyrotechnics and told him stories of the stuff she and I had made for KISS and other bands. Cubby was impressed, and determined to outdo us with his own achievements. He was nothing if not competitive.

Cubby came home from Mexico with a new interest that elbowed aside Pokémon and Yu-Gi-Oh! cards once and for all. I was proud of what he'd learned, but Massachusetts just isn't a very fireworks-friendly place. By then, though, Cubby had discovered the Internet, and he'd learned that fireworks were legal only forty miles north, in New Hampshire. As soon as he found that out, the requests began: "Can we go get some, please?" He was very persistent, and he was just getting started. July 4 was coming, and there was no way he was going to let it go by without fireworks. The bigger, the better.

AMHERST

The rockets of summer came and went with the Fourth of July. When fall came, Cubby was headed for the ninth grade. He'd be a high school student. The idea was hard to imagine, but there it was. My little boy was growing up. One way I knew that was that he discovered Eminem, the rapper. I had never even heard of the guy, but now his music filled our house: loud, punchy, and belligerent. All of a sudden, I understood what a generation gap sounded like. It was Cubby's first expression of musical taste—a sure sign of a developing mind. Houseplants and dogs, after all, do not choose the stations on the radio, though chimpanzees sometimes do.

Soon the *Star Wars* posters came off his walls, to be replaced by crude, brutish images of thugs in gold chains. Gangsta. If only it had stopped there.

I had become accustomed to delivering Cubby to his mom's on Tuesday and getting him back on Saturday in essentially the same condition as when I'd handed him over. Eminem changed all that. One day when I arrived to pick him up, his hair had turned yellow-white and was twisted into points. "Wow," I said. "What happened to you?"

He had become a little Eminem, just like the poster in his room. "My mom helped dye it," he said proudly. I didn't know what to say. Clearly, my parental influence was waning. I had never had white spiky hair, nor had I ever recommended such a thing for him. The closest I had come was suggesting that we point his ears Vulcan style, like Mr. Spock on *Star Trek,* and he declined that. As we drove home, he began reciting the lyrics to the latest rap, which he had proudly deciphered and was now bound and determined to share with anyone who would listen. His mom was probably relieved that I was taking him away.

Meanwhile, another decision point regarding Cubby's schooling had arrived. He'd outgrown Montessori and ended up at South Hadley Middle School, which he hated. With his time there at an end, we had an opportunity to put him in a high school he might like a little better, or at least hate a little less. However, bad as South Hadley was, we still weren't sure we should try our luck elsewhere. Maybe the new school would be worse. Other people might have embraced change, and jumped into a new educational program with both feet, but we were not that way. Neither, it seemed, was Cubby. If anything, he was more a creature of routine and habit than either of us.

We had both seen how he thrived in the Montessori environment, but there was no Montessori high school within driving distance. So Little Bear visited almost every private school in the area in hopes of finding a place Cubby could be successful. They had names like Hartsbrook School, The Common School, or Deerfield Academy, and every one followed a different teaching philosophy. At least that's what they claimed. When you read about them, each school had a slick set of arguments for why their method was best. I'd never have guessed there were so many ways to run a school. Like many dads, I had taken school for granted. You put your kid in as an ignorant toddler, and he emerges twelve years later doing reading, writing, and arithmetic like a champ. If only it were that simple.

With all the educational variety we looked at, none followed the Montessori method, and we had no idea how Cubby would do in them. I looked at the school materials briefly too, but seeing pictures of smiling kids in school sales packages just made me mad, as I thought about my own failures years before. So I mostly left school selection to Cubby's mom.

She jumped into the task with both feet, but she ran into some fundamental problems right away. We had been thinking so hard about what school we would choose that it took a while to dawn on us that the school had to choose us back. To my dismay, I learned that Cubby had to apply, and that he might be rejected. Still worse, we found out that we were long past the application deadline. *How full can they be?* I wondered. They charged the price of a nice car for a season's tuition. At those rates, I figured they'd take anyone who came along, if the parents were willing to pay. To my shock, half the places we looked at were full.

In the case of the ones that still had room, we now faced the ugly prospect of Kid Assessment. *Was he good enough?* I had known all along that Cubby would have to compete if he wanted to get into a good college. Every sixth grader knows that Harvard and MIT only admit a few of the kids who apply. But competing to get into high school? The mere suggestion sounded crazy to me, and when I met some of the parents who drove their kids to go to those places, I decided they were not for us.

Not that there was anything wrong with those moms and dads, but they exhibited a strong surplus of what I'd charitably call "competitive spirit" on behalf of their kids, and with that sentiment totally lacking in me, I did not see a possible fit. I had as much desire as anyone to see my kid succeed, but the idea of calling my son's history teacher and bullying her because she only gave Cubby an A-minus was alien to me. Actually, Cubby getting A-minus grades was alien too, and that made the whole thing moot.

I wanted him to do well and go to college, but my desire only took us so far.

There was also the possibility of homeschooling, but Cubby's mom ruled that out. She was finally on track to earn her doctorate at UMass, but she had run out of time extensions, and taking on the job of teaching Cubby would have meant throwing all that away.

By then it was August, and we did not have too many choices left. One or the other of us could move somewhere with better public schools, or we could keep him in the South Hadley school system. Mom was in no position to move, but I was. I had no ties to Chicopee, and I liked the idea of a nicer home in a more rural setting. So Martha, Cubby, and I started talking about a new home. We wanted a town where we could all feel like we fit in—a place that accommodated geeks and freaks, was safe, and within commuting distance of Springfield.

By that point, my business had brought me into contact with people in most every town around us. I'd learned which ones had good schools and which ones were troubled. The towns with the best schools—Longmeadow, Wilbraham, and Amherst—were very different from one another. Longmeadow was a town of large traditional homes populated by business executives, doctors, and lawyers. Wilbraham was more rural with a similar population. Between them, those two towns seemed to contain most of the affluent people who worked in the Springfield area.

Unfortunately, I didn't identify with the denizens of those places at all. I might have serviced their cars, but I never saw myself as one of them. After all, I hadn't attended a fancy college, and I had failed in my efforts to play executive. I didn't play golf, and I was the farthest thing from a backslapping good old boy at the nineteenth hole afterward. I wished I could do some of those things, and I wanted to be a different person, but I knew I wasn't.

Then there was the problem of rules and regulations in those upscale executive neighborhoods. That became apparent as soon as

I began looking at property. "They have a neighborhood association here," one Realtor said proudly as I stood before a fine home smack dab in the midst of twenty more identical properties. "What does that mean?" I asked. She was quick to answer. "It means they keep the riffraff out. No vans with tradesman markings in the driveway. No pink flamingo or stable boy lawn ornaments allowed. No boats or campers parked out back. No fences or sheds or other structures allowed."

Jesus, I thought. *These people might think they own their houses, but they have no rights. No tradesman vans? What am I, if not a tradesman?* I fixed cars for a living. It didn't take long to conclude that neighborhood was not for us. After all, if I couldn't fit in myself, I surely wasn't going to be able to help my son fit in. As nice as some of the Longmeadean and Wilbrahamian homes were, I knew we had to keep looking for a place with less anal zoning regulations.

We found that in Amherst. The people who lived there wore tie-dye shirts instead of fancy polos. Many of them worked at the nearby colleges—UMass, Amherst, Hampshire, Smith, and Mount Holyoke. Others did creative work, like composing or performing music, writing books, or developing computer software. I didn't do any of those things (yet), but the eclectic mix of people made me feel more comfortable. Also, I had grown up there and Cubby's mom was finishing her degree at UMass. Cubby had attended Montessori right downtown and liked it the best of any school he'd attended. Some of his friends were now at the high school. Best of all, Amherst still had rural homes in communities with no obnoxious regulations. I would be free to do whatever I wanted, surrounded by woods. All that considered, moving to Amherst made a lot of sense.

The only thing that stood in our way was cost. Of all the towns around us, Amherst was the most expensive place to buy a home. A few towns away, you could buy a nice home for $150,000. That same house would cost three hundred grand in Amherst. That's the price you pay for a town with good schools. All the parents want to raise their kids there, and that drives the house prices up. It would be a stretch, but we decided to do it. We'd move to Amherst.

With our minds made up, all that was left was choosing a house. We began our tour the following weekend. Cubby was excited for the first half hour but quickly became bored. I didn't feel bored; I was just disgusted. By that time, I had a fair bit of experience fixing up houses. The house I'd moved into in Chicopee had been a wreck, but it was also inexpensive. The houses we were looking at in Amherst were worse wrecks for twice the price.

I was finding out that the premium for living in Amherst was even higher than I had thought. I compared the housing situation to the used-car market, because I was a lot more familiar with cars. If you want to drive a high-end car like a Mercedes, there are two ways to do it. You can go to the dealer and buy a new one. That doesn't require anything but money, but it takes a lot of that. More than I had. Alternatively, you can buy used. There are like-new cars with like-new price tags, and junks one step from the scrap heap at somewhat lower prices. There's always some do-it-yourselfer waiting to fix up those old beaters.

Finally, there were the cars with major problems, like a blown engine. Those cars sell for next to nothing, because most do-it-yourself bidders won't tackle projects that big. Those were the cars I bought for myself. I could always fix them up and sell them for more than they cost, and I did that for years.

After a bit of study, I concluded the same philosophy applied to houses. Indeed, we doubled the value of the Chicopee house through well-chosen repairs and improvement. Unfortunately, there were no suitable fixer-uppers in Amherst.

That left one more option that did not exist in the car-repair world. I could build a home on an empty piece of land. That would give me the chance to use my engineering skills to design the place, and my mechanical skills to put it up. I wasn't planning on hammering every nail myself, but taking an active role in the design and management could save me a huge sum of money. The more I thought about it, the more I realized that was really what I did at my car company. I didn't turn the wrenches there, but I planned the jobs and supplied the vision. That's what had made the money to buy our last home, and I hoped those skills would deliver us an even better home now.

That's what we decided to do. Just after Cubby's thirteenth birthday, we picked a lot on a tract of land one of my friends was developing. Then I got out a book of home plans and sat down with my AutoCAD drafting system to work out the details. I'd designed all sorts of things for work, I figured, so how hard can a house design be? Cubby would finish high school in the same school I had attended, thirty years before. I was very sure he would do a great deal better. And when we broached the idea with Cubby, he was actually enthusiastic.

Since we were building the house ourselves, I seized the chance to design in features that would maximize the chance of a happy outcome for everyone. For example, the new house would have radiant heat, which would make it much more comfortable in winter. I'd never lived in a house with radiant heat before, but many of our more affluent customers did, and they recommended it highly.

All my life, I had lived in houses that didn't have enough electrical outlets. I'd tripped over extension cords for lamps because there were no lights in the ceiling. I'd endured tiny windows that leaked cold air in winter and air conditioners that struggled to cool the house below eighty-five in summer. "We are going to address all those deficiencies in this new place," I told Cubby.

Most people think architects design houses, but that's not completely accurate. Anyone can draw a door or a window onto a plan, but it takes an engineer to ensure the structure will stay together and do its intended job. Architects deliver style, convenience, and many other things, but proper home design starts with engineering, which for our house meant me. "You have to think about what you might do in a room," I explained to my son, "and engineer the room to do that job. For example, if we want to be able to move heavy objects, we can put a steel beam in the ceiling to support a travel crane. We can have a miniature version of a shipyard hoist, right in our garage!"

Seeing his surprise, I realized my son had not foreseen the full range of uses the rooms of our house might be put to. "Why would we want that?" he asked. I reminded him that we use the lifts and cranes at my work every single day. Indeed, we'd be crippled without them. "If you have a travel crane, it will get used." He nodded his head, realizing the wisdom of that statement.

"We need to think through every nook and cranny of this house, and design in whatever features we may need," I said. I showed him the computer program I used to calculate the heat load for the air conditioner, and we looked through climate-control catalogs together. I told him that every kid needed to understand refrigeration systems, and he nodded thoughtfully. My son even helped work out the placement of light switches, water faucets, closets, and cabinets. We have allergies, so we designed in a central vacuum system, with pipes in the walls, outlets in each room, and a big vacuum in the basement. Whatever air and dust that system sucked off the floor got exhausted into the yard, not recirculated back into the room as with an ordinary vacuum. Our new house was going to be really special, and totally unique.

The pile of blueprints grew steadily larger. I opened a charge account at the architectural printer in town so I could keep the workmen up to date. As the months passed, one crew of tradesmen after another passed through. First there were framers, then roofers and siders. The most unique were the plasterers. Making walls out of lath and plaster is becoming a lost art in America, so my plaster crew was imported from Russia. They didn't speak English, but they read instructions, and they walked all over the house on stilts, telling obscene jokes, laughing, and spreading plaster on walls and our twelve- and fifteen-foot ceilings with big plastic trowels.

When they were done there was no sign they'd ever been there, and the surfaces were silky smooth. No one would ever guess that men on stilts had made it happen.

As the pace of work ramped up, we visited the job site every day. I brought Cubby with me as often as I could. He helped me answer the endless questions from the crew that was putting our new home together. Where should the electrical outlets go? How about shelves in the closet? When you walk through a finished home, it's easy to forget that someone had to make a choice about everything you see. For our home, the decision maker was me—with some help from Cubby and Martha.

His contribution to the construction was back in a corner of the yard. There he found a great big tree with a trunk two feet in diameter. Seeing it, Cubby had one of the workmen saw him a series of planks. He took them out back and nailed them to the tree, forming a ladder. Then he rigged some rope—hammock style—to make a platform. Then, below and behind the tree, he dug a six-foot-deep foxhole and surrounded it with stones. We could do what we wanted up at the house—he had us all covered from his fort in the back!

The plans showed three bedrooms on the main floor. One was labeled "Master Bedroom," and it was visibly bigger than the other two. "I'll take that one," he said as soon as he saw the choices. "No you won't," I answered. "I am the King of the House, and that is my room. You pick one of the others." Cubby snorted.

"I'll take the one in the corner," he said, and we set about laying it out. One of Cubby's friends had a seat built into the wall beside his bed. The top of the seat opened to reveal a large storage area. "Can we do that in our new home?" he asked. "Sure." Cubby and I drew a window seat into the plans. "Can we build a secret room in the closet, too?" So we did. That's the thing about building your own house—you can do anything you want. And that went for me, too.

"I want to keep track of what you're doing in that room," I told him. "Let's add cameras so I can watch you day and night." "No!" His objection was loud and immediate. I wondered what he was trying to hide. He was certainly changing as he got older.

We never installed those cameras, but we did build a walkway all through the attic and installed nice bright lights in the attic and the basement. No dark crawl spaces for me. If there was a storm, I told my friends proudly, I could walk through the attic and inspect my roof for damage from the safety of my walkway. I could not tell if they were impressed or puzzled. "I've never inspected my roof," one said quizzically. I didn't know how to respond.

Finally, I put in a platform, nestled in the rafters, four feet above the ceiling of Cubby's room. The platform was connected to the attic walkway above it with a short ladder and was designed to serve as a work space for anyone making repairs in the attic. I even had a pipe to the basement, in case we needed to pass electric cables from here to there in the future. The whole thing was rather nice, if I did say so myself. Cubby didn't agree.

"What's that up there?" he asked warily. He had become very suspicious of my construction suggestions, especially when they involved him.

"It's the Demon's Nest. If you can't handle cameras," I said, "my supernatural guardians will do the watching for me."

Because, well, you just never know.

PINE DEMONS

We put the Chicopee house on the market a few weeks after starting construction in Amherst. I felt a little anxiety about that, because I figured it would take at least six months to sell, and the builders were racing forward on our new place. My worst fear was that they'd finish the new house with the old one still unsold. *What then?* To my amazement, the Chicopee place sold right away for almost twice what we'd paid a few years before. I felt smart and proud, attributing its rise in value to my own fixing-up efforts. That was a few years before people began talking about the great housing bubble.

Unfortunately, our quick success selling the old place meant that we had only sixty days to move out, and our new house was nowhere near ready. On top of that, we discovered that there were very few houses for rent, and most required one- or two-year leases. "You should rent a motel suite," one landlord suggested helpfully. We finally found the place Cubby named the Interim House through a friend's son who knew a landlord with a two-story farmhouse. She was willing to rent out the first floor month to month, and I grabbed it, sight unseen. "How bad could it be?" I asked my family. "And anyway, we're only going to live there for a little while."

So we packed up the household and put it in storage, keeping only the barest essentials, and installed ourselves in the farmhouse, about four miles from our new home site. That was good. There were trails to walk on, and the setting was pretty. That was good too. Then school started, the students returned, and we found ourselves living downstairs from four girls who liked to stay up all night and party. That wasn't so good, especially when their friends got drunk and sang songs in the backyard.

"It's okay," I reassured Cubby and Martha, as revelers banged on the ceiling above. "We're only going to be here a few more months. We're better off putting up than starting over." There was a crash outside as someone or something upended a barrel. I didn't tell them there wasn't anywhere else to go, but it was true. In a college town, there are plenty of places to rent in summer, but once the school year starts, forget it. Every room in town is rented to students.

Cubby didn't seem to mind; after all, we were building him his own room in the new house, and meanwhile the Interim House was a lot nicer than the cabins at Chesterfield Boy Scout Camp. He was fine right up until the weather turned cold, a month or so after we moved in. That was when the rodents invaded.

Some rodents are bold, breaking down doors and taking over kitchen counters. The creatures at the Interim House were subtle and sneaky. So much so that I hadn't even known they were there until Cubby told me.

"Dad!" he shouted. "There's someone in here!" I ran to his room, ready to confront an attacker. There was no one there.

"Did you have a bad dream," I asked? He'd had dreams before, and woken up when the monsters grabbed him.

"No," he said. "Listen!" I stood still for a moment, and I heard it: a slow scraping, as though something was moving against the wall.

I shone my light in the direction of the sound, but there was nothing but bare floor. Yet the sound continued.

Was it coming from outside? Perhaps someone or something *was* breaking in. Or perhaps one of the upstairs tenants had fallen out a window and was crawling around drunk on the ground. Quickly, I ran across the room, down the hall, out the back door, and into the night. I crept quietly around the house, until I had Cubby's room in sight from the yard. I hit the switch on my flashlight and lit up the area, expecting to catch someone or something in the act. Nothing. I walked up to the house. There were no burglars, no drunks, and no footprints or tracks. Puzzled, I went back inside.

"There's nothing there," I told Cubby. But that didn't satisfy either of us; we'd both heard the noise. Then it started again. I put my ear to the wall. I opened the window and looked out from there. Whatever it was lurked within the wall.

Cubby dragged his bedding into the other bedroom, and we all went to sleep.

The next day we went exploring. It didn't take long to find the answer. Squirrels. I showed Cubby the evidence. "It's rodent central in the wall. They've eaten a hole through the siding, and they've tunneled into the house. There could be a whole rodent empire, right on the other side of your bedroom Sheetrock. Cool, huh?" Cubby was not impressed. He remembered my tales of superpowered squirrels living in the woods around our Chicopee house, and he had never been quite sure whether or not they were true. "You called them Pine Demons," he said accusingly. Then an idea hit him. "You should shoot these squirrels," he said with great certainty.

Most times, I was willing and able to accommodate his requests, but that time I couldn't. "Sorry, Cubby, it's a rented house and we can't perforate the walls with gunfire. We won't have a problem unless they eat their way through and into our space. But I don't think that will happen. Look at this hole. They've obviously been in there a long time. And there's no sign the inside walls have been invaded.

I'm pretty sure we are okay. I think they know enough to stay on their side of the wall."

"Also, squirrels are not carnivores. They eat nuts, not kids. You should be perfectly safe, unless these squirrels are mutants. Then you could be in trouble, so maybe you should sleep with a hammer next to your pillow."

He still wasn't reassured, but I had another idea. "Let's go to work and get a big piece of steel plate. We'll use your mattress and some boxes to press it against the wall. That way, if they eat through the wall, the steel will stop them. Even New York City rats don't eat through steel plate! You'll be the only kid in town with an armored bedroom wall."

Cubby liked the idea of the plate, but he still didn't like the house. "How soon can we move out of here?" he asked. I wasn't too afraid of carnivorous vermin, but I was eager to leave too. "Soon," was all I could say. Building a house was turning out to be a bigger job than I'd imagined, and winter had set in. The short days and cold nights really slowed us down. Three months turned into six, and six months turned to seven.

We reached an uneasy truce with the rodents—one that lasted through winter. They did not eat through the walls and attack us, and we did not shoot the house full of bullet holes to suppress them. They agreed to keep the noises in the wall to a minimum, and we did not explore what they were really doing in there. No one called the cops. As I told Cubby, some questions are best left unanswered.

Christmas came and went, and the days started getting longer. Construction of the new house was almost done, and Cubby had settled into the new school system. I had anticipated the beginning of school eagerly, with its promise of peace and quiet at night, as Cubby studied quietly and went to bed. Unfortunately, he didn't share my enthusiasm for school. For him, the resumption of school meant more adults telling him what to do, and schoolwork instead of chemistry and games. I just hoped we'd see the end of Cubby staying up till three in the morning and sleeping till noon.

Unfortunately, we were not progressing too smoothly toward that goal. For a whole month before school started, we'd been struggling to get him to bed on time and to wake him up at a reasonable hour. We'd sat down at the dining room table and had mature discussions about healthy sleep habits and responsibility. Unfortunately, translating that understanding into practice proved to be very difficult for my child. We went through the same ritual night after night. It began with me saying, "Cubby! It's time to turn the lights off!"

"Okay," he'd answer. "Just a minute." A minute would come and go, and the light would remain on. We would go back and forth five or six times, but that "lights out" minute never seemed to arrive. On rare occasions, he would actually shut down the computer, shut off the lights, and go to sleep. However, those nights were the exception, not the rule. Most nights we went around and around, with the talk getting more and more acrimonious, until one or the other of us gave up.

On the nights his mom had him, she didn't do any better. She tried a different tack to get him to sleep, but Cubby promptly turned it around on us. "Mom says I can stay up as late as I want, as long as I get up and go to school in the morning." When we tried that, he woke up at ten, halfway through the morning. A few weeks later, the notice came from the school: He had come in late too many times, and half the times he was late, he'd been with Mom.

Clearly, neither one of us knew what to do. Yet it seemed like such a simple problem. "Establish a bedtime," the parenting books said. Why couldn't we do that?

Cubby was turning out to be highly resistant to authority, and the situation got worse as he got older. He was so difficult, he actually reminded me of myself. Some nights I just got fed up and shut off his computer. That produced horrible howls of protest, but they usually subsided and he eventually settled down to sleep. Or else I fell asleep and didn't know what actually happened. After all, I had to work in the morning. He seemed to think school was optional. I knew work wasn't. I wished he'd learn that school wasn't optional either, but we didn't seem to be getting too far in that direction.

Cubby knew I'd had a hard time at Amherst High, so he would look at me and say, "You dropped out of school. Why do I have to go?" It was hard to come up with a compelling answer, though I knew his life would be better if he graduated. From his perspective, I'd thumbed my nose at school and done just fine. He didn't see how many doors had been closed to me as a young adult for lack of a high school or college diploma.

I tried to focus on the problems without getting mad and solve them one at a time, rationally. The first problem was figuring out whether he had really gone to sleep. When he was little, I just tip-toed into his room and looked. Now he hunkered down behind a closed door. The problem with bigger kids is that they want privacy. Ever since he turned thirteen, Cubby had insisted on closing his door. This made sleep verification next to impossible. I could not tell if his light was off and his computer put away unless I looked inside. However, he objected to my looking, even briefly. In fact, he began locking the door, which provoked a series of arguments that culminated in a standoff. I would not remove the door, and he would not lock it. I would knock before entering, and he would not jam things in the doorway to block me. That wasn't very conducive to nighttime sleep monitoring. Finally, I realized I had to give up. I had to trust that he was going to bed, and if he wasn't, I had to leave him to face the consequence of being tired.

For someone who was accustomed to being King of the House, Wondrous Dada to his son, it was a sorry turn of events, and a fateful shift in the balance of power. I told myself that's what happens to all parents. The kids get bigger and stronger, until one day, you throw them out.

A NEW NEST

In the midst of our tug-of-war with Cubby, spring arrived and our new house was finally finished. The rodent army was still alive and well in the walls of the Interim House, and we were more than ready to leave. The very day that the building inspector gave us a certificate of occupancy for the new home, we split, hauling mattresses and clothes across town on my utility trailer. A week later, after a lot of hard work and a little professional help, we were settled into our new home among packing material, boxes, and furniture.

The dog spent the day walking around, sniffing his new place. He hadn't liked the Interim House at all, because the upstairs tenants' noises woke him up constantly. He was getting old and cranky, and I hoped he'd be happier here, because he barked when he woke, and that aggravated all of us.

The one thing we did not bring with us was the vermin. In fact, we took secret special steps to make our new home as resistant as possible to unwelcome envermination.

Cubby had never been in a brand-new house before. It was a unique experience, sleeping in something we had just created—sort of like being a dog, nesting in a freshly dug burrow, except we weren't dogs, and our burrow had heat, light, and running water. We spent several contented hours walking around and exploring our new yet familiar home.

The following Monday, Cubby and I walked together to the bus stop. I had high hopes that he'd like Amherst High School better and get on a good schedule in this new place, but that was not to be. The fight to get him up and moving continued. As the school year progressed, Cubby won the battle of bedtime by default. I was tired out from working, moving, and the stress of argument. I left him in his room, door closed, and went to sleep. All I could do was warn him that wake-up time would be coming soon. And that was the next battle.

Six o'clock would come, and I would wake to the sound of Cubby's alarm, beeping away through the closed door. "Cubby! Get up!" I'd pound on his door, but he had practiced ignoring both the alarm and me. I don't know if he ignored those alarms consciously or he just slept like the dead. We bought him every loud and obnoxious alarm we could find, and none woke him up. Most days, I faced a choice of going off to work and leaving him asleep with a blaring alarm, or going in and waking him up. Eventually, with the threat of a bucket of cold water, he would acknowledge me.

"Out," he said, as he waited for me to leave the room before he would get up. I'd learned that was often a trick. If I went away and didn't follow up, he might just go right back to sleep. I tried everything I could think of to change this ritual, to no avail. Some said, "Make it his responsibility. Let him suffer the consequence of missing school." The trouble was, he did not care about the consequences of missing school. He was like me in that regard. The older he got, the less use he had for adults telling him what to do and trying to make him study boring dreck when he had his own topic in mind: chemistry.

If I'd left him alone, he would have happily slept till noon, and then woken up and studied chemistry and done experiments until two in the morning. More and more, I was seeing my own Aspergian traits in him . . . his obliviousness to other people, his rigidity, and his all-consuming obsessions. The psychologists who had examined him earlier had never suggested he had Asperger's, but of course Asperger's wasn't in the diagnostic lexicon when we started working with him and the school. And each report just built on the one before, which meant that we talked about ADD tendencies or problems with visual processing. All the while, the root cause—autism in the form of Asperger's—was right there under our noses.

When I look back on those years, I'm shocked I didn't see it sooner. He was so stuck in his routines, and his behavior was, in retrospect, totally Aspergian. It was his way or no way. Very regimented, and sometimes seemingly nonsensical. Like the fight over the bus on our first school day in the new house.

"I can't ride the bus. You have to drive me." He knew we expected him to ride the bus, just like every other kid. And he surely knew what I'd say when he objected.

"When I was a kid, I walked to school. You should walk too. It would be good for you."

"Dad! It's three miles! I can't walk!" I just looked at him. It was six miles from my parents' house in Shutesbury to the same school he was attending now.

"Of course you can. You're a kid. Kids are full of energy. Pretend there's a pack of monsters chasing you."

"Dad!" He was getting to the age where monster threats were more aggravating than scary. As we argued, he became more and more agitated, and meanwhile, the bus came and went. That left me with no choice but to drive him or leave him home. Abandoning him did not seem like a good way to help him succeed in his first year in the new school, so off we went.

That experience seemed to establish the pattern for much of the school year. We would argue, the bus would pass us by, and I'd take

Cubby to school. Then I turned south and headed for work. At least he was going to school, I thought, even if he didn't ride the bus. I hoped he was going to class.

I always wondered whether there was some reason he didn't want to ride the bus. Was he being bullied? When I asked, he said no, he just didn't like it. I finally concluded there was nothing more to it. Who wouldn't prefer to be driven? I wished I had the parenting skills to get him onto that bus every day, but judging from the line of cars dropping off kids, I was far from alone in that predicament.

Cubby wasn't doing extraordinarily well academically, but his ability to make friends was wonderful to behold. I'd been a total social failure, but he was downright popular! He didn't say much about friends to me, but I couldn't help noticing that when I picked him up at school he was always with other people. And once we were in the new house, he even started bringing friends home. By the time the school year ended, he was hanging out with friends at our house or in town most every day. First there was one, then two, and ultimately a whole pack. There were even girls. They'd come over and shoot paintball guns at the trees, or watch movies, or just sit in the living room and talk.

Of course, being Cubby, he also led his friends in some novel activities. "Check out what I just built," he told his assembled audience one summer afternoon. I observed the scene as I stood by my toolbox, across the garage. Cubby was pointing to a large white pipe on a wood frame, with wires leading from the pipe to a homemade box.

"What is it?"

"It's a cannon," he said proudly. "I built it from leftover plastic drain pipe, and I made my own black powder. It's fired by this electrical detonator, which sends a signal down these wires to a model rocket squib that I bury in the powder charge."

My friend Neil saw that and encouraged him further, sending

my son a magazine with plans for a hair-spray-propellant-powered potato cannon that could shoot spuds a quarter of a mile. Or so the designers claimed. Cubby immediately set to work building his own, which he assured us would be even better.

His friends looked at him with a combination of amusement, skepticism, and disbelief. Their expressions changed when he rolled his creation outside and set it off. With a roar and a great cloud of smoke, a plastic ball was launched across the yard. It was truly remarkable, the amount of firepower a chunk of common plastic sewer pipe could deliver.

Over the next few months, he refined his homebuilt artillery until he could shoot holes in plywood sheets from halfway down the driveway. Even my friends were impressed. I questioned him about safety, but he reassured me and pointed out how many other young people were involved in black powder competitions, potato cannon making, and even pumpkin chucking. "We should do that," he said excitedly. He got the idea that he'd like to compete in the world championship, and I almost went along until I found out it was held four hundred miles away, and the winners used home-built guns the size of the army's medium-size field artillery.

I looked at Cubby's experiments and marveled, and so did his friends. It seemed to me that I had a potential inventor on my hands. I thought of the sound effects and special effects I'd dreamed up in the music world, and envisioned him doing something similar with this. Never in a million years did it occur to me that his experiments would end up landing him in such hot water a few years later.

IN THE HIGH SCHOOL GROOVE

Impressed as I was by my son's ingenuity and newfound social skills, I still had worries about his academics. Indeed, his problems had already surfaced with a warning from the school: "Jack is not doing his assignments, and he loses or forgets them all the time." Those were the same sort of warnings he'd gotten in South Hadley; it was one of the problems we'd hoped to escape. With a dull sense of dread, I imagined my own high school failure playing out with my son. I never did my homework as a kid, and his homework load was far greater than anything I had known. We tend to look back and think we had it harder as youths, but when it comes to homework I know the reverse is true.

The note didn't surprise me; I'd been primed to expect trouble. What did bother me was the news that he wasn't doing his work. In anticipation of the upcoming high school workload, we had gone out and gotten him binders for all his classes. We'd set up colored dividers to organize things and purchased a little book that he could use to jot down notes. Could all of our organizational assistance have failed him?

A look in his room might have provided a clue. All teenagers have messy rooms, but his was beyond normal. It was the kind of room they featured on TV shows and cleaned out with a front-end loader. The floor was so covered in clothes, toys, and books that you couldn't open the door all the way.

I guess we should have realized the inside of his head might look sort of the same. Unfortunately, we didn't make the connection between the mess in his room and the chaos elsewhere in his life. His disorganization was a sign of an executive functioning problem, something psychologists see in many autistic people. At the time, the best we could do was clean the floor when he wasn't there.

When he came home from school, we learned we had to check his homework and review what he was expected to do. Martha often spent hours sitting beside him at the dining room table, going over his assignments line by line. Every night, we said, "Have you done all your homework?" and he answered yes. The trouble was, when I asked to see his papers, they were invariably covered in illegible scrawl. But when I pointed that out, he looked at me as if I were nuts and read what sounded like articulate prose from the paper.

I wasn't sure what to do. Cubby had conquered the reading challenge on his own. Writing was another matter, and he was starting to struggle in math as well. With the addition of his organizational troubles, even I felt overwhelmed.

Not only did the school offer no constructive help, they acted as if we'd done nothing at all. Their indifference to Cubby's plight made me furious. I was so mad I could not go see them, and I had to turn over school communications to his mother and Martha. I was sure the school had failed us but uncertain exactly how it happened. Worst of all, I felt powerless to do anything about it.

Finally, Martha suggested we try tutoring. We were in a college town, and there were plenty of students looking for jobs. At first, it seemed to work. The assignments the tutors helped him on did get better grades, and he understood the work more fully. But the notes about lost assignments and poor organization continued.

Then we got the idea to try the Sylvan Learning Center, a place we passed every time we went through Hadley. We stopped by, and it seemed a friendly environment, populated by grad students from the university, local teachers moonlighting after school, and a bunch of jolly-looking kids. So we spoke to a counselor there and over the next few days Cubby completed one test after another. Interestingly, he didn't seem to mind. Apparently, he wanted help just as much as we did.

We returned to Sylvan the following week to talk about the results. Cubby was two years behind his grade level in writing and math. The good news, they said, was that with intensive work on both, and help with organization, Cubby could be up to grade level or better in six months.

The idea that we might fix his academic issues in one school year sounded too good to be true, but the Sylvan people had a plan, and we decided to give it a try. Every day after school Cubby would go to Sylvan, where he'd do handwriting assignments and get help organizing his assignments. On some days he'd get math tutoring. Instead of doing his homework at home, he'd do it there, and a teacher would make sure everything was complete before we brought him home.

I was stuck at work when school let out, but Martha had more flexibility. She shuttled him back and forth from school to Sylvan to home. I worked harder to make the money to pay for the program. The results were visible right away. His grades went up, and the threatening notes from the school tapered off and finally ended altogether. In a matter of months, he had advanced two grade levels in math, and his handwriting had improved dramatically. We were both shocked and thrilled by the speed and magnitude of the improvement. It was the same sort of change we'd seen years before, with reading.

My hopes of Cubby graduating from high school returned.

Unfortunately, his academic success wasn't self-sustaining and our financial resources were not unlimited. When we stopped bringing him to Sylvan, his grades plummeted. We weren't sure why, because he retained everything they'd taught him in math, and his handwriting and grammar didn't deteriorate. He just seemed to stop getting things done. *It must be the organization,* I thought. We'd watched them walk Cubby through the steps to complete an assignment, and he followed the tutor just fine, yet he was simply unable to follow the same routine on his own. Every time I got mad, or decided he was just lazy, I reminded myself of that day the Yale shrink had drawn a tic-tac-toe game on the blackboard and my son was unable to copy it on paper. Then I remembered how we could tell him which boxes to mark, and he'd do it right every time. I wondered how that translated to his present-day trouble, but I never found the answer.

(Today, almost ten years later, I serve on the federal committee that makes the government's strategic plan for autism research. Simple as my son's issues sound, I now know the best scientists in the world have yet to find all the answers to problems like these. A few new behavioral therapies can help, but they only take us part of the way. The mind is a complex thing, and the simplest observed behaviors may have complex roots.)

We signed him up for another round of help, and another after that. All was well, until the bill came due. We'd spent ten thousand dollars, and we weren't even halfway through the school year! With a shock, I realized Cubby's tutoring was costing as much as a good college. I did some quick calculations. At the rate we were going, it would cost a hundred grand to get our son through high school. What then? We couldn't afford it.

I had just built us a house in what we believed was the best school district in the area. Before moving, I'd gone through the calculations of what the house would cost, the value of a better education for our son, and the other alternatives. The idea that he'd need costly coaching in addition to school had never crossed my mind, but even if it had, it wouldn't have made any difference. Forty or fifty grand a year for educational assistance wasn't in the cards, wherever we lived.

Today, there is a whole industry built around advocating for services. Lawyers and consultants hire themselves out to parents to force school districts to provide the support the law says they must deliver. Schools might fight tooth and nail, but the lawyers usually prevail. However, it never occurred to us to pursue a legal remedy. We assumed we were on our own. Little Bear had fought with the schools back in South Hadley, but all she got was an agreement that they would pay for Cubby to be tested. And I had never looked to others to save me or anyone in my family. The way I saw things, from the moment I left home as a teenager, I worked or starved. There was no safety net. It never occurred to me that things might be different for my son.

I sure wish I'd known a little more and hired someone to fight hard for Cubby. Twenty hours a week of one-on-one coaching might have made a world of difference for him. But I didn't know, and it didn't happen. I told Cubby we had to cut back on tutoring. Instead, Martha volunteered to help with organization. She accompanied him to Sylvan and watched carefully to see what they were doing. His coaches were happy to help her and offer advice. It seemed pretty straightforward.

Unfortunately, it wasn't. His grades dipped again, and stayed that way. The admonishing notes resumed and their tone made me feel as if our fitness as parents was challenged right alongside our son's poor academic showing. At first we didn't know about the warnings, because Cubby came home before us and he took to looting school correspondence from the mail. Weeks went by with no word from school, and I thought we were on track. The report card we pried from him set that notion straight.

I felt sad and scared and powerless. I could not afford the kind of help he needed, and the help I could afford didn't seem to make any difference. The worst thing was, my son was losing interest in school. With every nasty note, he lost a little more hope that he'd ever actually graduate. At the same time, he saw his budding success with chemistry, and thought the same kinds of things I'd thought about school versus electronics many years before.

"If I'm never going to graduate, why should I stay? I'm doing just fine learning chemistry on my own. What do I need high school for?" I tried to tell him how hard it would be to land a job as a chemist with no academic credentials.

"You did fine," he responded.

"Cubby, the situation was totally different. I joined a band, and used success there to get a job designing sound effects. And look at me now! I fix cars! Where's the brainpower in that!"

If he wanted to be a chemist, I told him, he needed to go to college. In fact, college wasn't even enough. His ambition was to do something big, like invent a new explosive or design a new antidepressant. To do that kind of work, I explained, he'd need a doctorate from a top-tier university.

He still didn't give in. "I could invent things, like Bob Jeffway. If I bring a big company a chemical process that works, they aren't going to ask where I went to college."

I didn't know what to say, because he was basically correct. Bob was one of my oldest friends. We'd been engineers together at Milton Bradley almost thirty years before. Back in 1979, Bob and I both earned a great living as engineers and thought we had it made. Yet the wages we earned then seemed like peanuts compared to the royalties Bob made later, when he went back to those same companies as a game inventor and designer. Cubby knew that. There was no personnel officer scrutinizing the credentials of inventors when they walked in the door. If someone brought Milton Bradley a winning game, they grabbed it. It didn't make a shred of difference whether the designer walked out of a Florida swamp or graduated with honors from Harvard.

"It's a hard road, Cubby," was all I could think to say. "Being a freelance inventor, with no one bankrolling your lab or your lifestyle—that is a hard road to follow. No matter what you say now, life as a chemist will be a thousand times easier if you get a good education. I just want you to make the right choice." All I could do was hope he was listening.

A DIFFERENT ANIMAL

Teenagers are very different animals from little kids. Little Bear and I found that out when Cubby was about fourteen or fifteen and began making plans of his own with his new Amherst friends. We parents weren't included. Actually, we weren't even consulted. Cubby simply began riding the bus to his friends' houses, or getting rides, and staying late into the evening. On days when he was supposed to be with his mother, he'd call her and say, "I wanna stay late. I'll have Dad pick me up, and I'll stay with him." Over the space of a year, he went from staying with Martha and me three nights a week to living in Amherst five or even six nights a week.

There were times when his mom got mad at that arrangement. "I need to get a lawyer," she would say. "You're undermining our equal-custody agreement." She thought I was conspiring to take Cubby away from her, but I wasn't. I told her so over and over, and eventually she realized it was true. Our son was old enough to make his own decisions, and he was choosing friends and community over us. He might have spent more nights in Amherst, but I didn't see him all that much either. If he was at home, he was in his room with the door shut, on the phone or on the computer.

If he was out with friends, I didn't see him except briefly on the ride home.

With every passing day, he was becoming more and more determined to run his own life. Parents who were once founts of knowledge became dumb as rocks overnight. Not only were we stupid, we were uncooperative, embarrassing, and totally useless. It was nice to be needed.

"Dad," he would say. "I need a ride." That became our principal conversational exchange. I wasn't sure how to go beyond that. I realized I relied on Cubby to start and maintain conversations. He'd always launched into monologues when I picked him up after school. I'd spent countless hours learning about schoolmates, Beanie Babies, Yu-Gi-Oh! cards, or whatever else was on his mind. I didn't have to do anything to keep the flow going; the challenge was making it stop. When that suddenly changed, I didn't know what to do.

Being Aspergian, it did not occur to me to say, "Hi, Jack, how was school?"

Being a geek himself, it did not occur to my kid to expect any questions.

When we got home he'd go into the kitchen, wash his hands five or six times, look at them, and wash them once again for good measure. Then he'd head for his room. His hand washing—sometimes as much as fifty times a day—was the most visible of his compulsive behaviors, now that he had outgrown brushing the hair off his head. I thought it was mostly harmless, except when he washed his hands so much the skin turned raw. We went to the doctor, who prescribed creams, but we never found a treatment for the underlying behavior.

Despite the hand washing, for a long time he had a powerful aversion to the shower, and he'd stay out of it for a week at a time. Then something changed and he went to the opposite extreme, taking hour-long showers with the water on hot. He'd ignore my yelling through the bathroom door, and I'd get so annoyed at the waste of water that I'd shut the lines off in the basement. Then he'd emerge, swearing.

"Run the shower all day when you pay the water bill," I told him. We learned to get along the best we could.

Maybe his eccentricities don't need treatment, I thought. *Not everything does.* My dad had many Aspergian traits and he also washed his hands compulsively. Now that he'd gotten older and stopped drinking, he was okay and functional. My real concern was staying engaged with Cubby as he got older. That was hard to do when he stopped talking to me except to yell.

Of course, Cubby's sudden lack of interest in friendly conversation didn't stop him from pointing out my many defects and character flaws. Every week I'd hear some variation on, "You're acting like a weirdo freak, Dad, all my friends think so!" I had known about my Asperger's for a number of years, and I was willing to accept that perhaps I was somewhat different from the other dads in the area. However, I didn't think that was what he meant. Sure enough, a bit of observation made it clear that the times he said I was weird, or a bad parent, or the worst dad of all were when I declined to do what he wanted. Thinking that through, I concluded that he had no idea if I was bad or not. How could he know? I was the only adult male he had ever lived with. He had no idea what his friends' dads did, and they no doubt described their parents with the same pugnacious derision he reserved for me.

That insight certainly made me feel better. After all, I did want to be a good parent. But it didn't change what I had to deal with. All Cubby knew was that I wasn't fulfilling his every wish. For that I was deemed worthless.

I tried to take it all with good humor. He was still my Cubby, and I liked him a lot. Even when he was totally obnoxious, self-centered, and combative. For now, I controlled the house, the car, and the money. He would have to act nice and deal with me until he could move out. I wondered how soon that day would come.

Thinking about that, I realized he had abandoned parents for friends. The year before, I'd wondered how long my little boy would remain a boy. Suddenly and without warning, I knew the answer. He wasn't a boy anymore.

"But he's not a man yet, either," my friend Bob told me. My buddy Neil had a better response. "This is when you chain him to a tree in the woods, and bring him a sack of food once a week. He'll either get nicer and come home, or run away."

Yet he wasn't always nasty. There were times he'd still snuggle up to me and listen to a story, especially when he was going to sleep. I'll bet he'd be embarrassed to admit it today, but there was still a little boy hidden deep inside.

Cubby had always been resistant to discipline. The more he moved from the parental orbit to the wider universe of his teen friends, the harder it was to obtain behavioral compliance. He was constantly testing us. "Call for a ride by eight," I'd say, "or get yourself home by nine." Sure enough, 9:05 would come and the phone would ring. "Come get me, I need a ride."

What do you do in a situation like that? You can't leave your kid at some other parent's house. You have to get him. What then? The parenting books made it sound so easy, but it wasn't. If I refused to get him, I ended up with a snarky parent in my driveway, pissed off that he had to bring my kid home. "Tell him to walk home," I'd say, but they never did.

Cubby became a master at playing me and his mother against each other, too. That made it very hard to impose consequences or levy any sort of punishment. We agreed that we wouldn't whip him or cut off his ears, so what did that leave us? Cut off his allowance? All that got was a call to his mother, or my mother, or my brother, and someone would replace what we took away without our ever knowing. He'd learned to circumvent us very nicely.

The same situation applied for his other behaviors. When he rode that bus to his friends one time too many, he'd call Little Bear and have her get him instead of me. He'd stay at her house a day or two and hope I'd forgotten his previous transgression by the time he came back.

Like most teenagers, he was difficult to raise.

"You need a job," I told him. "A working kid is a happy kid, and everyone knows children are born to the yoke." He just looked at me, wordless.

Jolly fun parenting had come to an end.

41

NICOLE

In the spring of his fourteenth year, Cubby did something extraordinary. He got a girlfriend. Others may take girlfriend acquisition for granted, but for geeks like me and my son, romantic success is far from assured. I knew that from personal experience and years of loneliness. When I was Cubby's age, I had only dreamed of holding hands or kissing a girl. My kid actually pulled it off.

Of course, I didn't find out about the girlfriend because he told me. I had to deduce it from his behavior.

The first thing I noticed was that he stopped coming home from school on the bus. Instead, he began walking into town and hanging out with friends. At least that's what he said. I didn't mind him doing things after school, but I did mind the phone calls. "Dad," he would say, "come get me. I missed the bus." The first five or six times, I believed him. But when it became a daily thing, and I found myself picking him up at a café half a mile from school . . . something was up.

I began paying closer attention when I went to retrieve him. Sure enough, he was always with the same group of kids. There were half a dozen of them, a mix of guys and girls. In fact, as he got more comfortable asking for rides, he even began offering my services to drive his friends home. I wondered if I could induce them to pay me.

I turned to the first kid we drove home and held out my hand. "That will be three dollars." He looked at me with a shocked expression, but he didn't say or do anything. "Dad," Cubby said. "Don't be a jerk. Just drive."

"Ignore my father," he told his friend. Then the two of them began yapping about Grand Theft Auto and the Age of Empires game as if I wasn't even there. As long as I kept the vehicle moving, I could have been invisible.

The idea of parents as friends, or even parents as part of the conversation, was a nonstarter. We were at the point where he knew everything, and Mom and Dad were embarrassments to be hidden away until needed for a ride or some money. Indeed, ride requests became a daily occurrence. There were rides after school, rides to the mall, and rides to friends' houses. And of course there were rides home at the end of the evening. In no time at all, transportation became one of the more onerous duties of parenthood, and the principal way I interacted with my kid.

I began to see a pattern. Most evenings, I found myself summoned to a parking lot in South Amherst to follow a set of cryptic instructions, as if I were dropping off ransom money or doing a huge cocaine deal.

"Turn in the first entrance. Go to the second parking lot. Drive to the back, flash your lights, and wait. I'll come out. Stay in the car." He was directing me to a parking area in the middle of a good-size housing complex. It looked nice enough, but there was no telling who lived there or what they were doing.

"I want to see where you are. Stay there. I'll come up." My desire to see what he was doing seemed pretty normal to me. Not to him. "No! Remain with the vehicle. I'll come down." Jeez, I thought, listening to him is like listening to some hopped-up policeman who panics when he pulls you over and you get out of your car.

Yet I was so impressed that he had friends to hang out with that I failed to ask any more about them. I wondered to myself when I waited in the car, but when Cubby appeared, he began yapping excitedly about his games or his chemistry, and any questions I had were quickly forgotten. It's also possible I didn't think to ask because I'm autistic, and I often miss stuff like that. Either way, we drove home with me none the wiser.

When we got home, he'd go immediately to his room and close the door. He'd done that before, but these days it was different. Now he began talking on the phone as soon as he was inside. I couldn't tell what he was saying, but I could hear murmurs. He was up to something.

The final tip-off was school. He had struggled and fought against going. Now, all of a sudden, he went willingly. Yet his grades were as poor as before—worse, actually.

Either he was selling drugs to his classmates, I concluded, or he'd gotten a girlfriend. I watched him closely for signs of drug use or drug dealing, and I didn't see anything. He didn't look high, and he never wore any of the gold chains, diamonds, or other bling that I associated with successful drug dealers. That left a girlfriend as the only possible explanation. When I asked, he spoke right up.

"Her name is Nicole. She's a year older than me. She's from France, and her dad teaches French at Hampshire." When I was a kid, French females were the stuff of movies—beautiful, desirable, and exotic. I had no idea there were such people right here in our little New England town, with parents who taught at Hampshire College.

"Perhaps I could meet them the next time I pick you up," I suggested.

"Okay," he said. "But you have to behave." I agreed, bearing in mind that my definition of *behave* probably differed from his.

The next day, when I went to retrieve him, he came out to the parking lot and led me back to a condo. "This is where she lives," he said. "Be nice." I snorted.

Nicole was a pretty girl, thin, shy, and quiet. Later he told me that they first met in front of the high school when Nicole was talking to one of his friends, and that they had walked into town together. I was never able to determine who chose whom; I finally concluded it was a mutual thing. For the first year, they were inseparable. Cubby went to her house most every day, except on days they stayed in town or went to our house.

With a girlfriend and an interest in chemistry that might really lead to a career, my son was growing up. It was striking how fast this change took place. The Beanie Babies and Pokémon cards were left in the dust of childhood. I wondered if all teens went through something similar, or if Cubby was somehow unique. The same thing seemed to be happening with his friends. When they came to the house, they watched grown-up movies and talked like adults.

Nicole never said more than fifty words to me, but I didn't make much of that because lots of teenagers are uncomfortable around strange parents, and I knew I was stranger than most. A few years later, when she told my son she had Asperger's too, her behavior made sense. Boys with Asperger's—like my son—are criticized as weirdos and freaks for their social ineptitude. Yet many of those same awkward behaviors—avoiding eye contact or missing social cues—are often dismissed as shy and cute in girls.

Cubby and Nicole would sit together for hours, talking or watching television. Seeing them reminded me of the same period in my own life, when Little Bear and I would walk and talk and the days went on forever. We were not romantically involved in those years—neither of us knew how to take that step, even though we saw others doing it and we read stories in books—but we had hopes and dreams and we shared them endlessly. I suspected things had progressed further for Cubby and Nicole, because I saw them holding hands and snuggling, something his mom and I had never done as teens.

I wondered if I should talk to him about sex and teen pregnancy, but I'm embarrassed to say I was just too shy. Whenever I thought about Cubby and sex, I recalled my teen years, when my social disabilities kept me clear of sexual entanglements more effectively than any conversation could have, and I convinced myself that he too was enough of a late bloomer that I didn't need to worry. In the end, responsibility for "the talk" fell to his mom, and I never asked him what was said.

Still, there would be times that the little boy would reappear. He didn't ask to be tucked in anymore, but he'd still say, "Pet me, Dad," if I happened to sit down beside him on the sofa at night, just as he had when he was little. And he still smiled at my Gorko stories and the talk of fire lizards and other fanciful creatures, though he no longer watched for them in the forest outside.

Now, when Cubby searched in the woods, it was for a place to test his latest concoctions. He shot his drainpipe cannon into the brush beside the house, but I complained about the noise, so he began ranging farther and farther to find remote spots to safely stage his explosive experiments. That was a new source of worry, because he was out of my sight, which meant out of reach of help should something go wrong.

His answer to that was his friends, who accompanied him on his tests. "They're always with me," he'd say, "and we check carefully to make sure no one is around."

His guy friends did accompany him, but Nicole didn't care much for Cubby's experiments. She preferred to immerse herself in reading and studying. In the beginning, he didn't care, because he was so consumed by the drive to learn and create. Both of us expressed our worries to him, but he didn't perceive our concerns either. It's funny . . . looking back, that too is a classic trait of Asperger's, but being that way myself, I totally missed it in him. I guess the adage "it takes one to know one" isn't always true after all.

Despite his dismissals, I continued to prod him. "It's great that you do your test explosions far away from people," I said, "but what if you get hurt?" Cubby dismissed my concerns in the superior way teenagers do. "Dad! My friends are with me, and I'm always safe. I'm not going to get hurt." It was hard having a kid who professed to have all the answers. Proud as I was of his chemical prowess, I worried about accidents. My own teenage interests never had the potential to blow off an arm or leg.

He always filmed the results of his experiments, and he showed the videos to anyone who would watch, including my parents. "That's very impressive, Jack," my father said carefully. "I'm just worried that you'll get in trouble. You be careful now."

Cubby assured my dad that he took all possible precautions. He was very sure of his technical knowledge.

My mother felt the same way. After a while, he decided they were not his most receptive audience. He decided to upload his videos to the Internet instead. "Are you sure that's wise?" I asked him. "Yes," he said. "I have an Internet bulletin board, and people write in with their own thoughts and advice. There's a lot of dangerous stuff online, and I want people to see things done safely and smart."

Only three months earlier, he had told me he was starting a website where he could talk about chemistry with other students. Now he had a whole community, with hundreds of members and thousands of posts. I was shocked by how quickly it had blossomed, thanks to social media.

Once again, I was stymied by my teenage son's impeccable logic. I might not have liked it, but the days when I could tell him what to do were receding fast. Any thoughts that my son might have an intelligence deficit were long gone. He was at least as smart as me, and clever to boot. I told myself that by way of reassurance: Any dad would have his hands full with a kid like Cubby.

Shortly before Cubby's fifteenth birthday, we got bad news. My dad was sick. He went into the hospital, came out, and went back again. By Christmas, I knew he wasn't going to get better.

He died in the last days of winter, a month before Cubby's birthday. The following weekend, Cubby and I drove Grandpa John's old car in the St. Patrick's Day parade. He was awfully proud of that Jaguar. We missed him a lot.

The month passed, and the pain of loss receded. Cubby turned fifteen, and that reminded me once again of my dad. He'd always been there for Cubby's birthdays with a cake and a spyglass or treasure chest or some other exotic present. Cubby felt the loss too, but he was distracted. He had a girlfriend, and after a quick bite of cake with us, he was off to celebrate with her. Those days, he was with Nicole and the gang six nights a week, and I hardly ever saw him. Some weeks, he didn't go to his mom's at all, and she had to meet him in town just to see his face.

Despite all his new interests, he'd maintained his membership in the South Hadley Boy Scout troop. Every four years, the scouts hosted a big get-together they called the Jamboree, and that spring he announced that he wanted to go to it. He'd missed the previous one when he was in Mexico, and the next one wasn't going to happen till 2010; he'd be done with scouting long before that.

Jamboree happened at the end of August, and Cubby did have a lot of fun. However, the thing that made Jamboree most memorable to me was what happened after—Cubby decided to move to Amherst full time. The school year was about to start, and he didn't want to shuttle from house to house anymore. Needless to say, Little Bear was very unhappy about that. I had mixed feelings myself. As much as I loved having my son around, it was nice having a quiet house once or twice a week. That never happened when he was there.

Still, I had to agree it made sense. Cubby was enrolled at Amherst High School now, and his mom lived half an hour away in

South Hadley. In years past that had been fine, because she was in school there too, at the university. Now she'd graduated and gone to work teaching school. She couldn't spend two hours a day driving him around. In any case, he wasn't thinking of his parents. He was interested in his new girlfriend and the new circle of friends he'd made.

All we parents did was provide money, transportation, and food. And we paid the cell phone bill.

DECLARATION OF INDEPENDENCE

The next milestone of Cubby's teen years was a big one: getting a driver's license. He'd been driving for years, but not legally, and not on public roads. All that changed when he turned sixteen. "Dad," he said, "you need to take me to get a learner's permit."

When I didn't respond to his demand fast enough, he called his mom. "Can you take me to get my permit? Dad won't do it." Since he had started staying in Amherst, his mom felt she hardly ever saw him, so she grabbed every chance when he called. The following afternoon, when I was at work, Cubby and his mom drove to the registry and emerged a few minutes later with a crisp new permit.

I discovered his new status that evening, when he volunteered to accompany me to the gas station. "I'll drive," he said confidently as we walked to the car. Then he took out his permit and handed it to me proudly. I looked at the road and back at him. Why not? He had been driving for years, in the woods. How much different could driving on a road be?

A lot, as it turned out. For one thing, speeds were higher. Before getting the permit, Cubby had practiced driving our John Deere garden tractor around the neighborhood. Most people don't think of a lawn mower as something that speeds and slides on the corners, but Cubby drove the thing like a dirt-track racer. Unfortunately, he misjudged his momentum and dirt-tracked my tractor right into the side of Martha's car. Seeing the damage, I wondered if Cubby would be able to navigate the roads. "Maybe he'll be more careful, having had his first accident," Martha suggested hopefully. I wasn't so sure. Those worries were foremost in my mind as I got into the passenger seat for his first foray onto a public highway.

"Dad," he said with some exasperation, "it's not my first time driving on roads. I've driven on roads a lot already." Where? I asked. And when? I remembered times when I was sure my car had moved since the last time I parked it in the garage. I decided it might be best if I did not pry further. Instead, I focused on making sure my seat belt was tight and the doors were secure as Cubby pulled onto the road with a twist of the neck and a chirp of the tires.

We made it to the gas station just fine, but his success with my vehicle was short-lived. That was a shame, because I was very proud of that car and I liked it a lot. It was a brand-new Mini Cooper S, British racing green, with a sunroof and racing stripes on the hood. It even had British flags on the mirrors. It was exactly the sort of machine a geek like me would drive.

I'd had the car two whole weeks when I asked Cubby to move it out of the garage. He immediately said okay and bounced out the back door. He was always quick to do anything involving that car, especially if he got to drive it. The car had come with two keys, and he had taken to carrying one of them in his pocket all the time. That made me feel like I needed to chain the little Mini to the floor anytime I was away, just like a bicycle.

People in the city, living where everything is in walking distance, might not understand that need to retain access to a motor vehicle. For us, living five miles from town on a backcountry road, motorized transportation was essential. And I was not about to have my kid make off with my wheels.

I heard the car start, followed almost immediately by a squeal of tires as he got it moving. Cubby's coordination never failed to impress me; that was one of the few observable benefits of his hours of video gaming. I knew he'd have one hand on the wheel, the other on the gearshift lever. His left foot was on the clutch and the right one was on the gas. All moved independently, but he missed a step. A solid thump rattled the house. Glasses and china clinked in the cupboards. Looking into the garage, I saw my son had backed the car out of the garage, just as I'd asked. He had even opened the garage door first, just as he should. However, he had failed to close the car door. When he launched the Mini in reverse, the driver's door embedded itself in the back wall of the garage. He'd hit it with enough force that the garage wall was caved in and the door was pretty well torn off the car.

"Cubby," I shouted. "You wrecked my new car!"

"Sorry," he said, tail between his legs. He looked down at the floor as I walked out to assess the damage. It looked bad from a distance, but it was actually much worse up close. It was bad enough that a stricter dad might have had him shot, but I just called his mom.

When I reported what had happened, all she said was, "Is Jack all right?"

"Of course he's all right. It's the car that's wrecked. If Cubby ran into the garage door, he'd get better all by himself. The car has to go to the body shop, and it will cost thousands of dollars!"

Little Bear was not sympathetic. "The kid is all right, and that's what's important." Well, I thought, the kid was all right the whole time. It's the car that got damaged. Clearly, she and I did not see things the same way.

Driving practice was delayed a few weeks, while the body shop reconstructed the mutilated Mini. While we were waiting, I took some time to read the requirements for getting a license in Massachusetts. It seemed they'd evolved a bit since I was a teenager. The most obvious change was the driving school racket. In the past, hopeful drivers simply went to the Registry of Motor Vehicles with a permit and a car, and took a road test. If they could drive on the road, parallel park, and do a three-point turn without terrorizing the inspector too badly, they got a license.

Now kids had to attend driving school and get a certificate of completion before they were allowed to take the road test. Clearly, our state had a strong special-interest lobby—one that paid off big-time for the Association of Massachusetts Driving Schools. The nearest such school was in downtown Holyoke, a place Cubby had not visited since he was two—the day some lowlife tried to steal his mother's grocery cart from the parking lot with him in it. Luckily for us, he did not get stolen, but he hadn't gone back there to try his luck again either. Until now.

Driving school was scheduled to start in two more weeks. Meanwhile, we had a vacation planned. Every August, we go to Lake George in the Adirondacks of upstate New York with my geek friends. We eat, lie on the beach, and ride around in boats. This year, Cubby had his own plans. "I could make some underwater fireworks, and we could toss them off the boat. It would be like in a movie!" I was proud of my son's prowess with chemistry, but I was not sure how wise it would be for us to lay down strings of depth charges in Lake George, and I suggested that we table that idea until the following year.

I headed for the Adirondacks after work on Friday. Cubby said he'd come up later that evening with his friend Luke, who had a driver's license and a car of his own. I thought that meant Luke would drive them up in his car. However, Cubby had a different understanding, as I discovered when they rolled into the motel parking lot driving my repaired and re-doored Mini. Kids in front, poodle in back.

"What are you doing driving?" I asked him. He just looked at me. "Luke isn't eighteen. You can't drive with him as a passenger. What if you got stopped?"

"They would have given me a ticket and Luke would have had to drive. Besides, I was extra careful, because I didn't want to get stopped. See? I got here okay!"

I wasn't sure what to say. I was secretly proud that he'd driven two hundred miles all by himself. He'd navigated country roads, busy interstates, and the heavy traffic around Albany, all without damage. Yet I could never admit that to him. He should have known better than to take a chance driving my car. I growled and snorted and wandered away.

But I didn't wander alone. I took the dog. And the reason I took the dog was another of Cubby's obsessions—he had decided that the poodle's fur "felt funny" and could no longer bring himself to touch him. Somehow fur that was soft and woolly became weird and bristly. I could not discern any change in the poodle's exterior texture, but Cubby was not budging. That left Martha and me to take care of the dog. Feeling Cubby had abandoned his pet, I suggested we give him to the Estonian family with the poodle acrobatic act in the circus, but Cubby objected strenuously. Clearly, he still liked Shenzi; he just didn't want to handle him. Just as clearly, the dog's fur hadn't changed a bit since we'd gotten him years before. Cubby's obsessions might have been harmless, but they sure could be annoying!

The next day I overheard the kids talking when they thought I wasn't paying attention. "There was one point where Jack drove over a bump and the whole car went into the air," Luke said excitedly. Clearly, Cubby had not learned sufficient restraint from the previous two mishaps. When the time came to go home, I drove the Mini and let him ride back with my friends. If there had been a bus, I'd have sent him on it.

Finally, it was time for driving school. It had been years since he was eager to go to any school, but he definitely wanted that license. Every day we took him there and picked him up when he was done. Then, armed with a certificate, he made an appointment at the registry. He wanted to take the test in my Mini, but it didn't meet the registry requirements, so his mom ended up taking him in her minivan.

He passed.

That left the matter of a car. Cubby helpfully offered his notion that a BMW Z4 would be great.

"They're nice cars," I said, "but I wonder when Kia started importing vehicles to the USA. I've heard the early models are really getting collectible. Hyundai has some nice compact cars too. You might even like a vintage Taurus or Escort."

"Dad! Be serious! You would really like a BMW!"

And indeed I would like a BMW, but that wasn't what he was proposing. He wanted me to buy one for him. However, there were more realistic options. He ended up with a ten-year-old Subaru wagon. Sensible yet slow, and not very sporty. It was a nice shade of blue.

Soon it was also a nice shade of dented. He rear-ended another car on an icy road, smashing in the whole front end. That event seemed to do the trick. From then on, Cubby drove with restraint and caution. At least when I was around.

I figured he'd drive his new car to school, since he hated the bus so much. That was one of the reasons we'd given it to him. But when summer ended, and Cubby's friends went back to school for their senior year, he announced that he had other plans. "Look," he said one evening. "They don't have any more chemistry courses at the high school, and I'm failing anyway. I think I should take the GED and enroll at Holyoke Community College instead. They have a chemistry lab class I can sign up for now."

I had really wanted my son to graduate from high school and go on to a four-year university. The idea of him dropping out sounded awful, and I once again reminded him how many opportunities I'd missed out on by making the same choice. He was stubborn, though, and I couldn't change his mind. He dropped out of school, took the GED, and aced it. Then he signed up for chemistry at Holy-oke Community College. He was seventeen years old, young for a college student, but he already knew more than any of the other students in his class.

"UMass won't admit me with a GED," he told me, "but HCC will, and I can get an associate's here and transfer to UMass with that, if I want."

"I've made it to college quicker than my friends," he said proudly, and I couldn't dispute that.

43

BLOWING UP

Things finally came to a head with Cubby's chemistry experiments in late 2007. He had turned seventeen that spring, and his interest in chemistry was looking like a real obsession. When you added the girlfriend, a driver's license, and a teenager's confidence in his own limitless wisdom, we were bound to collide. It would have happened sooner, if not for my own issues. My first book had just been published, and I was traveling all the time to promote it. When I was home, I was distracted by the demands of a budding writing career, which were piled on top of my existing responsibilities to my family and to Robison Service. With me away or preoccupied, and Martha's quiet personality, there was nothing standing in the way of Cubby's enthusiasm. He more or less seized the house and ramped up his experimentation in a major way.

Before, his experiments had been relegated to one corner of the garage. Now he took advantage of my absence to expand his operations into the house. Glassware, jars, and boxes with cryptic handwritten labels appeared all over the house, even in our refrigerator. Then there were the results. Friends who lived half a mile away would call and say, "Jack must be experimenting again. I heard him last night." Sometimes they were right, but not all the bangs were his. There were nights when I'd hear a loud bang from the landfill, yet Cubby was home in his room. I asked whether he knew who it was, but it was a mystery to him too. As far as I knew, none of Cubby's friends were experimenting with chemistry, but his own interest was no secret, and others could have been inspired. It was, after all, a college town with lots of geek kids.

When I was a kid no one noticed stuff like that. We shot rifles at targets right in the backyard. Nowadays, if we want to shoot some skeet, we have to call the cops first so they know what to say when the inevitable calls come in. That's what happens when rural areas get gentrified, I guess. We still have a right to shoot guns in the woods, but we have to be more careful if we want to keep the law at bay. Unfortunately, Cubby couldn't do that quite as easily. In most places in the U.S., you can still call the cops and say, "I'm shooting my rifle out back," but you can't call them and say, "I just wanna let you know that I'm going to be testing some explosives in the meadow."

I urged moderation, with only limited success. "You can't aggravate the neighbors," I told him. "If you get them mad, and they call the cops, you'll be all done. You should follow the same rules hunters use. No blasts on Sunday, and nothing in the dark. Those are the times people get annoyed and call to complain."

Noise was not the only concern. There was also the issue of space. Cubby had started out with a corner of the workbench in my garage. That fall, he expanded his territory to the whole bench, plus two portable refrigerators on the floor. He had salvaged them from the "free for the taking" junk pile in the Amherst recycling center. To my surprise and pleasure, he fixed both in short order. He was looking smarter and more useful all the time. If only he fixed things around the house . . .

Cubby scavenged parts from scrap appliances and reconfigured them to make a vacuum pump. Vacuum pumps were essential for some of the more sophisticated experiments he wanted to perform. "My pump pulls almost as good a vacuum as the ones in lab-supply catalogs for seven hundred fifty dollars," he boasted. I looked at the gauge readings, and he was right. He'd built a complex concoction of glassware, which had overspread the workbench and taken up a large area of floor. It looked like something out of *Back to the Future,* and it might well have had similar powers. But I had to be practical. Now there was no room for me to park an automobile inside the garage, and that would not do.

The problem was that any suggestion that the glassware be moved started a fight. And I was wary of moving things myself, because I did not know which liquids might explode and which might eat holes in my foot or the concrete floor. That's the problem with chemists—when you have one loose in the house you lose all confidence in the stability of liquids and even solids. A beaker of clear liquid could turn into white powder, or a ball of fire, just by lifting and shaking. The best course was to treat them all with caution.

Before Cubby became a chemist, the chemicals around me, at work and at home, behaved in a very predictable fashion. I had never worried that the chemicals stored in the garage would turn into something else or blow up. Cubby assured me that I didn't have to worry about spontaneous explosions. "Besides, all the chemicals in the garage change all the time," he said. "Paint catalyzes and hardens in the can. Spray solvents evaporate into the air. Everything changes. You just don't notice." I knew he was right. He didn't really introduce chemical instability into my life; he simply made me aware of the natural instability that surrounds us all. Very little truly stays the same. Even if it doesn't blow up or change visibly, everything changes at a microscopic rate, all the time. Geologists say even the land is in constant motion until it finds the level of repose—a state where everything has worn to gentle rolling terrain. Chemicals do that too, reacting until the energy is dissipated.

Even then, change can continue. Insects eat things. Rodents dig tunnels. Men drive bulldozers.

Thanks to Cubby, I see the whole world differently. In that way, I became a little like him, which is how it should be. Kids are our future; we parents can strive to be like them, but we should not try to make them like us. They are the next step, and we can't know what they will do until it happens.

Still, I missed that illusion of stability. It was troubling, always wondering if the shelf beside me would spontaneously combust. But of course that never happened, and when I admitted as much to my son he said, "See? You're irrational." At the same time, Cubby had gotten himself into a pattern of behavior that troubled me. His special interest in chemistry had turned into a total obsession. It would not have been so bad if he pursued it out in the open, but he did all his studying (or whatever he was doing) behind a locked door in his room. When he wasn't in there he was working in his garage lab. I hardly spoke to him at all, because he'd stopped eating meals with us and he wasn't awake when I got up in the morning. He was sleeping till noon and staying up all night. I was so frustrated that I began thinking Cubby might need to get an apartment of his own.

When I complained to a friend about Cubby's behavior, he told me kids were programmed to act that way. "When they're teenagers they turn into total jerks, so you don't miss them too much when you throw them out," he said. "He'll be better once he turns twenty-five."

Meanwhile, Cubby continued to be very active online. He was talking chemistry and explosives with people all over the country and possibly all over the world. Cubby was only interested in explosives for the science, but I wasn't so sure about the others. Of course, when I challenged Cubby, he dismissed my concerns.

"My videos don't show anything getting destroyed," he said. "All they show is explosives detonating on the ground. What's wrong with that?" He contrasted his videos with others on YouTube that showed old cars being destroyed and even houses being wrecked.

When I suggested that the FBI or the ATF (the Bureau of Alcohol, Tobacco, Firearms and Explosives) might still have a problem with his explosions, he disagreed. He kept insisting that there were far worse videos out there than his, and if the lawmen wanted to target people on YouTube, he'd be at the bottom of the list. It was very hard to counter his arguments.

"What law do you think people break, blowing up junk cars?" Hearing him, I had to agree. If it was your junk car, you had every right to destroy it. My son wasn't even doing that. He just set off explosives on the ground. Yet there were other laws.

"What about possessing the explosives? You already told me that's illegal."

Cubby's justification for that sounded quite a bit shakier. "I don't keep explosives around," he insisted. "All these chemicals I keep are just the ingredients. None of them are illegal at all. I mix them into a batch of explosive, carry it into the woods, and set it off. I don't have a stockpile of explosives." He was very rational, very insistent, and probably correct. However, it was increasingly clear that his notions would not protect us from a raid.

"Cubby," I pleaded, "how could someone from the ATF know any of what you are saying? If they see those videos of yours, how could they know you don't have a whole trunkful and you're waiting to go on a rampage? Just calling attention to yourself might be enough to get the doors kicked in by feds. Can't you see that?"

"Huuunh," he said. Sometimes it was striking how closely he imitated my noises. This time I wasn't amused.

I knew his interest was purely scientific, and I knew how it felt to be driven to experiment and refine something to make it better and better. That very trait had been the key to my success. However, I also knew he'd ventured into dangerous territory. The distinctive crack of fast-detonating high explosive is quite recognizable, even in an online video. If I could see it, it would surely be just as unmistakable to an expert, like the ones in law enforcement.

"Don't you think the ATF is watching you? How would they know you don't have a hundred pounds of homemade dynamite, ready to blow up the post office or your old school?" When I said that, Cubby just looked at me like I was nuts. He was so certain of the purity of his own scientific curiosity. The idea that he would blow up the post office was total nonsense to him, and he could not even conceive of the possibility that someone else might think he could do such a thing.

Instinct told me he was headed for disaster. But he didn't agree, and he argued his case with the greatest of eloquence. My attempts to change his mind went nowhere, and I could not decide on a course of action.

"Why put the videos online at all?" I asked him. That was the obvious question. By this time, he'd uploaded twenty-some videos to his own channel on YouTube. Cubby said he had worked hard to accomplish what he had, and he wanted to share the results with other chemists who might want to do something similar.

"What you don't understand, Dad, is that there is a lot of bad science online. There are lots of how-to videos that show procedures that would kill you if you tried them at home. I want to show people safe science." I wondered what would have happened if he'd followed hints in any of those "bad science" videos he talked about. Did his intelligence protect him, or was it just luck? Plus, "safe science" in the context of home-brew explosives sounded like an oxymoron to me, but he assured me it was not. "People make explosives for all kinds of reasons," he said. "Look at mining companies. They mix their own charges all the time."

Cubby's experiments and his videos put me in a very difficult spot. I wanted to encourage him in his passions, but I did not want to awake one morning to find my home surrounded by federal agents with tanks and helicopters. I also did not want to get a phone call one day, telling me that Cubby had blown his arm off. I knew he was smart and careful, but there was no margin for error in what he was doing. He did stick to small charges most of the time, but when he showed me a video of one particular test in the swamp behind the house, I was frightened almost as much as I was impressed. The blast tossed water twenty feet into the air, and I knew it would have injured him badly if it had gone off when he was placing it. Yet he dismissed my concerns once again.

"We're talking about water, Dad! I can throw a big rock in the swamp and blast water just as far, and no one gets worried. I'm not blowing buildings into the air!" Once again, I had to concede he was right, but it didn't make me feel any better.

When I challenged the risks of handling his explosives, I got a lecture on how stable the various chemicals were and how the explosives couldn't detonate without an initiating charge. And I did know that dynamite wasn't very sensitive, and that it was perfectly safe to handle under normal conditions. Blasting caps were safe too, until you connected the electrical wires to trigger them. They didn't go off spontaneously. You had to make a mistake to get hurt.

But those were commercial explosives. Cubby was making his own explosive compounds, and if he made any mistakes formulating them, they might well be unstable in ways none of us could predict. That is the nature of experimentation. So what was the risk?

I tried to put what Cubby did in perspective. Other kids did skateboarding tricks, and the risks they took may well have been greater. Kids joined ski clubs and hit trees. High schoolers got concussions playing football. Cubby was thoughtful, careful, and performed all his experiments well away from people or houses. Logic told me he was less likely to sustain damage than many of his peers, but I still worried.

My biggest fear was the speed with which he was racing forward in his research and experimentation. He had started out imitating the work of others—mixing chemicals to make mildly explosive compounds like flash powder. From there, he had moved on to blending simple rocket fuels. Then he took a big leap: He went from mixing to actually reacting. He mixed chemicals, extracted a product of the reaction, and mixed that with other chemicals. Those multistep processes were what yielded the sophisticated high explosive he was so proud of.

And he didn't stop there. He read extensively and learned how compounds like PETN or RDX were made. Then he came up with ideas to improve them and to synthesize them more easily. In the space of a few months, he had progressed from doing reactions he read about to inventing his own.

I was proud of his technical brilliance. In addition, I knew his ideas could be very valuable. He might well have patentable inventions, at age seventeen! At the same time I worried about the legal ramifications. He said he didn't keep explosive material around, but I suspected the sophisticated stuff he was learning to make was seriously illegal. Keeping black powder and flash powder was not much different from having a bag of firecrackers. But having PETN or C4 in the fridge was more like having a stick or two of dynamite, and the Feds had outlawed home stocks of dynamite a long time ago.

Something had to be done. Cubby was supposedly attending classes at Holyoke Community College, but as far as I could tell he wasn't making it to class on time, and he wasn't doing his work. He avoided showing me his grades, so I suspected he was failing. The Educated Cubby Who Does Better Than Dad plan was going seriously awry.

I tried to tell myself that I'd been the same when I was Cubby's age. I lived with a bunch of guys in a band, and I often played music till one in the morning, ate breakfast in the middle of the night, and slept until noon. The difference was, no one was going to put me in jail for music and electronics. At least, that's what I told my kid. He, of course, turned that right around.

"You told me you got arrested for drugs when you were with a band," he said. He was right. They weren't my drugs, and I did get acquitted, but I spent Easter 1976 in jail in Montserrat.

"You told me the ATF was looking at your special effects, too." That too was correct. The ATF never raided any of the bands I was with, but they certainly looked askance at some of our more spectacular effects. My first effects were unique, and they must have escaped notice. The longer we did it, though, the closer people looked. By the time I quit the business, the ATF had come to see a rocket-launching guitar as about the same as a rocket-launching tank destroyer. That's why you don't see effects like the ones we did in the seventies on stages much anymore.

Whenever I thought about that, I got even more worried about Cubby. As sound as my son's arguments about science and research and mixing the chemicals before the experiment were, I feared the government would see things differently. The risks were just too great.

A few days after Christmas, I finally had had enough. I told Cubby that everything had to go, that he could not keep his lab in my house. "Cubby, you need to be doing your experiments in a university lab, with a professor and grad students to help you. I'm terribly afraid you are going to get hurt. I am scared you are going to get raided. I can't handle those worries anymore. I'll get you a storage unit, and you can keep your lab stuff in there until you have a place of your own. I am really scared you are ruining your life, and I can't let you drag me down too."

Then I called his mom and told her what I had said. "Whatever you do," I cautioned her, "do not let him set his lab up in your house. He is headed for disaster. I just know it." She listened to what I said, and I thought she took it to heart. But ever since he'd moved in with us, she'd lived alone, and she was lonely. And, just as I feared, she told him he could bring his glassware to her house. Once he got it there, she didn't stop him from setting it up in her basement.

I called her again and urged her not to let him experiment in her basement, but I didn't get anywhere. She was always stubborn, and my suggestions were just more unwanted advice from an ex-spouse. If anything, my words probably made her more determined to stay her course with Cubby.

I didn't talk to either of them for a little while. In some way, I was relieved. I know Martha was relieved. But I was also deeply saddened. The house was calm and quiet, but I'd lost my Cubby. He was gone a month, through the coldest part of winter.

February 15, 2008, dawned like any other day for me. It was a raw winter morning in New England, with gray skies and temperatures just above freezing. Fridays are always busy for me, as we bill out the week's work on the projects in our shop.

At two o'clock I got the call.

"Dad, there are three ATF agents here at school," Cubby said. "They want to search my mom's house." He spoke slowly and cautiously, as if people were listening. He sounded scared but firm.

It was the call I had feared every day since I'd tossed his lab out of my house. Even if you expect such a thing, there is nothing you can really do to prepare. *They have your kid.*

44

A VISIT FROM THE ATF

Knowing he had a hard time getting up in the morning, Cubby had arranged his school schedule so that his first class was at 1 P.M. Even then, he usually arrived a few minutes late. According to my son, the professor didn't care. Most days, he slid in and sat down quietly. As soon as he opened the door, he knew this day was different. His professor looked right at him, stopped what he was doing, and headed for his desk. *Uh-oh.* Cubby remembered that today was exam day, and he wondered if that was a bigger deal than he'd imagined. He was, after all, new to college.

"There are some people waiting to talk to you, Jack. Come with me."

As they walked back toward the door, Cubby considered what kind of trouble he might be in and why. Classes were going okay, as far as he knew. He didn't drink or do drugs, and he was never involved in altercations. Yet his professor's demeanor was unmistakably serious.

Maybe it was a joke, Cubby thought hopefully as they stepped into the hall. Then he saw them: two serious-looking men in suits and a college policeman in uniform. Lawmen, waiting for him.

They introduced themselves.

"Hello, Jack, I'm Chief Gould from the college police department."

"Jack, I'm Special Agent Peter Murray from the Federal Bureau of Alcohol, Tobacco and Firearms." He stepped forward and shook Cubby's hand. Agent Murray was polished, tall, and trim in a dark sport coat. He radiated the look of frugal refinement that some federal agents are known to cultivate.

The third man held out his card. "Gerald Perwak, from the Massachusetts State Police Arson and Explosives Unit." Where Agent Murray sounded friendly, Perwak's tone was all business. He was a stocky, dark-haired fellow of indeterminate middle age—the picture of a solid plainclothes trooper. You could see him on the street and know him immediately for a cop, even at fifty feet.

By handing Cubby their business cards, as opposed to flashing badges or handcuffs, Murray and Perwak set the tone of the exchange. It was a smart move on their part. Cubby slipped the cards into his pocket. He regretted not having a card of his own.

Agent Murray gestured toward an empty classroom as Cubby's professor backed away, a little fearfully. "Can we talk?" His tone was friendly, and you could hear the question mark at the end of the words, but it wasn't really a question, as Cubby well knew.

"I guess you know why we're here," the agent said. Between the YouTube videos, his online postings, and his test blasts in the Amherst woods, Cubby knew there were a number of possibilities, but he was smart enough not to give anything away.

"No, I don't know. Why are you here?" I had taught him not to volunteer anything to police officers, but always to be polite.

Cubby paid very close attention, and he was nothing if not careful. He was well aware that even innocent-sounding questions could lead to criminal charges, and that they were not simply curious. Yet he also knew that a legitimate scientific interest in physics and chemistry was not against the law. He was very firm in his conviction that he had done nothing criminal. Therefore, he thought fast and spoke slowly. Just as I'd raised him to do.

After a few more conversational circles, the federal agent finally gave up. "You know what kinds of cases the state fire marshal and the Bureau of ATF investigate, don't you?"

"Yes. Are you here to talk about the videos I posted on You-Tube?"

"We are," Murray answered. "We'd like to talk about the explosions you filmed. Tell us what you've been doing out there in the woods." His voice was friendly, but firm.

I'd warned Cubby this day might come, and now it had arrived. As much as Cubby had argued with me, he had known too, and he was ready to tell his story. But first he needed to know where he stood. He knew they had not read him his rights, and he wasn't sure what that meant. He wasn't even sure if he *had* to talk to them, or what might happen if he didn't.

"Am I under arrest?" That was the obvious question, and Agent Murray assured him he was not. "Jack, you are free to go anytime. But if you walk out, we will just get a warrant and search without your consent. So what's it going to be?" He stayed seated.

"We have teams waiting to search both your parents' houses. You can talk to us now, or we'll search the houses and talk at the police station afterward." Were they for real? There was no way for Cubby to know. Everyone knew the ATF from their debacle at Waco. For all he knew, there were fifty agents and a tank waiting to pounce on our family. We might not even have a house when they were done. It was a scary prospect, not knowing who the good guys were, or indeed if there were any good guys at all.

To this day, I don't know whether Agent Murray was bluffing or not.

Cubby asked if he could call his parents or talk to a lawyer. The answer was the same. He could do that, but as soon as he called someone else, they would launch the raids and all bets were off.

That wasn't how it happened on the TV shows. There, when you said "I want a lawyer," you got a lawyer, not a bigger raid.

Cubby decided he was most afraid of parental fury over having our homes torn up. The threat of looting and pillaging lawmen sounded a lot worse than just talking to the cops right there. Whatever their suspicions might be, he believed in his innocence, and he decided to talk for a while.

When I heard the story a few hours later, I was very upset. None of the lawmen had read him his rights. They had not told him what he might be charged with as a result of their talks. They had threatened him when he asked about calling his mother or me. The whole interview was carefully orchestrated to get all the information they could out of him while revealing nothing of the risk he took by talking.

They knew Cubby lived at home and they knew he was seventeen. His age made him an adult in the eyes of Massachusetts courts, but a child in the federal court system. So what did they do with that knowledge? They hid; they snuck around behind my back. Even worse, they took advantage of his teenage immaturity. Instead of calling me and saying, "Mr. Robison, we'd like to talk to your son," they went to his school when they knew his mom and I were at work. Once there, they isolated and intimidated him into talking, hoping he would reveal something that might send him to prison without the benefit of either parental or legal advice.

Why did they do that? It seemed obvious to me: It was easier. They suspected I'd ask hard questions before agreeing to anything. Any dad would. Once parents and lawyers got involved, casual conversation and innocent-sounding fishing came to an end. That would sharply reduce their odds of a score; no lawyer worth his salt would let my son hang himself with his own words. If they had any evidence with which to arrest him, they would have done so right then.

I raised that question as soon as we hired a lawyer. To my surprise, he said what they had done was not considered improper. "The police only have to read you your rights when you're in custody and being questioned," he explained. Technically, Cubby hadn't been in custody, so that let them off the hook.

The cops gave him a chance, after a little intimidation, to see if he'd hang himself. Fortunately, that's not what happened. Cubby was smart. They said his Internet activity was the reason they were there, but he knew there was nothing to find outside of what he'd posted himself. He'd never been in trouble with the law. There were no trips to Iraq or Yemen in the past six months. None of us owned a missile launcher, or even a heavy machine gun. He'd seen those ads for paramilitary training in *Soldier of Fortune,* but he never signed up. Those were good things, he reassured himself. But it also made him something of an enigma to the investigators. Like most teenagers, he had yet to leave his mark on the world.

Agent Murray did most of the talking at first. He said they'd driven past his mom's house and mine, but that didn't worry Cubby. He knew there wasn't anything to see outside either place. My house was set back in the woods, and his mom's was in a development. Both were quiet suburban homes. There were no razor-wire fences, and no guard dogs in sight. We didn't even have security cameras.

Murray and Perwak took turns asking him about the explosions, and Cubby kept talking. He didn't say much about the most recent explosions, though. He wanted to tell them about science and the wonders of the natural world. Later, the investigators told me he spoke with surprising eloquence about chemistry, his passion for the past five years. They heard about the Estes model rockets he built with his mom. Estes engines use solid propellant, and he explained what that meant and how it worked. He told them about the school rocket club that he'd founded when he was thirteen years old. He sketched out some chemical reactions and explained the scientific shorthand that described what had happened.

"What kind of reactions did you do? What did you make?" The agents asked questions, but mostly Cubby just rambled on his own. They tried to bait him with talk of terrorist attacks, but Cubby wasn't biting. The investigators began to understand that Cubby did not have a revolutionary agenda at all, just scientific curiosity.

"One of the first things I learned to make was sucrose rocket engines," Cubby told them. "I made my own—it's easy. You just heat sugar till it melts and stir in potassium nitrate. It comes out looking like peanut butter. I used to roll tubes from kraft paper, fill them up, and I'd have an engine. They're just like the engines Estes sells, but a lot cheaper. I could make them as big and powerful as I wanted. I did that when I was about thirteen."

"How did you get the ingredients? Aren't chemicals like that hard to come by?" they asked.

"Potassium nitrate is stump remover. They sell it in cans at Walmart. And sucrose is just pure cane sugar. I got that at the grocery store. I used my allowance."

"Did your parents help?"

"No, I did it all myself. I studied the chemicals, figured out what I needed, and then researched where to get it. My parents took me to the store, but I picked out everything and used my own money."

The idea that a seventh grader could make decent rocket fuel all by himself was sobering. But he had not stopped there.

"I was really interested in energetic materials. That's the term scientists use for explosives. They are really just chemicals that release lots of energy fast when they react." Rapid energy release is what sets explosives apart from other chemicals, which are comparatively tranquil in nature.

That was what they'd come to hear about. Both Murray and Perwak leaned forward.

Whenever you mix things together, the result is some kind of chemical reaction. Most of the time, the result is something tangible that we eat or work with or use in some part of our lives. At work we might combine chemicals to produce anything from Coca-Cola syrup to automobile rustproofing. Farmers mix nitrogen into the soil when they put down fertilizer.

In most cases, the chemicals just mix quietly. For example, when you pour chocolate into a bowl of white cake batter, the mix turns dark brown. That's it. It doesn't get hot, crackle, steam, or blow up. At least, it's not supposed to. You put it in the oven—adding heat—and the liquid batter changes into its familiar form: chocolate cake.

Cubby wasn't very interested in those kinds of reactions, because they were not very exciting. He told the agents how his success with rocket engines had led him to even more energetic materials. His time in Mexico had exposed him to fireworks, which professionals call low explosives. Low explosives burn fast enough to make a flash and a bang, but they do not burn faster than the speed of sound. The technical term for fireworks exploding is *deflagration*.

Cubby found deflagration really interesting. Who wouldn't? It was the bang that rocked you back on your heels, as opposed to the hiss of a rocket launching into the sky. He described to the agents his first experiments with flash powder, which entailed taking stump remover and mixing it with fine powdered magnesium.

"Where'd you get powdered magnesium?" they asked. "They don't sell that at Ace Hardware."

"EBay! You can go online anytime and buy a pound of magnesium bar for twenty bucks, maybe less. I used magnesium fire-starter sticks at first. I just clamped them in a vise and filed them into powder."

When he told me about that later, I remembered Cubby patiently filing bars to dust as he made flash powder. I also remembered him testing the powder in Bic pen barrels. "Why Bic pens?" I asked him one day. "Why not straws?" He explained that straws fell apart and Bic pens did not. Furthermore, they held exactly 1.8 grams of powder, so he could compare different compounds knowing the charge size was always the same. The charge wasn't big enough to do much harm if it went off when it shouldn't. And finally, the tapered end where the point once protruded was exactly the right size for the fuse.

Cubby told the investigators he was just sixteen when he progressed to making sophisticated high explosives, which are totally different from flash powder. High explosives burn faster than the speed of sound. When they go off, it's called detonation, and the blast is far more powerful than that of any low explosive. The shock wave of a focused detonation can cut steel like butter, or throw an artillery shell over the horizon.

The first of the high explosives he experimented with was nitroglycerin, or nitro. Most people have heard of nitroglycerin, which was invented in 1847. It was the first high explosive to be created, and it revolutionized the world. Most people think of explosives in the context of weapons, but nitro was the tool that allowed us to dig the great railway tunnels of the nineteenth century. It's what brought the Union Pacific Railroad through the Rockies. Nitro dug the foundations for the new steel skyscrapers at the turn of the twentieth century. Before then, all builders had was black powder, a much less potent low explosive.

A few years later, Alfred Nobel mixed nitroglycerin (an unstable and dangerous liquid) with diatomaceous earth (known today as kitty litter) to create dynamite, the first safe, stable high explosive. My son followed in his footsteps, as fast as he could.

Cubby wasn't interested in blasting, so he did not bother to make sticks of dynamite. He preferred to master a chemical process and move on to something more complicated. There was always a next reaction, and nitroglycerin was just one of many stepping-stones for him.

By the time he turned seventeen, Cubby had taught himself how to make a wide variety of military-grade explosives, mostly by reading books from the University of Massachusetts library and studying texts he found online. Not only that, he had taught himself to use an inexpensive point-and-shoot camera to record the blasts and he'd even succeeded in photographing the fast-moving shock waves from his test explosions.

Those things would be significant achievements for a college student working in a well-equipped lab at a university. Modern-day grad students have written master's theses based on less. For Cubby to have achieved that and more in a home lab, with household chemicals as a starting point, was most impressive. And when you consider that he did it all as a kid with no formal education or training, it was nothing short of amazing.

I imagine the cops didn't know quite what to make of Cubby. His was not the voice of a bomb maker or someone who laid deadly traps. He was obviously a scientist, albeit a young one with unusual credentials. The investigators had been expecting an older person in the background, perhaps a chemistry professor with keys to a well-equipped lab. To hear that Cubby had mastered so much on his own would have been unbelievable, but for the way he told the story.

The investigators interrupted his narrative occasionally with questions, but mostly they just listened, amazed. One subject they kept coming back to was his raw materials. Even as trained explosives investigators, I think they were shocked at the variety of chemicals he'd found on the shelves of ordinary stores. And whatever he couldn't find in town, eBay offered in abundance. Like most people, the investigators had assumed the chemicals needed to formulate sophisticated high explosives could only be obtained from chemical supply houses—places a sixteen-year-old would not be expected to shop.

However, all of Cubby's so-called precursor chemicals were totally legal, unregulated compounds that are common in homes, garages, repair shops, and farms. The longer they listened, the more obvious it was that Cubby was not a criminal. The compounds he had created might well be dangerous, but Cubby had no malice in him as he made them.

Still, for people charged with preventing bad guys from making bombs, my son's answers were troubling. He had created state-of-the-art explosives with raw materials from Rocky's Hardware, Stop & Shop, and Amherst Farmer's Supply. Ingredients included liquid cleaners, powdered detergents, drain cleaners, hand warmers, and of course bleach and ammonia.

There were still more questions.

"Did you ever experiment with trip wires or booby traps?" they asked.

"Of course not!" said Cubby. "I'm a scientist, not a bomb maker!" His speech was always extraordinarily precise.

"So there aren't any bombs in the house?"

No, Cubby told them, slightly annoyed at such a ridiculous question. "I never had any bombs, just experimental explosive compounds." Cubby did his chemical reactions in the lab and stored the results in test tubes or plastic containers until he was ready to test them. When they asked where he did his lab work, he explained that he had set up a lab in his mother's basement.

The longer they talked to Cubby, the more relaxed the agents became. In fact, they began to reassure Cubby, who was feeling pretty anxious himself. Agent Murray said this did not look like a criminal case, at least from the federal point of view.

"You've got, what, a hundred grams of homemade explosive? You'd have to have more like a hundred *pounds* of PETN to get prosecuted by us. And we're looking for bombs, not chemistry experiments," he said. Trooper Perwak chimed in, saying, "You haven't described yourself committing any serious crimes. I'm not arresting anybody right now." Promising as that sounded, *right now* wasn't *never,* and he was still in their clutches, so he only relaxed a little.

After threatening him in the beginning, when he wanted to call his parents, they had turned friendly and encouraging. I guess they realized the easiest way to see his lab was with his help. Cubby was already cooperating, but his mom had no idea what was going on, and she owned the house. It was time to call her. But first, they needed to give Cubby a task.

"Can you write us a description of what you've been doing?" Agent Murray asked Cubby in the friendliest of tones. My son had seen spy movies in which the fascist police have their victim write his confession, which they subsequently use to convict him. Then they have him shot. With a sinking feeling he agreed—what else could he do? He was careful not to write about anything that could be even vaguely construed as a crime. Of course, the people in the movies probably had the same notion while writing their confessions, and they got shot anyway. Cubby wondered where he would be at that time the next day.

A few minutes later, he handed his inquisitors this summary of their conversation:

My interest in explosives began when I was very young. I had read on many websites simple formulas for black powder and sugar rockets. I was intrigued.

I was unable to perform experiments due to a lack of a bank account until about the end of 9th grade. Once I got my own account, I quickly ordered a few pounds of potassium nitrate (from eBay) and began experimenting. For a while I tested "candy" rockets, which are made from cast sugar/potassium nitrate. These were moderately successful. I also made sugar/nitrate smoke compositions. Gradually, my experiments grew more complex. After a while, I began experimenting with magnesium flash powder. That was a fantastic success. I made the powder by filing down campfire starters.

Then I began researching high explosives. I studied the reactions and the properties of many common explosives before I even considered experimenting with them myself. After several months of research, I performed my first acetone peroxide reaction. The yields were not great, but I learned a fair bit. All the precursors came from the hardware store and the pharmacy (drain opener, hydrogen peroxide, and acetone). I never used the TCAP alone; I always mixed it with ammonium nitrate to increase stability. I also never stored it dry.

After a few experiments with acetone peroxide, I decided to attempt my first nitration. I followed a common process for the production of picric acid from aspirin, battery acid, and potassium nitrate. This was by far the most interesting reaction I ever performed. I was fascinated by the color changes as it progressed. In the end, I wound up with a decent amount of picric acid.

While he was writing, the agents sat in the next room, planning their visit to his lab. The school day was over by then, so Special Agent Murray called Little Bear. At that time, she was teaching at a high school in Dalton, a bit more than an hour's drive from home. After introducing himself, Murray said they'd been talking to Cubby, who said he had explosives in the house.

"We'd like to see the lab and make sure it's safe." He was polite, but there was no putting them off at that point. I don't know if they could have gotten a search warrant earlier, but no judge would turn down their request now, after what Cubby told them.

That was when Cubby called me.

45

THE RAID BEGINS

I felt like I was under siege—an attack on Cubby seemed like an attack on me. I'm sure many parents would feel the same. Turning to our service manager, I said, "I gotta go, kid emergency" and zipped out the door. Driving on instinct, I headed for home. I knew Cubby was at school with the cops, but what would they do next? Were they planning to tear up his mom's house and mine? That sure seemed likely. If so, I'd better get home to protect my rights.

I called Martha right away to warn her and report what had happened. Shocked and scared, she looked out the windows. There were no lawmen visible. If they were outside the house, they were well hidden. If they weren't outside, I knew they might arrive any second. When they came, would they knock politely or break down the door? We had no idea what to expect, especially from the ATF, which had recently been characterized as "jackbooted government thugs" by the executive vice president of the National Rifle Association. I could almost hear the helicopter gunships circling as I drove.

With Cubby in the hands of the police and raiders headed for his mom's house and maybe my own, I knew it was time to find a lawyer. Luckily, I have a number of friends in the legal community, and they were unanimous in their recommendation: David Hoose. One of my friends called him and made the introduction. He called me back immediately and left me his cell number. But there was little more to say until I got there and learned what was really going on.

With the lawyer question settled, my thoughts returned to my house. Had Cubby left anything illegal there? Were there explosive materials on the workbench in the garage? At times like that, you realize how much you may not know about your own home and family. I also wondered what, if anything, I could say on the phone. Were they tapping my line? Years ago that would have sounded like paranoia, but thanks to the new Patriot Act, I knew it was entirely possible.

I was glad I didn't do drugs, raise fighting dogs, smuggle guns, or do anything else obviously criminal. But in today's climate of fear who knows what's legal and what's a felony? Just two weeks before I had been accosted by a Boston policeman, who claimed it was illegal to photograph subway trains in the city of Boston. What kind of crazy talk is that? He was good enough not to arrest me, and I went home and looked up the law. To my disgust, he was right. Freedom slips away by inches, while we aren't looking, with little things like that. Nothing had really happened yet, but already my neck muscles were tight from stress. I called Martha again and told her about the lawyer and my fears about Cubby and being raided and what might become of us.

Worried as I was, all was quiet when I turned into my street. There was no invasion army in the cul-de-sac, and no troops visible in the woods. If they were out there, they were singularly well hidden. At that moment I was glad for winter, because the ground was snow covered and I could see that the terrain around my house was untrampled.

Later, when I described my worries, some people dismissed them as alarmist. I felt vindicated when I talked to the investigators during the trial and they told me they had visited my house before the raid but they didn't see anything suspicious so they didn't approach too close. When I asked why, one cop said, "We didn't want to leave tracks and call attention to ourselves if something was going on. We watched, but nothing happened there."

Opening the door, I was relieved to find an intact home. I wondered how long it would stay that way. More than that, I wondered how Cubby was doing. I dialed his number, but he didn't answer.

He would have called if they'd arrested him. I was sure of that. *What was going on?* Finally, he called back. He was still free, and alone in his car. "They've been asking me questions for the past two hours. Now we're going to my mom's," he said. "They want to see my lab. They were impressed at what I told them," he said. He sounded pleased with himself, which was crazy, because he was in the clutches of the police.

"Just be careful," I replied. "These cops are not your friends. They are asking questions to see if they can build a case against you. If they do, they'll try and send you to prison." I didn't want to make him any more worried than he already was, but he had to know what was at stake.

"I told them everything was at Mom's house and there was nothing at your house. I think they'll leave you alone. My mom is pretty upset, though." Cubby sounded stressed.

Knowing my own house was intact and that the Feds were headed for South Hadley, I decided to go to his mom's myself. I told Cubby to say as little as he could and trusted in his judgment. He was the one on point, and it was all we had.

It was an anxiety-filled drive. I made sure there was nothing troublesome in my car before I left, just in case. I didn't have a gun, but I did have a very powerful flashlight. At that time, they were still legal.

Cubby was the first to arrive, with the investigators in tow. Agent Murray had told Cubby's mom that four plainclothes cops would conduct the search. Amazingly, he'd suggested that the tour of the lab would take only fifteen minutes.

When she arrived, they were waiting, just as they'd promised when they called her. They had not broken into the house, and they had not brought an army. There was just one new person: Special Agent John Murray, also of the ATF. At first I thought I'd heard his name wrong, but I soon realized it was a bizarre coincidence. Of all the federal agents who could come calling, who'd have imagined the ones we got would have the same last name? It was like meeting Darryl and the other brother Darryl, from the sitcom *Newhart*. At the time, though, it didn't seem funny. After asking Little Bear to sign a form allowing them to search the house, they left her in her car in the driveway while Cubby showed them his lab. And so the circus began.

First a South Hadley police cruiser pulled into the yard. Then another, and a third. They'd gotten wind of something from the state police, and they wanted in. After all, it was their town. But Agent Murray was firm. They could guard the driveway, but they weren't getting inside. "No sightseeing," he told them. As they sat there, more cars and trucks from the state police began to arrive. Then the fire department appeared with their ambulance. The street in front of Little Bear's house filled, and new arrivals lined both sides of the road. Neighbors wandered outside to see what was going on. Someone called the news, and vans full of reporters appeared.

Inside, the cops were deciding what to do. Cubby had walked them through the house and shown them to his lab. He pointed out every jar and tray and beaker, and what each one contained. Knowledgeable and cooperative as he was, the list was long. Some of Cubby's chemicals were packed in commercial containers; others were in glass or plastic containers, labeled in Cubby's handwriting. A few weren't labeled, but he knew what they were.

The vast majority of Cubby's chemicals weren't explosive or even dangerous. The explosives he'd made were in very small quantities, and stored separately from all the other chemicals. There were no bombs, detonators, or anything else scary.

Now the investigators' job was to verify what Cubby had told them, and to carry off and dispose of any explosives. It was taking some doing for the cops to decide exactly how to go about that task. The bomb techs were accustomed to simpler scenes, where there was a box of dynamite, or a grenade, or even a cache of weapons. Cubby's lab, with a hundred different chemicals in bags, jars, and bottles, was unlike anything they'd ever seen. Frankly, the array of compounds he had was way beyond their range of expertise. They were trained to recognize weapons, but there were no weapons to be found, just chemicals, and they weren't chemists or engineers.

If they insisted on testing everything, cataloging individual samples, and removing the contents of the lab bit by bit, we knew it would become a very long job. However, that's what they chose to do. The bottle may have said Drain Cleaner, but they tested it just to be sure. Lots of guys made good overtime that weekend.

As they would soon discover, every chemical my son had bought for his lab was legal and unregulated. Nothing was spilled and nothing was leaking. There was no cocaine hidden in the sugar. Despite that, the state police called for more bomb techs and what they described as a "Tier One hazmat response." That meant another squad of technicians had to be summoned, with bags of Speedi Dri (an absorbent cleanup product), and many more forms to be filled out. It was shaping up to be a long night.

46

THE LOCUS OF THE INVESTIGATION

Cubby's mom lives in a 1950s-era subdivision, one of a hundred Cape-style houses on orderly landscaped lots. Her neighbors are a solid conservative bunch, and the neighborhood is generally quiet and peaceful. Not that night. When I pulled in, the South Hadley cops had the street blocked off, and flashing emergency lights were everywhere. It was a Friday night, and there was more action on that street than anywhere else in western Massachusetts. Maybe all of New England.

What are all these people doing here? I was shocked at the scene I encountered when I drove up. Cubby had said he was heading to his mom's house with a few plainclothes cops following. What went wrong? For a moment I feared Cubby had something really bad in his mom's basement—something I knew nothing about. Suddenly scared, I talked my way past the barrier and drove down a street clogged with people, police cars, fire trucks, ambulances, and finally Cubby's little Subaru. I saw my son, standing with his mom in the yard, and felt a huge wave of relief. If he had anything awful in there, he would not have been walking around loose. I parked and got out of my car.

There were uniformed people everywhere. Some were cops, some were firemen, and others were not so easily identified. They flowed in and around the house and gathered in clumps in the street. Two cars had spotlights trained on the side door, which stood open to the night air. The whole thing was like a scene from a horror movie, where they light up the doorway and some slime-dripping monster walks out. But these weren't monsters. They were the ATF.

After a moment, Agent Murray and Trooper Perwak walked over and introduced themselves. They'd been talking to my son for a few hours, but this was the first time I'd seen either of them. To my surprise, they did not seem monstrous at all. Perwak impressed me as a solid plainclothes trooper, the kind of fellow who might visit my company, seeking help in an investigation. I wasn't too worried about him. It was the Feds who scared me. I turned to Murray, shook his hand, looked him up and down, and my first sense was of . . . relief. He struck me as a reasonable, intelligent, and articulate guy. Both of them were polite, respectful, and professional. There were no guns in sight.

"We're in the process of evaluating your son's lab," Agent Murray told me. "Your son has been very cooperative. He's given us a list of what's inside and our technicians are in the process of checking it out. So far it's going well." I looked over at the house and wondered how "checking it out" required the army of people I saw tramping in and out. Unfortunately, the raiders had complicated matters tremendously, all in the name of procedure. The house had perfectly good lights, but they'd shut the power off as a precaution. Someone noticed the gas stove, and that scared them, because gas causes explosions. So they shut the gas off too. That meant there was no heat, and everyone had to work in bulky coats. With the electricity turned off, fifty flashlight beams pierced the darkness and lights illuminated the house from a generator truck outside.

Standing in the yard, I could not help being shocked by the massive deployment of resources for what seemed to me a fairly trivial incident. The scale of the raid made for an enormous waste at a time when town budgets were already stretched too thin. The raid was also frankly very scary for everyone in the neighborhood. The sight of all those cops, with no one answering questions, must have led the neighbors to think there was something truly awful in that house.

One of the things that troubled me most was how the response had escalated, till it was crazily out of proportion for a teenager with a chemistry lab. The trouble was, every responder had a tiny and well-defined role, which made their individual tasks sound reasonable. All of them defended what they did by saying, "We're just doing it by the book," or "We're being careful." If I challenged the need for any of them to be there, the response was always that they knew best. Yet somehow those well-meaning individuals had added up to an invading army, with dozens of vehicles clogging the streets and countless men and women in uniforms trampling the house and the neighborhood, each one just doing his or her job. As I watched, I kept reminding myself that Cubby had brought everything there in the trunk of his car and set it up all by himself. This massive response was of their making, not his. One of the first things he'd done was offer to carry everything in his lab outside if they were scared or worried about entering. "I'll do it for you. There's nothing dangerous," he said, in a spirit of innocent cooperation. They'd chosen a different path.

As the night wore on, people got tired and communication broke down. Tempers flared as mistakes were made. At one point, an explosives tech emerged from the basement in a panic. "Guys! We gotta get out of here! There's a mason jar full of acetone peroxide ready to explode." Everyone turned on Cubby in anger. "You lied to us!" the bomb tech shouted at him, and everyone ran out of the basement and backed away from the house, as if the whole thing was about to detonate.

Cubby kept his cool. "There's no jar of explosive down there," he said calmly. As the cops got over their initial panic and the house remained standing, Cubby looked at their photo of the "jar of explosive." It was a mason jar, but it wasn't full of acetone peroxide. It contained a harmless mix of water and baking soda. Cubby had told Agent Murray what was in each jar, but the techs who copied Cubby's list made mistakes, confused themselves, and got scared. Who knows what would have happened if he wasn't there to set them straight?

As Cubby explained over and over, there was no special hazard in his lab. He knew exactly what was down there. He repeated his offer to walk downstairs and bring the materials up for them. But they were determined to do it their way. A bomb technician put on a Kevlar suit, walked ponderously down the stairs, and retrieved the results of Cubby's teenage chemistry experiments as if they were booby traps in a war zone. Later, one of the cops claimed the technician had risked life and limb to clean up the lab. It seemed laughable to me, but I guess they didn't know any better.

It got worse. Over the next two days, two Kevlar-suited techies would make twenty-plus trips up and down the stairs, bringing up one little bottle at a time. Each one was carefully placed in the back of a dump truck, covered with half a ton of sand, carried to the South Hadley landfill, and blown up with sacks of government-supplied explosives.

For training purposes, it was great. For doing the job that needed doing with Cubby's lab, it was like killing a gnat with a bazooka—a classic example of government in action. Rather than letting one guy change his own lightbulb, they called in a crew of fifty workers and twenty supervisors to do it for him. I was very concerned that I was the guy with the "lightbulb problem," and that these people were going to expect me to pay for their "assistance" changing it. But I kept those thoughts to myself.

I asked Murray if Cubby was going to be arrested, and his answer was cautiously reassuring. "I can't say what will happen, but at this moment I am not seeing any reason to arrest your son. He has cooperated with us all along, and everything he's told us has proven to be true." I walked to the house, but the cops at the door shooed me away. As I turned around, a huge ten-wheel truck appeared, and it morphed into a Mobile State Police Command Center right before my eyes. They were taking over the neighborhood.

I felt a new flash of fear. Could Cubby have a lot more explosives than I realized? Leading him away from the others, I asked him again how much explosive material was inside.

"A few hundred grams," he said. "There's about as much explosive as a bag of fireworks. Certainly less than a couple sticks of dynamite. I told them everything that was there." I wondered if I had underestimated the hazard of what he'd made, so I asked again. He thought a minute. "Obviously, the stuff I made is dangerous if it goes off in your hand. But if it went off in the house and you were out here, nothing much would happen. It would make a bang, and maybe break a window. That's about it. It would blow up the shelf in my lab."

"Do they know that?" I asked. "Yes," he said, "I told them several times."

Hearing that, the reaction we were seeing seemed totally inexplicable, especially when I recalled the ATF agents saying, "Everything your son told us is proving to be true." I didn't know what else to say. Apparently, the raiders didn't know what to say either, because they had gone into their command center and started making phone calls at ten o'clock at night. First they called John Drugan, the state police chemist. Whatever he told them wasn't enough, because they then called Kirk Yeager, who heads the FBI's explosives lab in Quantico, Virginia. I started getting worried again.

It was time to call the lawyer. To my surprise, he actually answered the phone late on a Friday night. He was at a restaurant in Northampton, but he stepped outside to talk to me. He sounded smart and confident, two traits that I value. My lawyer friend had told him what he knew of the story, and I added what more I had found out. It was too late for a lawyer's standard advice—don't talk to the cops—but he did tell Cubby to say as little as possible. "Call me immediately if they arrest anyone, no matter what time it is," he said. I noted he left the door open by saying *anyone*. At this stage of the game, he didn't know who the potential defendants might be.

After repeating the lawyer's advice, I gave Cubby his cell number. "If they grab you and I'm not around, call him." Cubby nodded soberly.

Everyone's emotions remained on edge. It was a "big response," in the words of one cop; they were used to covering crime scenes and they were constantly on the lookout for the "big crime" on any given night. Every time someone new entered the house, there was fresh potential for misunderstanding, which led to shouts and gesticulation among the crew. We cringed whenever that happened, because we suspected anything bad for them was likely to be twisted into something even worse for us.

One of the explosives techs tried repeatedly to bait Cubby, but he didn't bite. The fellow could not let go of the notion Cubby had a meth lab, even though there was no evidence he did. Nowadays, meth is mostly cooked in big superlabs in Mexico, but lawmen everywhere dream of finding a drug factory in their backyard. It's the stuff promotions are made of, but it was not to happen this night.

The tech pointed to a vodka bottle and sneered, "Do you swig that stuff while you're cooking meth?"

"No," Cubby said, "and you shouldn't swig it either, because it's not vodka. It's refined ninety-nine percent alcohol, and it would kill you to drink it. I use it in a recrystallization reaction."

If only he'd known what recrystallization was, the tech might have had a wiseass response, but he was smart enough not to look like a bigger fool. The quiet didn't last, though, as he saw another container a few minutes later. "That's a lot of Xanax you have there," he said, pointing smugly to a container sitting on the shelf below the sink.

The label was clearly visible, and it said Xylene.

"I think you must be confused," Cubby answered patiently. "Xanax is a prescription pill. Xylene is a cleaning solvent. They sell Xylene at Ace Hardware." Cubby couldn't tell if the guy was ignorant or just dumb, but he left him to speculate to himself about the remaining chemicals. Out front, the bosses knew the real score. So far, everything was what Cubby said it was, and where he said it was located. But they were far from done.

They kept working, and we stayed anxious. Our biggest worry was that we had no idea whether the authorities were honest. Would they report what they found truthfully, or would they "discover" a case of dynamite and a pound of meth just in time for the late-night news? Murray, Perwak, and the other leaders seemed like standup guys to us, but we didn't have the same confidence in the under-lings, like the troll who'd baited my son, hoping to discover a meth lab. We knew the cops would get mad as hell if we challenged them, and if they were liars, they wouldn't admit it anyway, so we decided to watch and judge them by their actions.

By nine o'clock there were sixty people on site, and all three local television stations were outside the police line, hoping to catch a story. None of them really knew what was going on, and we cer-tainly weren't talking. Gawkers who'd been drawn to the flash-ing lights stood behind the police line, bandying about rumors of a drug lab; others said there was a spill of hazardous chemicals in the basement. Only a few people knew that they were investigating a teenager's home chemistry lab.

I'd heard the old adage *any publicity is good publicity*. Well, I turned down plenty of publicity that night, and I'm glad I did. There are times when tried-and-true advice is wrong, and that was one of them.

To this day I feel a debt of gratitude to most of the local newspeople for not broadcasting any of the wild speculation that was rampant at the scene. Only one of the television stations succumbed, saying that "police were investigating a possible meth lab and guns" on their eleven o'clock news. Everyone else stuck to the facts, as given out by the police. They told reporters they were investigating a possible chemical spill (mostly true—chemicals were involved) and that no one had been arrested. Little Bear and I didn't say a word; in fact, we stayed well clear of cameras and reporters the whole time they were there.

Most of the emergency responders had never been on a raid like this one, and they'd never been near an "explosives lab," so I understood their excitement. Yet I knew from Cubby that there was only about the equivalent of a stick of dynamite in homemade explosive in his lab. It wasn't packed into containers to make bombs. It was just loose, in plastic bags and trays. There were no weapons of any kind, anywhere. There was no propaganda and no political ideologue. Most important, there were no victims, and no complaints, at least not until the cops arrived. The truth made a pretty dull story.

The idea that an army was needed to remove that material and protect the neighborhood was just crazy. The same was true of the evacuation; the only hazard to Cubby's neighbors was the invading army itself. His explosives were never a threat to any of them.

Things were only just beginning, but I could see where they were headed, and it did not look good. I had the two ranking agents telling me Cubby didn't look like a dangerous criminal, but there was this huge response going on, and someone was surely going to be blamed.

Eleven o'clock came and went. More vans and more people had arrived. They now had a mobile lab parked in the driveway, where they were testing the compounds removed from Cubby's lab. Most of the time, the tests simply validated what Cubby had told them. There were a few tense moments, when they thought they had found something unanticipated, but those results turned out to be lab errors and everyone relaxed.

Seeing a lull in the activity, I searched out Peter Murray and asked him what was happening. I guess he was feeling a bit better about things, because he smiled and said, "Every year, somewhere in the United States, ATF runs across a Boy Scout genius with a chemistry set," he said. "I guess this is your year." He then proceeded to tell me the story of David Hahn, the seventeen-year-old Boy Scout who tried to make a nuclear reactor in his parents' shed. "I don't know about the state, but I can definitely tell you the ATF has no criminal interest in your son. At this point, I just want to see the mess cleaned up."

Encouraged by that, I sought out Gerry Perwak in his unmarked car. He said about the same thing but added that cops just decide who to arrest. They don't make the decisions about who to prosecute. That's up to the district attorney. Perwak's words didn't offer much comfort, and I drove home to a troubled sleep. At least I still had a house to return to. Cubby and his mom didn't. They had to stay by the scene until the cops finally sent them to find a motel room a few miles away in Chicopee.

That was when they remembered Catto, their cat. When the raid started, the cops had locked her in the bathroom. Now they let Little Bear in briefly to retrieve her. When she went into the bathroom, she saw the medicine cabinet door opened a crack, so she looked inside. Every one of her pill bottles had been moved, and some of the lids were half open. She felt violated and wondered what else they had rummaged through.

When she went back outside, she ran into the hazmat chief and asked him how much longer they would be there. "I don't know," he said. "We still don't know how we're going to get all the chemicals out of this place. We may have to blow the house up and cover it with dirt." She looked at him as if he were crazy, but he made it plain that he was serious. There were no words to say in response.

She took the cat and snuck her into the motel with Cubby. They cried themselves to sleep as Catto bounced from bed to bed, energized and wild after an evening locked in the bathroom amid all the clamor.

I got home in time to discover that my son was the lead story on the eleven o'clock news, on all three local stations. With horrified fascination, I switched from one newscast to the next, wondering what they would say. To my surprise and pleasure, the reporting was remarkably balanced. "Police are investigating a teenager's chemistry lab in a South Hadley home," ran one headline. None of the news stories identified my son by name, presumably because he was still a minor. Walking around earlier that evening, I'd over-heard all sorts of wild speculation from reporters at the fringes of the scene, each one hoping to get a scoop. I was relieved that their fantasies of meth labs, guns, dynamite, and more hadn't made it into the news. I wondered how long that would last.

47

THE CIRCUS MUST GO ON

The news crews were still there the next morning. The raid was on the front page of that day's newspaper, complete with photos of the house and police cars. The headline read: "Possible Chemical Spill in South Hadley Home!" Disturbing as that was, it was a hell of a lot better than "Drug Lab Busted," or any of the other rumors that bystanders had been feeding the reporters. I was glad to see the newspaper editors had followed the precedent set by the previous night's television reporters; they stuck to what the police had told them, my son wasn't mentioned by name, and there was no sensational speculation.

The newspaper's online forums, however, were filled with all sorts of far-out innuendo. I'd heard some crazy stuff from spectators the night before, but the comments in the paper's discussion area put all that to shame. Cases of explosives, toxic waste, nuclear accidents—"people in the know" revealed it all. *The National Enquirer* could have taken lessons from the people who posted there. I wondered what we should do.

Meanwhile, my son had more pressing concerns. He'd given the cops an exact list of what he had, and so far, every test had proven him right. With all their talk of meth, there was not a single narcotic drug on the list. The only illegal chemicals were the small amounts of explosive he'd told them about in the initial interview. But the technicians kept making mistakes, or imagining things that weren't there, and whenever that happened, they jumped on him. We were now in our second day of that, and he was sick of their sloppiness and the repeated accusations of trickery. Walking down the street for privacy, Cubby called the number I'd given him the night before. David Hoose was cross-country skiing that afternoon, and he'd stopped to rest at the top of Northfield Mountain when his phone rang.

As soon as he answered, my son introduced himself, then asked, "Are you my new lawyer?" Cubby sounded a little hesitant, but Hoose was hesitant too. He had not met any of us and knew next to nothing about my son or what he might have done. Criminal lawyers are asked to represent all kinds of people, and every attorney draws a line somewhere. For all Hoose knew, Cubby could have been the next Unabomber. He decided to ask.

"If I take your case, I'm not going to find out that you are affiliated with the Nazis, skinheads, or any other hate group, am I?" It was a reasonable question, given that Cubby's lab was now dominating all the local news channels.

Cubby was taken aback. "I'm a scientist, not a terrorist! I'm not involved with wackos like that! I don't always agree with the politically correct people in Amherst, but that's about as far as it goes." With that established, Cubby had himself a lawyer. Hoose gave Cubby the same advice he'd given me the day before. "Say as little as possible to the police. Don't volunteer anything, but be cooperative when they ask questions. If anything blows up, call me!"

From that moment on, Agent Murray became Cubby's guardian at the scene. He'd been fair all along, but now he really looked out for Cubby's rights. For that he has my commendation and gratitude. He knew Cubby was represented by counsel, and that my son had chosen to help them voluntarily. Whatever the bomb techs thought, Murray was clear: They needed Cubby's knowledge. He made sure the meth lab taunts came to an end, and that people treated my son with respect.

By Saturday afternoon, the police had inventoried everything in the house and there was agreement about what Cubby had. To my great relief, Murray and Perwak still felt Cubby had been completely truthful with them. There had been some surprises but no evasions or deception.

Cubby's mom spent a second night in the motel around the corner, and Cubby went back to Amherst with me. I felt a little comfort, having him back home. The shock of the raid had left him pretty subdued, and he realized parents might be good for something after all. Meanwhile, having been evicted from her home, his mom was alone and scared. I knew she felt bad, but there was really nothing more any of us could do. So we went to bed.

Sunday morning arrived, and with it day three of the cleanup of Cubby's lab. I stayed home to catch up on work, and Cubby went to meet his mom. The scene was much quieter, as most of the people who'd been there the first two days slipped away. The State Police Command Center was gone, and the tent in the street had vanished with it. The bomb techs had finished blowing up Cubby's chemicals in the South Hadley landfill. The rest was up to the hazmat people.

Exactly what the hazmat crew was doing remained a mystery. They were still keeping everyone out of the house. Seeing there was nothing more they could do, Little Bear and Cubby drove to Northampton, where the three of us had a date to meet our new attorney.

Cubby was holding up pretty well on the surface. In the year or so before the raid, I'd been happy to see my son outgrow some of his more obvious compulsions, like the hair brushing and hand washing. I hadn't watched him get dressed for the lawyers, but now I couldn't help but notice his hands were scrubbed raw. I felt so sad for my little boy. I wished I could wash all this away for him, but I couldn't. I hoped the lawyer could help.

David Hoose was a tall, trim fellow, balding, with close-cropped hair. He had a ready smile and a firm handshake. He looked like exactly the kind of lawyer you'd want to see if you were locked in a jailhouse cage full of criminal deviants and freaks. There was little doubt he'd stand up fine to the likes of Murray and Perwak if push came to shove.

Actually, I was mostly just relieved he'd agreed to meet us, because we all felt pretty traumatized, and I knew he must have had better things to do on a Sunday afternoon. I sure knew I'd rather be somewhere else, but keeping my kid out of jail was pretty important. After all the trouble I'd gone to raising him, I did not want him to end up in some state prison cell.

Even though we had not met before, I had seen Hoose's face in the paper several times. Whenever there was a big criminal case, his name always seemed to appear. If he was picked to defend people in life-or-death situations time and again, it seemed to me that he had to be good. I hoped Cubby's case would be easier. I hoped it would cost less, too.

We talked together, and then he and Cubby spoke alone. Cubby had his laptop, which he used to show off his videos. He was still at the point where pride of creation outweighed fear of incarceration, but Hoose took steps to change that right away.

He cautioned Cubby that he could not destroy any of the videos without risking a charge of obstructing justice, but at the same time he told him in no uncertain terms that it was time to shut down the website. No more posting of videos and no more discussions on his forums on any topic, given that law enforcement would surely be monitoring his every word online.

Cubby looked chastened, but he agreed to do what he was told. With a few reminders and a subtle jab from his lawyer's sharp stick, Cubby's stuff went offline, and to the best of my knowledge, it hasn't returned since.

The seriousness of the situation still hadn't completely sunk in for Cubby. An ordinary kid would have been terrified at the prospect of going to jail, but my Aspergian son seemed mostly worried that the cops might damage his expensive laboratory glassware. Then he started wondering whether they would confiscate it. The idea of being sent to prison was simply not on his radar. At least, that's how it seemed to me.

In fact, throughout most of these events, he remained completely oblivious to the way other people might perceive him and his lab. All he could see was the purity of science. His inability to grasp others' point of view was typical of people on the autism spectrum. It was a stark reminder of how powerfully Asperger's had affected him, and how invisible to others those effects had been.

But I had to keep my focus on the here and now, where the threat of prosecution remained. I tried to get some reassurance from our new lawyer about what might happen next, but he didn't know any better than I did. After listening to our stories, all he could tell us was that whatever happened next was in the hands of the DA, and that he hoped she wouldn't press charges. It was the same refrain we'd heard from the cops.

There was nothing to do but wait. Hoose told us he'd send a letter to the DA telling her he was Cubby's lawyer and asking for a meeting. At that time, I still believed prosecutors listened to defense lawyers and cases got worked out quietly in back rooms, without the aggravation of court. If only that were true.

After the meeting, Cubby's mom returned to South Hadley. There was no one at the house but the hazmat crew, and they had turned friendly. The previous day's talk of "blowing up the house" was forgotten. Little Bear did her best to put fear and frustration aside as she waited them out. Finally, at 3 P.M., they left, and she was alone in the mess of a house. She began the process of putting her home back together. The first step was regaining the right to live there from town officials.

When the bomb technicians had the gas and electricity shut off, the utility companies notified the town inspectors. The building inspector said, "You can't live in a house without heat or light, especially in February!" The health inspector saw a wreck of a house with junk and clutter everywhere, and no utilities. He didn't need any encouragement to slap a Condemned notice on the door. Little Bear could not stay in a condemned house without utilities. The earliest she could get them reconnected was Monday, so she was stuck in the motel for yet another night.

Meanwhile, there was the matter of the cleanup. Little Bear has a problem with housekeeping; some would say she has great hoarder potential. When we were married, I thought she was just messy, but much later we found out that she has autism too, and her organizational ability is seriously impaired. In Little Bear's case, she has trouble completing tasks she begins, and she has terrible difficulty keeping things neat and orderly. Most people store their clothes in drawers or closets. She didn't have closets, because she'd taken them out while renovating her house in order to create more living space. But she had yet to replace the closets with other storage space. So she filled the drawers and stacked clothes and belongings on every flat surface. Then, rather than give stuff away, she installed a portable chin-up bar across the hall and hung that with clothing that should have been in a closet. When the raiders entered on Friday, the bar stood between them and the basement door, so they pulled it down and tossed it and the clothes aside. Over the next two days, innumerable boots trampled the clothing, which together with the other junk on the floor became one giant, muddy mess.

The result was definitely not for the faint of heart. Little Bear cried as she gathered her muddy, torn clothing into hampers for bulk cleaning at the Laundromat. Bags of trash were hauled out and taken to the dump. The following day, town inspectors signed off on her occupancy permit and she was back in her nest—sad, scared, and wounded.

Now the authorities were gone, but there was still a clamor in the media. The most visible outcry was in the Internet forums of the *Springfield Republican,* our local newspaper. There, in the South Hadley bulletin board, a self-described group of "Dartmouth Street neighbors" were whipping the Internet crowd into a frenzy. They were actually talking about banding together to sue Cubby's mom. It wasn't clear what they would sue for, as she had not done anything to them, but it was deeply upsetting to her.

It was also puzzling, because the neighbors she spoke to in real life were for the most part understanding. She and Cubby had gone from house to house the day after the raid, calming fears and apologizing for the disturbance. Even if they were annoyed, no one had given any indication they wanted to rise up and sue.

Yet the anonymous crazies in the forums were quite outspoken and sure of themselves, even when they were dead wrong. One stated with certainty that my son had an arsenal of guns, while another had the real scoop: It was a meth lab. There was talk of crack addicts mixed with mentions of Boy Scouts, nearby schools, and any number of popular conspiracies. It could have been a comedy routine except it was my family they were talking about. Our lawyer had said not to comment on the case, but I knew something had to be done. Whatever my son was accused of, I'd worked hard to build a reputation in that community, and I aimed to keep it.

That night, we paid visits to two of the three network TV stations serving our area. The news directors put Cubby on the air, where he introduced himself as the teenager who'd caused all the uproar. Then he apologized for all the trouble he'd caused and assured viewers that there were no bombs, drugs, or anything else to be afraid of. For a kid who was still terrorized by the raid, his composure was remarkable. I was glad they'd offered him the chance to tell his side of the story. He said the same things the following day in the Springfield newspaper.

In a perfect world, news reports would be impartial, but in

this world, they're not. One result of Cubby's outreach was that the Springfield paper—the biggest in our region—gave Cubby a fair shake, while the reporters for the Northampton local wrote as if they were in the district attorney's back pocket. The same thing happened on TV. He made a friend at Channel 3, where the news director told him his own son had Asperger's, while one of their competitors demonized him in a play for ratings.

None of the reporting made a shred of difference to the people on the forums. Although Little Bear's real-life neighborhood seemed to have returned to normal, forum activists announced that a "mass meeting" was going to take place at the local Polish-American Club. Supposedly, a lawyer would address the group and dispense advice. With some trepidation, not knowing whether she'd be at all welcome, Cubby's mom drove to the meeting at the appointed time.

No one was there except a film crew from the TV station that had been airing the wilder rumors since the night of the raid. A few old men sat at the bar, nursing drinks. The bartender didn't know anything about a meeting and didn't care. There was no lawyer and no advice. That was the last she heard about "community action." I don't know if all the traffic on the forum was the result of a TV reporter trying to stir up a story, online bullies, or some weirdo's fantasy. Whatever it was, nothing came of it.

As the story of the raid faded from the news, I realized that the goodwill I'd built up in the local business community had paid off in an unexpected way. Most of the newspapers and television stations had respected our privacy and reported the story fairly. No one mentioned that I was an author and local business owner, or that my brother had written *Running with Scissors,* a massive bestseller. My brother and I remained in the background, anonymous. Unfortunately, the same was not true for Little Bear. It was her house that had been raided, and there was no keeping her name out of the stories. Even today, people ask her if our son is "still in jail."

I guess the raid got so much attention that people assume he must have been arrested.

I'd never thought of myself as "connected to the media," but the events of that week showed me I was. Employees, managers, and even owners of every local media outlet had bought cars from me over the years, and brought them to my company for service. Several reporters had family members with autism, and they'd attended my talks at Elms College and elsewhere. When Cubby got into trouble, I didn't say a word, but many good-hearted people looked out for us anyway. No one convicted us in the news, spread rumors about us on the wire services, or sensationalized my teenager's misjudgments. I'll always be grateful for that.

Just when we thought things had quieted down, Little Bear got two letters from the government. The outfit that runs the dump for the Town of South Hadley sent her a bill for ten thousand dollars, claiming that she was responsible for the cost of opening the landfill on a weekend to dispose of "a chemical spill." At the same time, the state hazmat people billed her for an additional twenty thousand dollars for "cleaning up" her basement. Cubby's mom answered them both politely, pointing out that there had been no chemical spill to clean up. Everything in the lab was stored securely in containers, which the raiders had chosen to seize and carry to the landfill. Nothing was leaking, and anything they had spilled was their responsibility, not hers. They had made the choice to take Cubby's chemicals and dispose of them in the landfill. If she had any financial responsibility for that, she wrote to them, it would have to be determined by a court of law. Until then, she wasn't paying. Then she talked to her brother Ted, an attorney in Oregon. From his perspective, the situation seemed clear.

"They can go pound sand," he said.

48

THE DA

Cubby was never arrested, but Trooper Perwak had warned me that there was still the possibility that the DA would read the police reports and decide to press charges. That was very worrisome to us, especially when I began reading up on the prosecutor.

At the time of the raid, Elizabeth Scheibel was in her fourteenth year, and her fourth term, as Northwestern District Attorney. DAs are elected in Massachusetts, and she had run unopposed, as a Republican, in the last few elections. Her work on behalf of children was widely praised, and she had received accolades for her support of people with disabilities. Offsetting those good points were the many critics who described her office as capricious, heavy-handed, and unreasonable. By the time Cubby's lab was raided, the local media had become quite vocal in their criticism of her. The consensus was she'd been in office too long and the power of the job had gone to her head.

Cubby's case was assigned to an assistant DA named Alice Perry. I don't know whether she asked for the case or whether it was just handed to her. Either way, she seemed to take a vigorous interest in it, and warning bells began to ring in my head.

The first sign of trouble was Perry's refusal to give our lawyer a straight answer about anything involving the case. Then, when attorney Hoose offered to bring Cubby in for a meeting, she declined. That spoke volumes to me. It told me that she didn't want to learn who Cubby was, because the reality might differ from the image of him she'd already formed. In my experience, people often refuse to meet when they've closed their minds and don't want to face the possibility that they made a bad call. Wars have started that same way.

Well, if she wanted to fight, we'd fight.

Outside her office, the clamor about the raid had subsided pretty quickly. A week after the raid, the South Hadley police chief told the local paper he didn't think Cubby would be charged with anything at all. *If only he knew,* I thought. Many of the first responders—the cops, firemen, and others on the scene—had become sympathetic to Cubby's plight. They told him they'd experimented with explosives as kids too, but times are different today. Once they realized he wasn't a dangerous criminal, most everyone was on his side.

Everyone but the people in the DA's office, that is. When Hoose questioned her, Perry just said, "David, you don't realize how serious this is!" She talked to him like he was a child.

To me, it was obvious why they didn't let go. A Google search on Scheibel's office brought up a ton of bad press and very little praise. Their reputation had tanked, and they needed a slam-dunk, high-profile case to redeem it. Throughout the past year, their office had been under siege following one misjudgment after another. First there was what the media gleefully referred to as "Pottygate," in which the DA convened a grand jury to investigate a court clerk's alleged theft of the prosecutors' private bathroom key. Her actions earned Scheibel a stinging rebuke from superior court judge John Agostini and ridicule in the *Boston Globe*. Then there was the case of Jason Vassell, a student at UMass Amherst. One night, two belligerent drunks invaded his dorm, threatening him with racist slurs, and he stabbed them in self-defense. The result? The invaders were free, and Vassell was facing felony prosecution. The community was outraged, and many believed that Vassell was only charged because he is black.

With Vassell sympathizers calling the DA a racist and Pottygate making them look like wastrels, the prospect of being hailed for saving Amherst from a crazed bomb maker must have been a powerful temptation. A high-profile court victory could be a step toward higher elected office. That was my biggest worry—that my son would end up as a stepping-stone toward someone else's desire to advance her career.

Cubby's mom worried even more than me. It was, after all, her home that had been trashed by raiders. She began having panic attacks and grinding her teeth, and waking up with nightmares and sweats.

Meanwhile, Cubby was gaining more and more supporters. When people first saw the army that descended on his mom's house, they thought he must have a ton of high explosive in there. But when they realized that ATF and the state had sent fifty-plus people and dozens of cars and trucks to remove a couple of pounds of homemade explosive, they were as flabbergasted as me. Chemists from both the University of Massachusetts and Mount Holyoke College wrote to express sympathy over his plight. The Mount Holyoke chemist told Cubby about his own experiments with explosives fifty years earlier. "All chemists try that stuff," he said. The UMass professor invited my son to come check out the chemistry program at his labs in Amherst.

It took some people longer to come around. During the raid, a few of Little Bear's neighbors became agitated, thinking she had put their lives in danger. However, most soon realized that was not the case, at which point they focused their annoyance on the authorities for the size of their response to a kid's chemistry lab. They were understandably upset that the neighborhood was invaded in midwinter for what was essentially a huge training exercise. In fact, that's exactly how the hazmat guys had described it as they packed up to leave.

So what would the DA do? The prosecutor's behavior implied that she was trying to build a criminal case against my son. But it was not obvious to either our attorney or us what they might charge him with. A month and a half passed, with no word. By then, the story had vanished from the news and Little Bear's street was totally back to normal.

Then, in late March, Cubby got a phone call. His friend and high school classmate Alex had been summoned to appear before the grand jury on April 1. Alex was scared, and so was Cubby. A call from the lawyer confirmed Alex was not the target of the grand jury, but that was scant reassurance, because he already knew they were after my son. He'd never been called before a grand jury—none of us had—but we knew they only investigated serious crimes. For Cubby and me, that was a chilling thought. I felt like we should be doing something to prepare to defend ourselves, but we could not attend the grand jury session or speak to the jurors, and its proceedings were secret. It was a horrible, stressful time.

I spent some of the time educating myself about the Massachusetts legal system and what might lie in store for us. The first thing I learned was that grand juries aren't "grand" at all. Like many people, I assumed a "grand jury" would consist of leading figures in the community, people who wanted to get involved and provide the prosecutor useful guidance. Nothing could be further from the truth, at least where I live. Grand jurors are just ordinary people, selected at random from the voter rolls. Their principal qualification to serve: the ability to take time to appear in court, over a period of months, to hear a procession of cases presented by prosecutors. By state law, grand juries must approve all felony indictments, which are then tried in superior court. Of all the places Cubby might have ended up, that was by far the scariest. District court sends drunk drivers to county jail for six months. Superior court sends murderers and rapists to state prison for life.

We trusted Alex, and we knew he'd try to present Cubby in a positive light. But we didn't know if that would matter. We had no idea what other witnesses they had called. We didn't even know what charges were contemplated. All we knew was, Cubby had offered to meet them himself and they refused. No DA who wanted truth or fairness would have done that.

As I said, we could not attend the grand jury session, but we did get a complete transcript a few months later. I was able to review the record, and it just made me furious, the way the prosecutor presented a totally one-sided picture to a group of people, leading them to do her bidding, and return criminal indictments. The word *jury* implies people who consider all sides and render a decision, but our grand jury did nothing of the sort. The first witness called was Trooper Perwak, who told the jurors how Cubby first came to the attention of the police. To my surprise, Perwak said it was an informer. The person who turned Cubby in to the cops was Kevin Goyette, a surplus and salvage huckster Cubby had encountered on eBay. Cubby ordered glassware from him, and when he did, he revealed his name, e-mail address, and home address. That information was his undoing.

Goyette Googled Cubby and found his online discussion forums and the videos of his explosions on YouTube. I never understood why a glassware merchant would investigate a customer, but whatever his motives, he called the South Hadley police and told them about Cubby. The South Hadley cops looked at Cubby's videos, but they did not have any expertise in explosives. They turned to the state police, which was how Gerry Perwak became involved in the case.

Perwak proceeded to show the jurors fifteen videos Cubby had made the year before. Most of them showed small amounts of explosive being detonated on the ground. Some of the experiments didn't even work; all they did was fizzle and smoke. A few were more dramatic, as Cubby set off blasts underwater and geysers erupted ten or twenty feet into the air.

Perwak related all that in a very matter-of-fact way, without any embellishment. He had a reputation as a tough but fair cop, and it showed. If he thought Cubby belonged in jail, he would have said so. In fact, he did not say one word about malice, criminal intent, or property damage. To convict Cubby of any serious charges, the prosecutor would have to prove all those things.

As I read the transcript, I was deeply troubled by the prosecutor's distorted presentation of the evidence. Grand juries are supposed to govern themselves. A prosecutor may bring in and question a witness, but a juror has the right to decide what additional questions to ask him or her. Cubby's prosecutor ignored that rule. At one point, Perwak read some of the comments on Cubby's videos, and a juror asked whether any of the people who discussed explosives with my son had been investigated. It was a reasonable question, but the prosecutor cut it off, dismissing the juror out of hand.

No one gave the jurors any perspective on what they were seeing and hearing. No one pointed out that any Massachusetts resident could drive over the line into New Hampshire, where fireworks are legal, and buy far more explosives than Cubby was accused of making. Thousands of people do that every Fourth of July. They return home, crack open a cold beer, and start lighting 'em up. They drop fireworks in the water and toss them on the ground. Some folks even throw them at people, and blow up whatever they can find. Yet those individuals don't become the subject of grand jury investigations.

Even today, a YouTube search for explosion videos produces half a million hits. Cubby is far from alone in his interest. But no one told the jurors that. His handful of homemade videos were presented as if they were unique in the world.

After Perwak stepped down, Alex took the stand. He told the

jurors about making one of the videos Perwak had just shown them. "We had walked out behind Jack's father's house . . . through a patch of woods next to the landfill, no other houses nearby. Jack had this little thing, probably about that big." With his hand, he indicated that it was about the size of a golf ball. "It was for a fuel air experiment. He had taped it to a tree and set it off. It smoked and didn't really work, as you can see in the video."

The prosecutor then asked Alex about Cubby's lab, and he said, "Yes, I knew about the lab he had in his mother's basement. He was willing to try a few things out and he, of course, now regrets it being that he is in so much trouble, but this was simply just a test of chemistry." Alex was nervous and a little rambling, but he stood by Cubby with every word.

Perry got a more useful witness in the form of Frank Hart, another state police detective. He eagerly described the chemicals in Cubby's lab. Unlike Perwak, who stuck to the facts, Hart happily supplied a terrorist purpose for every substance he mentioned. Ammonium nitrate was no longer just fertilizer. It became the material that "wiped out" the Alfred Murrah Federal Building and "killed 168 and injured 800 people." Triacetone peroxide, or TATP, became "the weapon du jour of terrorists," as well as "Mother of Satan, the type of device that Richard Reid, the Shoe Bomber, was trying to ignite on an airplane."

By analogy, if Hart had discovered a jug of gasoline in someone's garage, he would have said that it's known far and wide as the principal ingredient in Molotov cocktails. That might be true, but it's an awfully misleading way to describe unleaded premium.

When Hart told the jurors about Cubby's ammonium nitrate fertilizer, he forgot to tell them it was still in its original packaging, the very same bags in which it's sold to gardeners all over the world.

"Fifty pounds of ammonium nitrate" sounds a lot scarier than "a sack of 34–0-0 lawn and garden plant food."

Then Hart focused on the hazards in Cubby's lab. With great relish, he told jurors how his technicians put on Kevlar bomb suits and "walked very slowly" to carry Cubby's TATP out of his basement lab. He told them how they carefully loaded it into a "huge total containment vessel" and carried it to the landfill for destruction. He said, "We had to put people in there at the risk of life or limb to remove this stuff," which sounds very brave. He didn't say that my teenage son had offered to carry it out for them, but the bomb techs declined because they preferred to "handle the situation with standard procedures."

The small amount of TATP Cubby had could have been detonated right on the basement floor with no hazard, but Hart didn't say that either. At first I thought he was being deliberately deceptive, but I concluded he just didn't know. He was a lawman, not a scientist. He had no idea how powerful the explosives were, so he put on a bomb suit and hauled them away in a two-ton containment vessel. That's a lot of special handling for the explosive power of a pack of firecrackers.

Perry pressed Hart about property damage—a necessary thing for serious criminal charges. She said, "Based on your training and experience, would the explosions that you witnessed cause property damage or damage?"

Hart hadn't witnessed any explosions, he'd just watched the online videos. But with no defense attorney to object to his speculation, Hart said, "Oh, yeah, without a doubt."

Later in the testimony, an inquisitive juror asked, "You said that the explosions that you saw in the same videos that we saw, that they did do property damage?"

"Mm-hmm," Hart said.

"What was the damage?" I found myself liking this juror.

Hart stumbled a moment and said, "Well, the woodlands and who knows what, you know, that water system, that water supply system what, you know, the contamination from those chemicals and so on and so forth. If you were an amphibian in that water I would think you'd say it was definitely property."

Clearly, at least one juror was dubious of the property damage claim. But there were twenty-three of them, and they did not need to be unanimous in their opinion. They began their deliberations, and a short while later, the jury foreman gave the prosecutor what she wanted: the go-ahead to indict my son.

Our lawyer had asked to be notified as soon as the DA's office made a decision. That seems like the courteous thing to do. Nevertheless, on April 2, Perry called a press conference, at which she charged Cubby with three counts of malicious explosion, without so much as a heads-up to our attorney.

Federal agents had concluded he was just a smart kid who wasn't a threat to anyone. The ranking state trooper at the scene had not seen fit to arrest him. But the district attorney—who was never at the scene, and never met my son—had decided to go for the big score.

49

ARRAIGNMENT

The next step was Cubby's arraignment. It was scheduled for April 8, just after lunch. Arraignment is a court proceeding, generally open to the public, in which the prosecutor and the defendant appear before a judge. The prosecutor briefly describes the case, and the charges are spelled out. Then the defendant tells the court how he wants to plead: guilty or not guilty. We felt fortunate to be arguing before superior court judge Judd J. Carhart, one of the most respected jurists in our state's court system, with a reputation for fairness.

Perhaps because there were reporters in the audience, prosecutor Perry seemed intent on getting as many inflammatory statements as possible on the record, whether they were true or not. She used the same scare tactics Trooper Hart had used before the grand jury—relating every chemical Cubby had to some kind of terrorist attack, even though there was not a shred of evidence that Cubby had any interest in, or connection to, terrorism. For example, she said that my son possessed the same explosive used in a 2005 terrorist attack in England and videotaped himself blowing up a flag bearing a Jewish symbol.

When I heard her words, I was so mad smoke sizzled from my ears.

Cubby had never blown up any flags, and certainly not any Jewish symbols. What he did do was make a matchstick figure, less than two inches tall, that he called a "suicide bomber." He blew up his construction on camera. Stupid kid behavior? Certainly. Offensive to some? Sure. But blowing up a flag bearing a Jewish symbol? Absolutely not.

Psychologists say boys with Asperger's tend to lag several years behind their peers in the realm of social judgment. That was a good example. It was nothing like what the prosecutor described.

Perry continued in the same vein as she described and "interpreted" the chemicals found in Cubby's lab. In addition to listing explosives, many of whose names she could not pronounce, she claimed Cubby's lab also contained the makings of lysergic acid amide (LSA), a chemical compound she likened to the hallucinogenic drug LSD.

In fact, there was no LSA seized from Cubby's lab, nor were any makings for illegal drugs seized. LSA is a Schedule III narcotic, so if any had been found, it would surely have led to additional criminal charges. I could not believe a sworn officer of the court would stand before a judge and state something that was patently untrue, but there it was, plain as day.

On four separate occasions, Carhart asked Perry to stop rambling and stick to her requests and recommendations. But she couldn't seem to switch it off. "Enough!" Carhart shouted in exasperation at one point. "This is a simple arraignment. We'll try the case later."

Finally, the charges against Cubby were read and filed. My son was formally charged with willfully placing explosives near property and with three counts of maliciously creating an explosion. Without a moment's hesitation, he pleaded not guilty to all the charges.

That took us to the next part of the hearing—what the lawyers call "bail or jail." At arraignment, the judge accepts the defendant's plea and decides what to do with him until trial. Most defendants are permitted to post bail, to ensure they don't just take off. Other defendants—the most dangerous ones, and those with no bail money—are held in jail till the trial. Cubby didn't go to jail. As a local kid with no prior criminal record, the judge let Cubby live at home with me until the case was resolved.

After a brief verbal scuffle between Hoose and Perry, Judge Carhart set some conditions. He decided Cubby had to stay in my house, not his mother's, which was no surprise. He ordered Cubby to check in with the probation department weekly. Next he said Cubby could not possess chemicals of any kind. That suggestion was nuts, and totally unreasonable and unenforceable. Toothpaste is a chemical. A CO_2 (carbon dioxide) cartridge to make fizzy water is another. We all use chemicals. Then he said, "No Internet." In today's world, there is no such thing as a college student who doesn't use the Internet, all the time. It took another hearing to get those last two points clarified and made workable. Cubby could be around household chemicals, but he had to keep his lab packed away. He could use the Internet, but only for school. He had to stay clear of chemical and explosive forums.

Even those conditions were aggravating, but they could have been worse. Still, on Hoose's orders, we didn't complain. Our lawyer gave a brief interview to the local newspaper, in which he called the release conditions "a complete overreaction" and said Cubby never had any malicious intent.

We were back to the waiting game. Meanwhile, life went on.

50

ASPERGER'S AND CUBBY

I had always taken pride in the idea that Cubby was more socially aware than me, but the events leading up to the trial forced me to confront the idea that perhaps my notion was wrong. Sure, Cubby had more friends than me, but he was totally oblivious to the ways other people might see his actions.

In fact, he was oblivious to others in some very basic ways. That was revealed to me gradually, as others told me stories of Cubby's behavior. For example, when Cubby was sixteen, my friend Rick gave him a summer job in his civil engineering lab at the university. One day, Rick watched Cubby run over another student's foot with a chair and not even notice when she howled. Most days, my son was so immersed in his work that he ignored the other students, and they were annoyed when he neglected them. They would talk to each other about their lives and local events, while he behaved as if he didn't know them and didn't care. Indeed, he probably didn't. It was as if they had formed a team and he was on his own. Meanwhile, Cubby had no clue they felt that way, though like me, he always felt he was an outsider.

He was the same way with his lawyer. Hoose had given Cubby

his cell phone number to call in case there was an emergency, and Cubby took to calling at odd hours whenever trial-related thoughts popped into his mind. Hoose would be at dinner or a movie, and the phone would ring. He had to answer, because it might be an emergency. But it wasn't. It would be my son, with some random question or comment about the case.

Having read my memoir about growing up with Asperger's and having gotten to know Cubby, Hoose was at first amused by his behavior. However, after a 9:30 call on a Saturday night while he was entertaining a houseful of guests, Hoose mentioned to Cubby that most people called on his business phone during regular office hours. It had never occurred to Cubby that there was anything at all odd about the nature or times of his calls. My son was shocked to realize he was being rude.

Was that Asperger's? I was afraid it was. One of the key markers of Asperger's and autism in general is blindness to the nonverbal signals of others. One of the ways that manifests itself is in self-centeredness. Folks on the autism spectrum don't behave in a self-centered way to be mean or take advantage; they do it because they don't "get" the signals others are sending. This trait has caused me a lot of trouble in life, and it looked like it was affecting my son the same way.

Shortly after the raid, Cubby and I went back to the psychologist Cubby had been seeing, who concluded that my son did indeed have Asperger's. In fact, Cubby and his therapist had often talked about "Asperger traits," but Cubby had never been given a formal diagnosis. Like the Yale psychologists who'd tested Cubby when he was small, this therapist was more focused on solving problems than affixing labels. Together they talked about friendship, organization, and other problems of day-to-day life. But now that Cubby's obliviousness to what others might think had placed his liberty at risk, it was important that we give a name to the overarching cause.

Going forward, the goal for the therapist remained the same—

how could he help my son navigate independent adult life? Simple as that is to say, it's a very hard problem to solve in practice. If you are blind to certain signals from other people, it's not easy to create emotional insight where there is none. It's a problem I have wrestled with for years.

Then, in the spring of 2008, my son accompanied me to Harvard Medical School and Boston's Beth Israel Medical Center, where we participated in several studies that use high-powered magnetic fields to both measure and change the brain. The measurement study confirmed that Cubby shares my brain differences and gave him new insights into his perceptual abilities.

Cubby walked out with another bit of good news too. After extensive testing at the hands of skilled and enthusiastic scientists, we learned his IQ is four points higher than mine, and he will never let me forget it.

But that wasn't all. The stress of preparing for the trial caused all of us to reflect and learn, and we learned that Cubby and I were not the only autistic Robisons. We realized that Little Bear is also on the spectrum. At the time of our divorce I didn't know, but when I look back with the benefit of the knowledge I have today, her behavior fairly shouts "autistic!" Most scientists believe there is a significant genetic component to autism, and our family history certainly supports that argument. My father died before any of this unfolded, but if he were alive today, he'd almost certainly be diagnosed on the autism spectrum. And when I consider family stories of eccentric ancestors, I suspect this difference has been in my family for a long, long time.

As we got ready for the trial, Cubby and I had several conversations about Asperger's and the role it played in this chapter of our lives. It was obvious to me that Cubby's Asperger's had blinded him to how other people might see his videos. His inability to imagine that anyone might be frightened or worried was a perfect example of what psychologists call *lack of a theory of mind.*

I realized that Asperger's had blinded me too on more than one occasion. My desire for Cubby to be "better than me" had been so strong that I failed to recognize one of the chief hallmarks of autism: his fixation on one thing after another: Yu-Gi-Oh!, Pokémon, and finally, chemistry and explosives. I always told myself that he had my gifts but that he'd magically escaped the disabilities. Now, on the eve of a superior court trial, I realized that was wishful thinking. The gifts and disabilities of Asperger's go hand in hand, and he has them both.

One of the things I thought about a lot was whether Asperger's had any place in the trial.

From the beginning, Hoose was opposed to mounting an Asperger defense because of the nature of the case. Saying my son did what he did "because he has Asperger's" would be tantamount to asking the court to excuse criminal behavior because he was disabled. Hoose didn't think that was necessary or desirable. Cubby was not accused of being oblivious or exercising poor judgment. As he said, the charges the state had filed required them to prove malice, criminal intent, and real, tangible damage to property. None of those elements were present in my son's actions. Hoose believed Cubby's peaceful nature and the absence of damage were the only defenses we needed. I prayed he was right.

51

IN LIMBO

It took more than a year for Cubby's case to make it to trial. First there was the two-month gap between the raid and the arraignment. After that, we had thirteen more months of delays and continuances till the actual trial. During that time, our stress level skyrocketed. I tried to soothe myself by studying the odds and contemplating strategy, though it was really out of my hands.

Did we have a chance of getting a fair hearing, and of Cubby being exonerated? It was impossible to predict, and Hoose could provide only so much reassurance. "I'll do my best," he told us, "but you never know with a jury. That's why a trial is always a last resort. Unfortunately, these people aren't open to any kind of reasonable bargain."

More than 90 percent of cases in the U.S. court system are resolved by plea bargaining, where the prosecutor and the defense attorney hammer out an agreement and the defendant pleads guilty to some lesser charge, thereby saving him the risk of trial and saving the state the cost. However, in Cubby's case, there was no lesser charge on offer. The only Massachusetts law he might have pleaded to was possession of fireworks, a misdemeanor that carried a hundred-dollar fine.

The DA's office had chosen to go for the big score, which meant he'd either end up a felon or be acquitted. Since there were four charges, he could win or lose on each one, and any one of them could send him to prison.

As far as I could tell, few people who appeared in criminal court walked away scot-free. I studied the statistics for our state's court system and discovered that our own county's conviction rate was a disturbing 75 percent. That meant most defendants settled, and of the ones who didn't, three-quarters lost. In the face of those numbers, all I could do was tell myself that broad statistics didn't matter for Cubby and me. Our only concern was whether *we* won or lost.

We were going to do everything possible to win.

Put in context, the threat of Cubby's experimental chemicals was trivial. A criminal with a gun presented an immeasurably greater menace to the community. Unfortunately, Perry could not see that because her mind had gotten stuck on criminality and danger, not reality. That happens when you're in a job too long. To a roofer, every house needs a new roof. To some heart specialists, every patient they see has a heart problem. I guess it's natural—you find what you know and what you look for.

Perry didn't know anything, in a technical sense. Not roofing, not cardiology. Certainly not chemistry. She couldn't evaluate Cubby as a chemist, but she felt confident condemning him as a criminal, based on the vague idea that the experimental explosives he made could have been a danger to the community. That was the essence of her argument.

For Cubby to be guilty of a felony, as she suggested, she needed to prove criminal intent, malice, and meaningful property damage. As the trial date drew closer, we remained mystified as to how she proposed to do that. Her statements during the months leading up to the trial did not hold much water. She said the peace and quiet of Amherst had been disturbed, and she characterized that as property damage. Yet it was legal for people to shoot guns in the same woods where the explosions took place. Amherst is a rural community; people hunt here every year. If the noise of gunfire is legal, how could the sound of Cubby's experimental explosions be a crime? It certainly wasn't any louder.

The argument that he destroyed property by damaging the woods was similarly thin. After all, people discard trash, cut trees, and even start fires in the local woods all the time, causing very visible damage. Yet few of those people face any sort of penalty, not even a citation for littering.

Perry also said his explosions had polluted the water and soil, but that ignored the facts of chemistry. In an explosion, the explosive is converted into heat, sound, carbon dioxide, and water vapor. Therefore, Cubby's explosives didn't leave any significant pollutants behind. Also, the quantities of explosive ranged from a thimble full to perhaps a few chicken nuggets' worth. No reasonable person would think a small handful of homemade explosive was a threat to the woodlands. All over America, millions of pounds of explosives are used in mining, quarrying, construction, demolition, and even farming every day. If pollution from the use of explosives were a problem, we'd surely know it by now.

We wondered if she had something up her sleeve, but try as we might, we could not figure out what it was.

For a while, I put my hopes in Judge Carhart. He'd struck me as fair during the pretrial conference, where he did his best to keep the case on track and didn't let the prosecutor walk all over us. Unfortunately, that conference was the last we saw of him. As the schedule shaped up, Carhart had a conflict and could not see our case through to the end. The court reassigned Cubby's case to Judge Bertha Josephson.

Josephson was fifty-five years old, with sixteen years on the bench. Before becoming a judge, she had worked in the same Northwest District Attorney's office that was now prosecuting my son. In fact, she and DA Scheibel had worked side by side for a few years under Judge Carhart, who also served as DA before becoming a judge. That discovery made the judges and prosecutors sound like a pretty tight little family, something I found rather unsettling as a defendant. However, our lawyer wasn't concerned. "Most criminal court judges are either former prosecutors or former defense attorneys. And you know, some of the worst judges I've known were former defense attorneys. Judge Josephson is fair."

When you hire a defense lawyer, you want him to win. Before this trial, I thought guilt and innocence were black and white. They aren't. If there was one thing I learned from Hoose, it is that winning means different things, in different times and places. I saw that when we talked about Cubby's guilt or innocence. "Just about everyone who appears in superior court is guilty of something," he told us. "The person might not be guilty of all the stuff the prosecutor is charging, and there might be extenuating factors, but the fact is, most defendants did something to put themselves on trial."

As that sank in, he continued his train of thought. "The trick is figuring out a fair and reasonable outcome in light of the facts as we see them. Most times, we don't expect an acquittal. We bargain for some more acceptable charge, or get a continuance without a finding. But in Jack's case we can't do that. We can't plead guilty to a series of felonies, and they aren't willing to consider anything less. So we have no choice but to go for acquittal. It's all or nothing. That's pretty unusual."

That was a sobering thought. My son had never disagreed that he was guilty of a small crime: being in possession of some homemade explosive. Yet somehow the prosecutor had spun that admission—which Cubby made in his initial interview and never wavered from—into a series of violent felony charges.

As the trial date drew closer there was more and more work to do. Case law had to be researched, and a defense strategy had to be formulated. We needed individual strategies with which to challenge every witness Perry would call. But before that, in November, our lawyer tried to get the whole case thrown out. He did that by filing a motion to dismiss all charges because the state had yet to show any evidence of either malice or property damage. A hearing was scheduled at which Perry countered with the ridiculous amphibian analogy Detective Hart had offered the grand jury, and on December 4, Judge Josephson agreed to let the case go forward.

I wondered if judges would be so quick to approve crazy motions like that if they had to pick up the tab when they lost. I made that point to Hoose, who reminded me that the state doesn't usually lose. The vast majority of criminal cases in superior court are resolved with some kind of guilty plea before the trial. From the state's point of view, all of those are victories because they exact some kind of penalty from every poor schmo, guilty or not.

It's a rare case where the defendant wins, hands down, but that was our only option. Anything else was just unthinkable. After the holidays, the clerk of the court set a preliminary trial date of March 16, 2009. Our anxiety built as the date drew closer. Then we got a call from our lawyer.

"The DA wants to move the trial," he said. "They have a schedule conflict with Kirk Yeager." I could not believe what I was hearing. Perry was actually bringing in the head of the FBI explosives lab to testify in a case about a teenager's chemistry experiments in the woods. Yeager was the guy who had been assigned to investigate the Oklahoma City bombing case. *Didn't the FBI have more important things to do?*

The prosecutor asked for a new date, April 6, but they moved that too, when Yeager had to investigate a real crime on the day he'd planned to be here in court. Finally, after everyone had had enough of continuances, the judge set a firm date of May 21. If Perry couldn't get her witnesses together by then, she would have to try the case without them.

We were ready to rock and roll.

52

THE TRIAL BEGINS

Like most trials, this one started with opening arguments. That's the part where the two lawyers tell the jurors what they are about to hear and why. The prosecutor went first.

As I expected, Perry tried to scare the jurors right away. She described Cubby as "a teenager with a frightening amount of explosives who likes to videotape himself setting them off." She told the jury Cubby had many chemicals in his basement lab, and that one of them was so volatile it could be set off by static electricity. "A gram of TATP in the cap of your Sharpie could blow off your hand . . . This is not about firecrackers," she said. When I heard that, it was all I could do to stay quiet. I hoped at least one juror had worked in an emergency room. Anyone who's spent time in an ER knows that firecrackers shred people's hands up all too often. Like Cubby's TATP, they are harmless when they're on the ground but bad news indeed if they go off in your hand.

When Hoose's turn came, he began with a simple statement. "This case is very much about who Jack Robison is; it's about his life in many ways." He let the jury know that it was up to them to decide whether my son was the dangerous criminal the state would have them believe he was, or a precocious teenager who loved chemistry. Then he told the jurors about Cubby's gymnastics and his years as a Cub Scout and Boy Scout. I wondered what jurors were making of the contrast between Hoose's remarks and the prosecutor's portrayal.

When he got to my son's education, he said, "Jack Robison dropped out of Amherst Regional High School at the end of eleventh grade. Now let me be clear with you, ladies and gentlemen, that Mr. Robison didn't drop out because he was not doing well in school or because he was failing, he didn't drop out because he wasn't smart enough, he didn't drop out because he didn't like learning. Mr. Robison is one of those young people for whom public school just wasn't working for him. In fact public school kind of bored him. He is, what my kids and perhaps yours would say, wicked smart."

He let the jury know that Cubby had a girlfriend as well as plenty of friends, some of them in the courtroom. At that point Hoose gestured to the gallery, and the jurors looked back at Cubby's supporters. At least a dozen friends were in the audience that morning. They'd all gathered around him and fussed over his appearance before walking into court. It was both sweet and funny to watch—a pack of geeky teenagers, all uncomfortable in nice clothes, standing around my son and squaring up his tie, touching up his hair, and making sure his shirt was tucked in smoothly. A few jurors smiled, and I took that as a hopeful sign. Psychologists say many seemingly complex decisions are made unconsciously, and I wondered if we'd won those jurors to our side already.

Hoose told the jury that Jack developed an interest in model rockets that led to a passion for chemistry. "A young man sixteen, seventeen years old, as you know from those of you who had children, . . . start thinking about careers, some boys at that age still have the fantasy that I'm going to pitch for the Boston Red Sox, some of them think I'd really like to be a police officer, some may want to be a firefighter, some may want to be a schoolteacher. . . . Jack Robison knew what he wanted to do: go to UMass and become a Ph.D. chemist." He explained to the jury that during visits to Mexico with his mother, Jack had been exposed to firecrackers, "which are legal down there," and that he'd come back and started experimenting.

He told the courtroom that all the chemicals Cubby had can be legally obtained. He said Cubby's own videos would show that he was careful to detonate his explosives at the Amherst landfill or on his father's land, where they would not harm property or people.

Hoose concluded by saying, "You won't see anything, ladies and gentlemen, to suggest that Jack Robison had any political aims, any anti-government aims, anything that would be of a nefarious nature, it's not there. What you'll see is just the opposite, just a kid who is experimenting and learning from something that is unquestionably potentially very dangerous, but you'll also hear that this is a young man that never did anything without educating himself, without learning about the substance he was dealing with and following through on his knowledge to do things in a safe manner."

With that, the trial was under way. The prosecution was up first, with Trudi Romonovitz of the South Hadley Police. She talked about getting the call from Kevin Goyette, the huckster who'd turned my son in to the police. It was Goyette who pointed her toward Cubby's online videos. She watched them and then called Gerry Perwak of the state police. He met her, and they drove around looking for the areas shown in the videos. They didn't find anything.

At the time, she didn't know anything about Cubby. He'd never had any dealings with the police. She did a little digging and learned that his mom and I were divorced. Finding out that I lived in Amherst, she called the police there and asked them for help figuring out where the videos were made. They had a little more luck. Knowing my house backed up on the old landfill, they looked out there and found a shed that had been visible in the background of one video. It was something a resident had abandoned, decaying quietly in a corner of the town landfill.

As she was beginning her investigation, Cubby was continuing his experiments. On February 4 he uploaded a new video, showing a larger test explosion in water. She was worried because the newest video showed he was still active, and it showed a bigger explosion than the ones before. She didn't know where it was or what it meant. She then handed the matter off to the state police.

I was surprised that she never thought of simply talking to Cubby the day she got Goyette's phone call. He was a local kid, living with his mom in town, not five minutes from her office. If she was afraid to talk to my son, she could at least have spoken to his mom. It's a sad state of affairs when a local police officer can't have a conversation with the parents of a kid who's lived in town his whole life. *This whole thing could have been avoided with a little more common sense and understanding,* I thought.

An hour had passed and the jurors looked bored. Fortunately, the next witness was a bit more dynamic. Gil Moring heads the Amherst Department of Public Works. His department runs the landfill where Cubby set off some of his explosions, among what he cheerfully described as "fifty-six acres of woodland, wetland, and trash."

I've lived next to the landfill for many years, and I've visited it even longer. I went there with my dad in the sixties, when we made our weekly run with the household garbage. Later, in the seventies, I went there to scavenge parts from junk cars, to keep my junks on the road and running. The open landfill is long gone, replaced with a neat transfer station. But thousands of people still come and go, dumping trash and scavenging for treasure, just as I had done years before. Some come by road, but plenty more walk in through the numerous holes in the fence that surrounds most of the property.

The prosecutor handed Moring a large photo of the front of the transfer station. Pointing to the photo, she asked, "Who can go into the transfer station and landfill? Can anyone get in there?"

Gil smiled slightly and said, "Anyone can go in. It's open to the public."

One of the rules every trial lawyer learns is this: Never ask your witness a question unless you're already pretty certain how he'll answer.

Having struck out with that question, she tried a different tack with the next one. "Who owns the landfill?"

He said, "It's town property, so I guess it belongs to all the residents of the town. Meaning the defendant and everyone else." He smiled at her and looked over at my son.

She didn't give up. "Isn't it true that you walked through the landfill with state police detectives, looking for evidence of the defendant's explosions? Can you tell us what you found?"

"We didn't find anything. It's a landfill. It's full of broken things. That's what it is," he said. Several jurors laughed out loud.

I needed a break, so I stepped into the hall outside the court. Over in the corner, I saw Gerry Perwak. He was scheduled to testify next. I walked over to him. "I'm sorry it's come to this," he said. "I never thought this case should go to trial, but I don't make those decisions. I hope it turns out all right for your son." I was touched by his thoughtfulness. I went back in and sat down as he began his testimony.

Perwak talked about the call from Officer Romonovitz in South Hadley, and his own investigation. He said he looked hard but wasn't able to identify any property damage from any of my son's explosions. Next he described meeting my son at his school. "The interview lasted almost three hours," he said, and my son seemed concerned, cooperative, and truthful.

He said Cubby led them to his mom's house in his car, while the investigators followed in their own vehicles. When they arrived at the house, they met his mom, who gave them permission to search the lab. When the search started, Perwak told the jury that Cubby showed them exactly what was in the house and where it was located. He stayed at the house till two in the morning that first night. Then Perwak reviewed Cubby's videos for the jury.

Finally, it was time for cross-examination. Hoose had a number of points to clarify, and I think he wanted to make the most of a somewhat cooperative prosecution witness. He began by asking Perwak to confirm that all of Cubby's glassware and beakers were standard lab equipment. "Yes," he agreed, "there was nothing illegal about any of it." Perwak remained on the stand for more than two hours, going over his findings and Cubby's videos piece by piece. As detailed as his testimony was, he did not say one word about malice, criminal intent, or property damage. In fact, he said the opposite, more than once.

That led Hoose to ask why Cubby wasn't arrested at the scene. "If you have probable cause to believe someone committed a crime, you arrest them on the spot, don't you?" "Yes. Absolutely," Perwak said, and the jurors all turned to look at my son. You could see the question in their minds. *If the ranking trooper hadn't seen cause to arrest Cubby, why are we all here today?*

The next witness was Michael Murray, one of the two ATF agents in the case. He described walking through the house with the state police bomb techs. He said there were so many different chemicals in Cubby's lab that he wasn't sure how to handle them. He called John Drugan, the state police chemist, who gave him advice and suggestions. Murray stayed on the scene till midnight and returned the next day.

Murray wasn't on our side, but he didn't have any really harmful testimony. The only scary thing he said was that he'd walked through the house in a Kevlar bomb suit, but of course nothing happened. So the suit was a precaution that was never needed.

I wondered what the jurors thought.

With that, the first full day of trial came to an end. Court adjourned for the Memorial Day weekend. It was a time of fun for some, but not for us. Cubby had started sipping Maalox by the bottle, and my jaw and shoulder muscles were so tense they hurt. All we wanted was for this nightmare to be over.

53

THE CRIME OF INQUISITIVENESS

Court resumed at nine o'clock Tuesday morning, after the long holiday weekend. I had the list of witnesses, and I knew who was up next. I was about to meet the rat who'd turned my kid in to the South Hadley police. The thought of people who do things like that just made my blood boil. I took a deep breath and waited for the day to begin.

"The commonwealth calls Kevin Goyette." I looked at him as he sauntered past and shook my head. I don't know what I had expected, but he was a pudgy figure in a cheap suit, the kind of specimen who might appear at your business selling supplies. He positively bounced into the witness box, looking excited to be there. Then, with a little urging from Perry, he told his tale.

He bought up scrap and salvage material that he sold on eBay and elsewhere online, he told the jury. Cubby had run across his merchandise while searching for flasks and beakers, ordinary glassware for any chemistry lab. Goyette had some nice-looking stuff at what seemed like good prices, so Cubby placed an order. In doing so, he gave Goyette's website his name, address, e-mail address, and credit card information. Armed with that, Goyette decided to go snooping.

He found Cubby's videos, watched a few of them, and called the South Hadley police. After that, he canceled the order. Cubby's lawyer asked Goyette if he made a practice of snooping on his customers. He just squirmed, and he was dismissed with no further questions.

Jeremy Cotton from the state police bomb squad was next. He was one of the troopers who responded to Perwak's call, arriving that first afternoon. He said my son's lab was more complicated than any explosives scene he'd been to before. There were lots of different chemicals, many of which Cotton did not recognize. "It was the defendant who explained to me what they were," he said. Most of the chemicals were not dangerous at all. The few explosives Cubby pointed out were loose, in glass jars and Tupperware containers. There were no "bombs" to clean up, just material in containers. That was an important point, because loose explosive in a lab tray isn't considered a weapon by most people, and the charges against Cubby implied he used explosives as weapons. "I'd never seen anything like it," he said. Cotton readily conceded that he didn't have "solid knowledge" of chemistry, so he called FBI chemist Kirk Yeager for guidance.

Like several previous witnesses, Cotton stressed that Cubby was very cooperative. He made clear that his main job was to put on eighty pounds of protective gear and carry materials from Cubby's lab out to the truck, which took them to the local landfill for disposal. There, the ATF agents blew it all up, with official government-issue explosives.

Next was Agent Peter Murray of the ATF. He was a local fellow, having served with the UMass Police before joining ATF eight years previously. He told the court about taking Cubby's statement at school and about touring the basement with Cubby. "I didn't see any explosives connected to a fuse or detonating device. All I saw were loose chemicals," he said.

John Dearborn of the Longmeadow Fire Department was the

next to be called. I hadn't understood why a fireman from a town twenty miles away was there at all, but he explained that he headed the state's District 14 hazmat team, which responded to situations all over our area. Speaking like a true bureaucrat, he told the court, "When I arrived, there were already multiple resources present." To him, every person and every piece of equipment was a "resource." I just shook my head for the hundredth time.

He first arrived on the scene at 8:30 Friday night, and stayed till 2:30 the next morning. The Red Cross was also there, feeding people, and the explosives techs had set up a mobile lab with a spectrometer to analyze the stuff my son was pointing out to them. With all those resources and all that activity, you would have thought there'd be nothing for him to do. Not so! He had a Geiger counter and went right to work. As he told the court in a wistful tone, "I did a radiation sweep, but there were no levels above normal background." I reminded myself that his crew had actually sent Cubby's mom a bill for their efforts. I characterized the hazmat response as a massive play date at the time, and Dearborn's testimony confirmed it.

When Hoose questioned him, he agreed they only saw two materials that were actually classified as hazardous, and those were legal and safely stored in containers. You could almost feel his disappointment as he told the court there was never a chemical spill. He even admitted that the hazards were only what you find in a typical residential garage. I could see he didn't like saying that, because he was essentially conceding that there was no justification for most of what his crew had done that weekend.

Most prosecution witnesses were announced without any fanfare. The last one was different. For him, Perry turned to the jury and the spectators with a great flourish and said, "The Commonwealth calls Doctor Kirk Yeager of the FBI." There was a pause, but no one applauded. She looked disappointed at our lack of response. I felt disgusted wondering who'd paid for Yeager to come up here and testify.

Yeager told the court he'd taught at New Mexico Institute of

Mining and Technology in addition to working for the government. He'd presented papers at sixty conferences and won several awards from the FBI. He was clearly a high-caliber fellow.

Then we got to the reason he was there: the call from the Massachusetts State Police, on February 15 of the previous year. He said he spent five hours on the phone, advising the techs on how to remove and neutralize the chemicals in the lab. As a budding scientist, Cubby had a much wider variety of chemicals than they were used to finding at crime scenes. Many were new to the technicians. Then he recited the same list of explosives we'd heard before, with a little elaboration. He told the jury how dangerous TATP was, and how a gram could blow off a finger, while a pound could kill. He told the jury Cubby had ETN, an explosive he had never before seen in the United States. Cubby's lab was unique, he said, because it had so many different explosive compounds. He said my son had a postdoctoral understanding of the physics of explosives.

He might have said all that to scare the jury, but I watched the jurors closely, and I think the point they took home was that possession of many different chemicals equals an experimenter, not a bomb maker. Yeager's comments about Cubby's knowledge simply reinforced that.

At that point, Perry trotted out her evidence bags once again. "Do you recognize these?" She handed him a few snack-size Baggies from the raid. These were the very same bags she'd been waving about the courtroom and passing among the jurors earlier, although they were new to Yeager. He took the bags from her and read their labels, then frowned.

"I don't know if I'd be passing explosives around in court like this," he said. She looked surprised. With all her talk of the incredible danger of Cubby's lab, she had been carrying his explosive compounds around in her big manila evidence folders for more than a year. She had handled them, the cops had handled them, and the jury had handled them and they'd done nothing but lie there, inert.

Among the bags was one containing TATP, the very same material that was, according to her opening statement, "so highly volatile that if you were to walk across the room and static electricity from this rug were to be emitted, it could set it off"!

The judge sent the jury out for a recess. The rest of us remained in our seats as she asked the attorneys to step forward. "Doctor Yeager, I wanted to ask you if these items are in a state that currently renders them safe in the environment that they're in for jurors and other court participants."

"Advising all due caution, anything that contains TATP I would get out of here immediately" was his reply. "There's only so much you can do to make it safe, and this material does not look wetted to me at all. The material in this amount is probably not going to detonate, it's scattered out, but it's going to create one nasty fireball if it decides it wants to go; and the person sitting in proximity to that is not going to be pleased."

With a look of annoyance, the judge had the prosecutor call a trooper to gather up her evidence bags and carry them out of the room. I could see people in the courtroom looking at one another and whispering commentary as this went on.

With the jury back in their seats, Yeager talked about analyzing videos of explosions, including Cubby's, and how it's sometimes possible to evaluate the materials and the damage done in the blasts. He told the court how he'd analyzed video from the attack on the USS *Cole,* perhaps in hopes the jury would draw some kind of analogy. I listened very carefully. He said Cubby's narrations and captions were consistent with what was shown, and the videos showed a steady increase in success and sophistication. That was especially true for the last video, where Cubby set a charge off underwater.

Yeager never mentioned a single instance of property damage.

Perhaps realizing that, Yeager tried to fill in with what might have been. "An explosion of that size could do substantial damage to a building, or even kill someone," he said of the underwater detonation. Of course, there were no buildings or people in sight when Cubby did his experiments.

As Hoose said later, Yeager was totally on board with prosecuting my son, but he really didn't have anything concrete to offer the court, as Hoose established on cross-examination.

"You never went to any of the sites, did you?" he asked. Yeager reluctantly conceded his involvement was limited to looking at images and talking on the phone.

Next he addressed Cubby's motives. "Not every kid who experiments with chemistry becomes a terrorist. Isn't that right?" You could see the sigh as Yeager agreed. Hoose tried to get him to admit his own students at New Mexico Institute of Mining might even experiment with explosives, but he wasn't having any of that. "Not in my classes, they don't!" He actually sat up straighter as he said it. The vehemence of his denial said more than further questioning. Yeager was a government chemist, with zero tolerance for breaking the rules.

Next they turned to PETN. Hoose said, "PETN as it sits on a shelf is sensitive enough to scare us, but not so sensitive it can't be handled or used." Yeager agreed. Yeager said PETN was widely used in weapons, but he agreed that all Cubby had was sample quantities of the material. So far, nothing new or striking had come out. I kept my fingers crossed.

Of all Cubby's chemicals, Yeager had been most critical of the TATP. Yet he said he'd made some himself in a government lab. Just experimentally, of course. In pursuit of science, not terrorism. Hearing of Yeager's personal experience with TATP, Hoose asked if things could be done to keep it safer in the lab. Cubby had kept his TATP covered with water. Yeager agreed that storing it in water made it safer and less likely to detonate. I hoped the jurors were paying attention.

Perry sure was paying attention. As soon as Hoose finished, she popped up with more questions of her own. "Dr. Yeager," she began, "your college students are not allowed to perform experimental explosions, are they?" He agreed they were not. "In your lab, you take all sorts of safety precautions, don't you?" He agreed with that too, but they couldn't take that line of questioning much further because Yeager had never been to Cubby's lab.

She changed tack, remembering Hoose's point about the TATP stored underwater. "TATP stored in tinfoil would be dangerous, wouldn't it?" Yeager agreed, but I saw some quizzical looks from the jurors. After all, wasn't it the same stuff she had handed them, with no comment, a few hours before?

When she was done, Hoose stood up again. They were both working Yeager for all they could get. Hoose reminded him of the TATP underwater and the other precautions Cubby had told them about. "Wouldn't you say Jack took the highest precautions possible in his experiments?" To my surprise, Yeager agreed.

With that, the prosecution rested. They had hammered us for two days with one witness after another. We had been buried in detail about what they found, where it was, and what they did with it. We had not heard anything awful, but we had been deluged with a torrent of testimony. I was reminded of the famous quote, "If you can't dazzle them with brilliance, bury them in bullshit." I was truly afraid the state would succeed with that very tactic.

All the gravest crimes in our area are tried right where we sat, in the Hampshire Superior Court. All those trials are open to the public. Most times, the audience consists of victims and their friends and family. There are often reporters, and sometimes families of the defendant. This was the first trial in years where there were no victims and no complaint. Consequently, the entire audience—other than the reporters—was my son's friends and supporters. Over the past few days they'd come to fill the courtroom. Many of his buddies from school and town were there. My neighbors and my family were there. My friend Bob, his wife, and even Bob's parents were in attendance. Everyone gathered around him as court recessed to offer a pat on the back, a cold soda, or words of encouragement for the next phase of trial. "Now it's your turn," they said. "You'll set them straight!"

That night, I did some thinking about what they had said about my kid and his chemistry. We'd heard from a slew of experts, and all of them had said the same thing: Cubby's lab was very sophisticated. He had made a lot of different compounds, and his understanding of the chemistry of explosives went way beyond what they ordinarily saw. Of course, what they ordinarily saw was the work of criminals. They didn't generally see the work of scientists, which was what Cubby wanted to become.

They had actually described a key difference between Cubby's lab and that of a criminal, though they hadn't spelled it out in so many words. In a scientist's lab, there are many different chemicals with which the scientist can conduct experiments. Even if the lab has a single purpose, like the development of a new explosive, the scientist might explore a number of paths to find a solution. Labs like that can be found in every college chemistry department, and in the research and development area of many large corporations.

Criminal labs are very different. Criminals are not interested in esoteric experimentation. They are interested in producing a particular substance. A criminal lab is not a vehicle for discovery and understanding; it's a factory for the production of banned chemicals. Whether those chemicals are recreational drugs, explosives, or something else does not matter.

A chemistry professor would not have been at all surprised by the variety of chemicals Cubby had on hand. Many of them worked with the same compounds on a daily basis. I heard that many times, getting ready for the trial. That's what experimenters do. Unfortunately, there were no chemistry professors involved in Cubby's investigation, only policemen of various sorts. None of them seemed able to escape the criminal lab fixation.

Not one of the investigators said, "This is a really smart kid.

What could we do to help him find a place where he could develop his talents?" Instead, in essence they said, "This is a really smart kid. What can we charge him with, to put him in prison?" I suppose you can't blame the investigators for thinking that way. After all, they investigate criminals all day, so everyone they see probably looks like some kind of criminal, or a potential criminal, after a while. But what about their bosses? Couldn't one of them have seen the path they were on?

Cubby had not been convicted of anything—yet—but it was already obvious how our society's misjudgments could turn good kids into criminals. Whether we won or lost, none of us would ever see the criminal justice system in America the same way again. I felt very sad.

We'd been hopeful in the beginning of the trial, when the witnesses were all on Cubby's side. However, the tide had turned with the later witnesses and the state's hammering on the idea of hazard and danger and threat. Cubby and I now had to consider what we'd do if he lost.

If he were found guilty, the next step would be a sentencing hearing. The problem was, any superior court conviction would leave my son with a felony criminal record, which would close many doors for him forever, no matter the sentence. I wasn't sure that we wanted to stick around for that outcome.

Cubby had the same thought I did. "We should leave the country and go somewhere we'd be welcome," he said. I wondered where that would be. Canada had welcomed draft dodgers in the sixties, but I doubted they'd welcome a teenage felon today. We pondered our options, none of which looked appealing.

The only clear thing was that we were in this together. If we lost this case, our lives as we knew them were over. Wherever we ended up, western Massachusetts would be left far, far behind.

54

DEFENDING CUBBY

After two days of prosecution witnesses telling a totally one-sided story, it was our turn to tell the truth about Cubby. The first witness our lawyer called was Alex Turner. Alex talked about meeting my son at Amherst High, going to school together, and doing the things teenagers do. Things like playing video games, surfing the Internet, and hanging out with friends at my house.

Alex also described some things most teenagers don't do, like watching TV while Cubby mixed chemicals or read chemistry texts. He talked about walking through the woods and looking for places they could safely set off test explosions, far from people or houses. With a trace of pride, Alex said he was present for several of Cubby's explosions. He made a particular point of looking at the jurors and telling them that no one and nothing was damaged. When he said that, the prosecutor looked downright venomous. He said Cubby just loved chemistry and science and wanted to learn more. Perry objected, and then it was her turn to question Alex.

When she stepped up to cross-examine Alex the whole tone of the courtroom changed. Until then, both sides had been respectful. Perry had been almost pleasant with her own witnesses, and our attorney had approached them politely, speaking in a friendly and conversational tone of voice. But as soon as the defense's first witness was on the stand, Perry attacked, with a hard, mean look and an edge to her voice that we hadn't heard before.

"You remember talking to Trooper Perwak last year, right?" Alex said he did. "Things got a little heated, and you had to apologize. Do you remember that?" Of course they had gotten heated. Perwak had tracked Alex down at school and questioned him aggressively in order to build a case and charge his friend with a crime. What teenager wouldn't get scared and maybe a bit heated over that? Alex was pretty uncomfortable, but he stood his ground for his friend, both when questioned originally and at the trial.

Two of our next witnesses spoke of Cubby's peaceful nature: Steve Roberts, his scoutmaster, and Mark Moriarty, one of his high school teachers. Bringing them in to testify hadn't been easy. When we listed them as witnesses, Perry challenged us, and we had a minitrial to decide if they could appear in the regular trial. According to her, Roberts and Moriarty had nothing relevant to say because they weren't there for Cubby's chemistry experiments or the raid. However, Hoose made a passionate argument for Roberts and Moriarty. "The reputation evidence [Jack] wants to introduce is essential to a fair trial," he said. "The state has done its utmost to portray a serious student with an interest in chemistry as a terrorist-in-training. This is a vindictive perversion of his character that can only be countered by the insight of people in the community who know him." That was a fine turn of phrase, I thought.

I'd been feeling down because the last few rulings had gone against us, but this time the judge ruled in our favor. "Malicious explosion is a violent crime, so the testimony of local residents is indeed relevant," she said.

We were counting on that very thing. For us, Cubby's reputation was the heart of his defense. We needed respectable people to say he was peaceful, nonviolent, and interested in science. If the jury agreed, there was no way he'd be convicted of the state's charges.

Steve Roberts was Cubby's first character witness. He'd known my son half his life and spent many hours with him. As scoutmaster, he'd counseled Cubby through all the levels of scouting, from cub graduation to Life Scout. If it weren't for the stress of the raid, we were all sure Cubby would have made Eagle Scout too.

"Jack was a popular patrol leader, and he earned sixteen merit badges, including one in chemistry. In fact, after earning his own badge, Jack taught the chemistry merit badge course to other scouts." Roberts told the court about the National Scout Jamboree, which Cubby attended the year he turned sixteen. He talked about community service, and how Cubby helped the other scouts and other people in town.

"Jack was always peaceful. He didn't get into fights or serious trouble," Roberts testified. As a scout leader, he made it clear it was his business to know which kids he needed to watch, and Cubby wasn't one of them. He spoke with great certainty, in a calm, measured voice.

"You don't really know the defendant," she charged. It seemed to me that she was grasping at straws.

He looked at her and smiled gently. "Yes," he corrected her firmly, "I do. I've known him since he was ten. We passed many nights talking by the campfire, at Chesterfield Scout Camp and at events."

The jurors watched the exchange silently. I was hopeful, but also nervous. It was becoming clear to me that Perry intended to bully our witnesses when their responses did not serve her case.

Retired Mount Holyoke chemistry professor Ken Williamson was our next witness. Jack first met him a week after the raid, after he received a letter in the mail from the older chemist. Williamson is a kind older man, seasoned by forty years as a college professor. After hearing his qualifications—which included a doctorate in organic chemistry, authorship of several chemistry textbooks, and almost fifty years on the Mount Holyoke faculty—Perry attacked his qualifications as a witness.

"How many courses on explosives have you taken?" she asked.

We had heard from the state troopers and ATF agents, all of whom were qualified as experts on the basis of government training programs. It takes a little more than that for a college professor to learn his trade. "Explosives are part of organic chemistry. I haven't taken courses on explosives per se; they are just one part of my training."

She didn't want to hear that. "So you have never taken any courses in explosives?"

He didn't know what to say. After a lifetime as a chemist, he didn't expect his legitimacy to be challenged because he hadn't taken a six-week bomb tech's course. He tried to explain, but she cut him off. The whole exchange was just revolting to watch, as she beat up the poor fellow unmercifully. I was glad when he stepped down.

She did the same thing with our next witness, Jack's high school teacher, Mark Moriarty. "I always knew Jack as a peaceful kid with a love of chemistry," he said.

"You don't really know him at all," she challenged. I realized there was no answering her questions. He said he did, and she denied the statement. It was a mean, ugly thing, the way she treated Cubby's witnesses.

The irony that she accused Cubby's friends and teachers of "not knowing him," when she herself had never spoken to him, was not lost on me. I wished there was a way to share that fact with the jury.

With Moriarty's testimony done, we had reached the end. We didn't have anything else to offer; there were no other witnesses to call. I'd felt good about our position earlier in the trial, but Perry's relentless assault and the sheer weight of testimony had me badly discouraged.

It was time for our best and last shot at winning—time to put Cubby on the stand. We'd talked about it before the trial, and we'd all been in favor of it, provided my son felt strong enough. "I can do it," he said now.

I hoped he was up to the task. Defense attorneys are always wary of letting their clients testify, because their words may open the door to unwanted questions that blow their own case to pieces. Hoose decided our best bet was to let him speak and give jurors a chance to see his peaceful, geeky self.

We had just watched Perry brutalize one witness after another, so Cubby knew it would be tough. He took a swig of Maalox and stepped up to the witness box. With a bit of a start, I realized this would be the first time the two of them had actually spoken. Taking his seat, he looked at the jurors and back at me. He was scared, but brave. Hoose stepped up to begin the questioning. He asked Cubby why he'd left high school.

"I wasn't really involved in the high school system, and I didn't like the courses that were being offered to me. I decided that it would be better to start taking college courses at HCC, so I took the placement test and started taking courses there. I started with calculus and anthropology."

I could see the jurors looking at him appraisingly. The real-life Cubby before them wasn't sounding like the monster portrayed by Perry over the past few days. They moved on to his interest in chemistry.

"I've been interested in some form of chemistry since I was very small. I first got interested in rocketry in elementary school. I learned about it from the History Channel, from my mother, and from doing amateur rocketry. There was a hobby store that sold rocket kits near us. Eventually, I started building my own rockets and I even started constructing my own engines as well as the rocket tubes themselves, and I stopped using kits entirely."

Then he talked about his other interests.

"I have an active interest in computer science and programming of various sorts. I have an interest in the outdoors like camping, hiking, and walking around outside. I've recently had an interest in biology and the mechanisms of antidepressants and antipsychotics." He spoke clearly and precisely.

He talked about going to Mexico with his mom and learning about fireworks down there. From there, they moved on to Cubby's online forums and how he taught himself the necessary web programming. He told the jury he called his forum De Rerum Omnis, Latin for "About Everything."

"I decided I'd like to have a website that covered far more topics than just chemistry—a universal science site. I had topics relating to the major fields of engineering and science, as well as other stuff like *Doctor Who* and cooking. I'm a big fan of *Doctor Who* and cooking." Some of the jurors laughed, but others looked puzzled.

"Who is *Doctor Who*?" his lawyer asked.

Cubby explained that it was a science fiction program on BBC television. "It's been on the air about forty years and I like it a lot." Any jurors who weren't smiling before were smiling now.

Hoose continued asking Cubby about his forums and the rules Cubby had posted to govern the site. He seemed puzzled by some of the forum rules. "In one of them, you said people must speak in proper English. 'The first letter of a sentence and pronoun *I* must be capitalized. If you don't do this you will not be allowed to participate on this site.' Why would you have a rule like that?"

Cubby was unperturbed. "Well, I like grammar, but also because of the type of conversation that was there, there's potential for misunderstanding somebody's post. In science, if you misunderstand somebody, you can have dangerous consequences, so I wanted to eliminate as much risk as possible."

From there, Hoose moved on to Cubby's chemicals and experiments. He asked how explosives were made, which Cubby was happy to answer in a long and technical narrative. I smiled as I saw jurors shaking their heads. Cubby told them how he kept his experiments safe, and then he talked about finding places to set off test explosions.

I couldn't tell what the jurors were making of Cubby, but he sure looked like a geeky science enthusiast to me, and I hoped they felt the same. When he talked about setting off blasts in my backyard I could see a few jurors nod. I hoped they were remembering that we still have some property rights in this country and we should be able to do what we want on our own land.

When Perry stepped up to cross-examine Cubby, she could barely contain herself. "Mr. Robison," she said, "you left Amherst High School because essentially you didn't like the kids there, is that right?" I wondered whether calling him "Mr. Robison" was an attempt to mock him, or perhaps hide the fact that he was still a teenager. And I wondered whether her comment about his not liking the kids at his school was an attempt to portray him as a loner. Later, in her closing statements, she would call him an "enigma."

Cubby just looked at her quizzically and said, "No. I left because the way the classes worked didn't really work with me, and college classes were much better suited to me."

The courtroom in front of him was full of kids; they were all Cubby's friends from Amherst High. A moment passed, and the judge called for a short recess. The prosecutor started walking toward the door. As she walked out of the court I heard a shout. "Jack does too have friends!" It was Cubby's girlfriend, Nicole, sticking up for him the only way she could.

When Perry walked back in and court resumed, she looked enraged.

"Isn't it a fact that one of the people that you have been communicating with goes by the username Bomb Boy?"

"No," Cubby said. I couldn't believe that she would bring up Bomb Boy. I knew, and I was sure she did too, that he was just someone who'd commented on Cubby's online forums; my son had never met him.

I could see the jurors' eyes moving from the prosecutor to Cubby, and to his many supporters in the audience. With each baseless accusation and each calm reply, you could almost see her case unravel. She must have sensed that too, and it seemed to make her even wilder.

At one point, she asked whether he had considered the "thermal heat scorching of people in the woods."

"People in the woods," Cubby repeated, puzzled.

"Yeah. People walk through the woods. Did you ever consider children playing in the woods when you're setting these explosives, sir?" She was practically shouting.

"There were no children present," Cubby said.

"You guarantee that, is that right, sir?"

"Yes."

Having failed to place children at the scene, Perry moved on to a red fox. "Now, you had some postings after this, sir, on the Internet, and one of the postings that you had, sir, was the detonation and explosion of a red fox, is that right?"

"That was not my video," Cubby explained. "That was a video made by a user on YouTube named Axstram from Australia." Even after Cubby had made it clear that he had nothing to do with the video, she pursued the question.

Perry's hostility stood in stark contrast to Cubby's placid geeky demeanor. I saw the jurors looking at the two of them, back and forth, and I wondered what they were thinking as she made each fresh accusation. I hoped they saw her for what she was. If they didn't, we were lost.

And then it happened. Until then, the witnesses' testimony had matched the written reports and my own memories of the scene. I knew because I had been on high alert, listening intently to every word. But as the prosecutor questioned Cubby, I heard her speak the words ". . . sitting on your bookcase next to a hundred pounds of PETN." A hundred pounds!

Cubby spoke right up. "Well, it wasn't a hundred pounds, it was a hundred *grams,* big difference in scale."

Was it an error or was it intentional? The fact is, there's a huge difference. One hundred grams is equivalent to a quarter-pound hamburger patty or a stick of butter. One hundred pounds of high explosive is a serious matter. A quarter-pound of powder in a lab tray isn't. The slip wasn't lost on the jurors.

The prosecutor looked furious and corrected herself.

In the end, if there was anyone who seemed oblivious to her own actions and to how she might be perceived, it was Perry. I couldn't tell whether she truly believed Cubby was dangerous, or whether she was simply trying to make a name for herself. Either way, I knew I would never forgive either her decision to prosecute the case or the way she had gone about it.

After what felt like hours of testimony, all of which kept the jurors riveted, the questions came to an end. The judge looked at my son and said, "Mr. Robison, you may step down." Cubby looked at the prosecutor, snorted slightly, and walked slowly back to his seat.

It was time for closing arguments, and for that Perry waxed lyrical. "If you close your eyes for a second and you think about the quiet and the beauty and the stillness of the woods, you can almost feel the sun on your face, that's a human experience that we all have, you're walking through the woods, you might have a child with you, and then there's a huge explosion. That's what this is about."

So there it was: My son had disturbed the peace and quiet of the Amherst woods, and for that she asked the jury to send him to prison with four felony convictions. I don't know how many explosions disturb the peace of Amherst every year, but it's a lot. We have steady blasting in two rock quarries just over the Granby line. We've got a couple of shooting clubs in town, and much of the land is rural, and walked by hunters every year.

Finally, it was the judge's turn. She turned to the jurors and thanked them for sitting through the trial. Now, she said, it was time for them to go to work. They had to discuss everything they had heard, and reach a verdict on each of the charges. To convict my son, they had to believe—beyond a reasonable doubt—that he'd done some sort of tangible damage to property and that he'd acted with malice. They filed out of the room to begin deliberations. We started pacing and wondering how long we'd have to wait for the verdict.

We weren't the only ones cooling our heels. The local television stations had camera crews lurking in the halls, and reporters from the newspaper had staked out two prime benches in the foyer. Thousands of cases move through our county court every year, but only fifteen "big cases" make it all the way to superior court trial. Cubby's case was one of them, keeping company with a murder, some robberies, and an arson or two.

THE VERDICT

At 3:45, the bailiff called us back to court and announced there was a verdict. As much as I wanted the trial to end, I cringed at those words. This jury had taken less than two hours to make up its mind, and I'd read that speedy decisions often signal conviction.

We took our seats as Cubby and the lawyers took their seats at the bar. The jury foreman handed a folded piece of paper to the bailiff, who passed it to Judge Josephson. The judge looked at it, nodded, and turned to the jurors. She would have made a world-class poker player; for all I know, that's what she was in another life. Her expression gave absolutely nothing away. At her nod, the bailiff spoke.

"Ladies and gentlemen of the jury, have you reached a verdict?"

"We have," the foreman answered.

"On the first charge of malicious destruction of property, how do you find?"

"We find the defendant not guilty."

"On the second charge?"

"Not guilty."

"On the third charge?"

"Not guilty."

We had reached the last charge, detonating explosives near people and property. I'd seen trials on TV where the defendant was acquitted of all but one charge and ended up in prison anyway, so I was right on the edge of my seat.

"On the fourth and last charge?"

"Not guilty!" The certainty was palpable in the juror's voice.

Cubby and his lawyers stood up and smiled. At that, the whole courtroom seemed to rise as one and burst into applause. My son turned to David Hoose, nodded slightly, and said one word: "Excellent." It was a most Aspergian reaction. The newspaper photographer popped up and captured the moment. Across the bench, Prosecutor Perry looked like she'd just swallowed a lemon.

The audience of supporters parted as we walked outside to share Cubby's victory with the reporters. Perry slunk out a side door when no one was looking.

The reporters gathered around Cubby and his lawyer and peppered them with questions. One of them asked my son how he felt. "I'm very pleased the jury was able to see through all the hype and the inflammatory testimony on the part of the prosecution," he said in a measured tone. When this process had started, he'd been a gawky kid. Now he was a strong young man.

His attorney spoke up. "Today Jack knows better than to tinker with such potentially dangerous chemicals." He smiled a little. "Part of being young is not being wise. It's time for Mr. Robison to go home to his family and friends and studies—a little bit older, but very much wiser for his experience."

It was finally over. Cubby, his lawyers, and a crowd of friends and supporters headed down the street to Fitzwilly's for the first of several victory celebrations. Many of Cubby's high school and college classmates had been in court that last day, and they all joined in, filling several tables in the back of the restaurant. My friends were there too. The restaurant was overflowing, and we were just getting started.

That night, we joined more friends for a victory dinner at my son's favorite restaurant in downtown Northampton. As we walked in the door, the people at a long table straight ahead of us turned our way. I recognized a number of senior officers from the Northampton courthouse and I was surprised as they looked at Cubby, smiled, and started to applaud. None of the folks at the dinner table had been involved with my son's case, but obviously they followed what went on in their courthouse closely. One of them walked up to my son and shook his hand, congratulating him on our victory. "Those people in the DA's office have gotten out of control with some of their recent cases," he said, adding, "We're all so glad you won!" I was amazed and moved by the depth of support I came to find in the community as news of Cubby's acquittal spread.

As we were driving home after our victory celebration, I turned to Cubby and said, "Now we can go to Australia as free-range Aspergian tourists and see the penguins you've always talked about. That's a hell of a lot better than going there as fugitives and hiding at some mining community in the outback." Cubby agreed.

"All you have to do is earn the money to pay for the trip, because I had to spend what I had to keep you out of jail." Cubby snorted. He never has paid me back, and he hasn't gone to Australia. Yet. But there is still time for both.

EPILOGUE

Five years have passed since that fateful visit from the ATF. Cubby's almost twenty-three now. We haven't heard from the Feds since his acquittal, but none of us have any doubt that they're keeping an eye on our corner of the planet, just to be sure.

The prosecutor never said a word to any of us before the trial, and she hasn't said a word since. You'd think the DA's office might have apologized, but I guess they don't see things the way we do. Anyway, the DA was voted out of office a few months after our victory, and the incoming DA replaced most of the staff. Good riddance to them, I said.

We won the case, but victory came at a high cost. The most obvious was the legal fees. I've been very fortunate to achieve enough success that I could afford to hire a top lawyer for Cubby's defense. Without that, we'd have had little choice but to cave in before the state's onslaught. Knowing that, I realize how wrong it is that there is no mechanism for holding district attorneys accountable for rogue prosecutions and the harm they can cause. Even if most people who enter the legal system are guilty of something, a few are not, and those people suffer irreparable harm even when they win.

Moving beyond the scope of local officials, I see what a terrible mistake our society has made by criminalizing so much that young people do. Activities that were once dismissed as pranks and "kids being kids" are now prosecuted with vigor. Fights between schoolchildren end up in court. Fights between drunken college students send youths to jail. Sure, those behaviors merit punishment, but in today's society the punishment is out of proportion to the action. That's true for so many felonies today. In the space of a generation, an activity that millions of kids have engaged in—experimenting with fireworks and explosives—has evolved from mostly harmless fun to being a serious felony. There's no doubt that the events of 9/11 went a long way toward building the climate of fear that has allowed our state security apparatus to run wild in this fashion, but I believe these changes have deeper roots than that, and began even before 9/11.

We think of our country as free, but we have the highest rate of incarceration of any developed nation. In 1980, five hundred thousand Americans were in jail. Today that number has ballooned to almost 2.5 million. Less well known is how many adult Americans have criminal convictions. The shocking truth is that one in thirty adults is behind bars, on probation, or on parole. That's more than seven million people. One reason for that is that we've criminalized so many behaviors. Americans end up with permanent criminal records for driving eighty-five on the interstate or for shoplifting at seventeen. I stopped to pee in a ditch by the side of a backcountry road in Alabama last year, and a cop pulled up behind me. To my disgust, he told me I could be arrested and that I'd be a registered sex offender because I was "exposing myself by the roadside." Is this the system we want?

What's even worse is the fact that our justice system often takes a poor person convicted of a "blue collar crime" like barroom fighting and sends him to prison for a longer term than a rich man who embezzles millions. It's hard to watch that, and go through something like my family went through, and still feel good about where our country is headed.

Little Bear was devastated by the consequences of the raid. Her house was wrecked, and she suffered the humiliation of having it publicly condemned. She's wrestled with organizational troubles all her life—a hallmark of autism—and her house was always a mess. That was okay as long as it was private, but she has yet to recover from the effects of having a hundred strangers tramp through it, exposing her belongings to damage and her psyche to ridicule. In addition to all that, she's still being harassed intermittently over the costs of the raid, even though she was never charged with any wrongdoing and our son was acquitted.

She's convinced that the publicity during and after the raid caused the administrators at her school to not renew her teaching contract. There's no way for us to know, but whatever the reason, it has proven very hard to find new teaching jobs and the sting of that rejection still hurts.

The stress took its toll on me too. I became very depressed and almost suicidal the winter before the trial. It seemed like everything we had worked so hard to build was crumbling. Our son was facing prison, and we underwent a ruinously expensive trial to defend him. At the same time, the nation's economy was collapsing and our resources seemed to diminish daily. All the gains I thought I'd made went up in smoke. It was all I could do to keep going.

When the trial ended, everyone applauded our victory, but I still had a mountain of legal bills to pay. My family and work life, which I'd neglected during the period before the trial, felt like a shambles. I was able to turn around the business, but my marriage came to an end. The years 2009 and 2010 were very hard ones for me. Three years have now passed and I have mostly recovered. Martha is doing okay as well. I'm remarried to a wonderful woman who came into my life with three kids, two cats, a fourteen-pound Imperial

War Pug, and a vegetable garden. We're looking forward to a bright future together.

But enough about us. We are just the supporting characters in this story. You want to know what happened to Cubby.

He's stayed well clear of all the activities that got him into trouble on that cold winter day in 2008. At the same time, he remains fascinated by chemistry. He doesn't have a lab at home anymore, but he's become the top student in all his labs at the university. I'm proud of what he's doing without worrying that he'll blow himself up in the process.

Cubby matured a lot as we prepared for the trial, and every year his intelligence shines brighter and brighter. In fact, the change from childhood is so profound that I wonder whether he's getting smarter or his innate intelligence is simply becoming more visible. Brain researchers wonder the same thing when it comes to autistic people. My next book will tell the story of scientists who are working to unravel the secrets of intelligence and perhaps make us all smarter. Autism is described as a developmental delay, and researchers at CMU/Pitt and elsewhere are now exploring the idea that autistic people may develop certain brain pathways much later in life than "neurotypical" people. I've always wondered how my son could be "nearly normal" in first grade, and "nearly a genius" on a different IQ test fifteen years later. The question remains to be answered.

I mentioned executive function and organization several times in this book. That's a big problem for many autistic people; indeed, it's a problem for many people of all sorts. Last year I worked with a team from Children's National Medical Center in Washington, D.C., and Ivymount School in Rockville, Maryland, to develop a book called *Unstuck and on Target,* which describes a new therapy intended to develop better executive function in kids. I wish something like that had existed when Cubby, Little Bear, and I were young!

My son had many friends growing up, but he had and has problems with teamwork. My troubles making friends were more severe, as were his mom's. One new therapy that addresses teamwork and friendship is PEERS, from Dr. Elizabeth Laugeson at the Semel Institute for Neuroscience & Human Behavior at UCLA.

I also describe many strategies for making one's best life in the face of difference in my second book, *Be Different*.

As Cubby has gotten older, a number of his Aspergian traits have softened. He's still oblivious to other people at times, but when he pays attention, he shows a kind and gentle side that makes me happy and proud to be his dad.

He still has the intense concentration he had as a kid with Pokémon cards, but it looks very different now that it is focused on grown-up interests. As a little kid, his fixations were strange, geeky, or even weird. As a young adult, his concentration and insight reveal an intelligence that went largely unnoticed throughout grade school. We first saw that when he became captivated by chemistry.

His mom would say, "I knew it all along," but that's certainly not something I heard from his teachers or anyone else at the school. More than anything, the "near-normal" description by that Yale clinician exemplifies the difficulty of testing kids who are different. What if we'd accepted that assessment instead of pushing to expand Cubby's capabilities? To a large extent, his mom is to thank for that.

Brainpower aside, my relationship with Cubby is in the middle of the evolutionary process all father-son relationships go through. Having long ago finished with the tuck-in and the homework stages, we're moving toward a time of equals. Except I'm still King of the House.

It did take a few years for Cubby to get back on track. The time between the raid and his victory in court was a lost cause, academically. He wasn't able to reenroll in classes till the following January, and when he did, he had to make up the courses he'd failed. Our state has a program through which people can graduate from community college and be guaranteed admission and reduced tuition to state university. That's what he's planning to do. We're hoping he will earn his bachelor's in chemistry from UMass in fall 2013.

Right now he attends classes but does most of his learning on his own, using the resources of the university to educate himself. That's pretty much what I did as a student. The difference is, he's likely to get a degree, and I didn't.

When he started in college his only interest was chemistry. Indeed, he's taken a few swings at the ball before he could get passing grades in college courses that weren't chemistry or math. However, in the last two years he's also become interested in libertarian politics, software, electronics, and mechanical engineering. He's especially interested in a developing subculture known as the maker movement. *Make Magazine* says makers "celebrate arts, crafts, engineering, science projects, and the do-it-yourself (DIY) mindset." That sums it up pretty well.

Cubby's interest in chemistry wasn't merely theoretical; he wanted to make things. He still wants to do that, but today he's also making things from plastic, metal, and wood. He's making electronics to run his creations, and writing software to run the electronics.

He recently started designing and prototyping a quadracopter, a four-rotor model helicopter built on a rectangular frame with propellers on each corner. Right away he ran into problems. Parts made from metal were too heavy to fly, and he had no way to make things from lightweight plastic. Enter the RepRap. An open-source wiki on the RepRap winningly describes the device as "humanity's first general-purpose self-replicating manufacturing machine." Put another way, a RepRap is a desktop device that extrudes molten plastic from a print head that moves in three dimensions. A

RepRap can print three-dimensional objects the way a conventional inkjet printer prints pictures on paper. It just takes a bit longer.

Another cool thing about the RepRap is that it's self-replicating. The wiki explains: "Since many parts of RepRap are made from plastic and RepRap prints those parts, RepRap self-replicates by making a kit of itself—a kit that anyone can assemble given time and materials. It also means that if you've got a RepRap you can print lots of useful stuff, and you can print another RepRap for a friend."

When Cubby learned about RepRaps, he had to have one. So he and his mom bought a "kit" with some plans for a few hundred dollars. It turned out to be little more than a few gears and rods and the vaguest of instructions. Turning those bits into something that rendered objects you could hold in your hand consumed many weeks and several kitchen tables, and involved the assistance of a small dog, but they did it. The two of them then joined forces with Cubby's girlfriend and a few buddies from school to form Robison Industries. Now they are creating and selling their own RepRap kits, including instructions that are a marvel of exactitude.

When I was a kid, a friend and I captured his little brother, stuck him in a mold, and cast him in sand. (Don't be alarmed, he emerged intact.) With the advent of the RepRap, kid duplication just got a whole lot easier. Now Cubby can take a picture, digitize it, and make a replica from plastic. What a remarkable development. By the time you read this book, you might be able to reproduce your own kid, fully formed, in white polystyrene. After buying a RepRap from Robison Industries, of course.

When that happens, Cubby will have made the Kid Store of his childhood come true after all these years.

Cubby's romance had faded by the time of the trial, and that spring he and Nicole went their separate ways. She headed for college in

Oregon, where she remains today. They still talk via e-mail from time to time.

Cubby was sad to see the relationship end, but he wasn't alone for long. Kirsten Lindsmith was dating one of Cubby's friends when they met in the fall of the year before his trial. He saw her again that summer and something clicked. "She's the first person who really showed an interest in all the things I do," he said. "Other kids might have thought I was smart, but they looked at me like an exhibit in a zoo. She's different. To her, I'm just me."

Kirsten is currently a biology student at the University of Massachusetts. She's a talented artist who dreams of being a medical examiner one day. She's very smart and introspective.

I enjoy watching them together, because they are so alike. A few months after they started dating, they moved in together, to an apartment Cubby had found in Greenfield. In an effort to better understand my son, Kirsten began reading up on Asperger's and autism. She soon came to the realization that she probably had Asperger's too. A formal diagnosis the next spring confirmed it.

Both of them had been socially awkward in school, and they share many geeky traits. They're a really cute couple, though he'd be embarrassed for me to say that.

Seeing my son struggle when he was growing up made me remember how hard being a kid was and gave me a desire to help other children and teenagers who felt like outsiders. That was one of the reasons I began writing—to show younger people that geeks and misfits like me could grow up to have good lives. My first book, *Look Me in the Eye,* became my way of saving others from the worst of that hardship.

I'm very fortunate to be invited to quite a few conferences on autism and Asperger's. Many times I am asked to speak or do workshops for young people. A few years ago, Cubby began accompany-

ing me to some of those events, and last spring he started talking
about doing something on his own.

That surprised me because he was so young, but it made sense.
After all, he was the impetus for many of the stories I wrote in *Be
Different*. He and Kirsten began with a talk to a group of middle
school students in New York in September 2010. Then they participated in an autism panel discussion at another school. They did
those things all on their own, without any input from me. That
May, Cubby joined me at the IMFAR autism science conference,
where he met up with Alex Plank, another young man with Asperger's who had founded Wrong Planet, an autism community on
the web.

They became fast friends, and Alex asked Cubby and Kirsten to
join him in a project he'd started called Autism Talk TV. The three
of them interview people in the autism community and discuss issues that matter to people on the spectrum, then post videos of the
interview at the Wrong Planet website. The episodes have a goofy
charm.

"You guys are like the *Wayne's World* of autism," I told them
when I saw the first cuts of their work. I meant it as a compliment—
the episodes are unpretentious, low-tech, informative, and funny.
As of this writing, they have accumulated hundreds of thousands
of views.

In December 2011, Cubby and Kirsten did their first all-day
workshop. They spoke to Aspergian teens at the Kinney Autism
Center, which is part of St. Joseph University in Philadelphia. In
spring 2012 they spoke to several autism societies and at the ASPEN
conference in New Jersey. They also did a workshop at Y.A.L.E.
School in Cherry Hill, outside Philadelphia. And in July 2012 they
were the hit of HOPE 2012, Hackers on Planet Earth. There's no
question that many people in that crowd are on the spectrum!

They talked about growing up different, but most of all they
talked about love, friendship, and finding each other. Those were

the things all the young people in the audience wanted to know about. You can see videos from their talks online.

I'm really proud of them all.

I'm not the only one to take notice of them. In fall 2011, *New York Times* reporter Amy Harmon called Cubby after seeing him in the Autism Talk TV videos. She was writing another install-ment in her acclaimed series on growing up with autism, this one focused on young adult relationships. Once Cubby and Kirsten had agreed to participate, Amy and her photographers traveled from New York City to hang out with them five times between Hallow-een and Christmas. She also interviewed Alex over the Thanksgiv-ing holiday. All told, she spent more than a week following them around, watching, and asking questions. She even attended their talk in Philadelphia and rode home with us in the car. By Christ-mas Eve I was really wondering where it would all lead.

The next day we got our answer. On December 26, 2011, her story filled the front page and two inside pages of the paper. Its title: "Navigating Love and Autism." It was the biggest piece the *Times* had ever done on autism, and it spread like wildfire.

In spring 2012, I got a letter from a musician asking me about the light guitars I'd made for KISS back in the seventies. "I got an un-finished light guitar body from Steve Carr's estate. Could you finish it for me?" I've gotten a steady trickle of queries over the years, but that one shocked me. *Steve's estate?* The guy was the same age as me!

I took a look, and sure enough, he had died. Steve Carr was the luthier who had done all the work to make my guitar creations play-able. He set up the frets and adjusted the necks and actions. He also refinished the bodies and did beautiful ornamental inlays. The news that he'd died was pretty shocking, but so many of the guys from that era didn't make it this far. Fast living, drugs, liquor, and

AIDS took its toll on us. It was a hard life, I guess, and I was lucky to get out, no matter how fondly I remember it.

I never patented any of my creations in those days. I always figured today's design could be replaced by a better one tomorrow, and that patents wouldn't mean anything anyway. So when I left the music business thirty years ago, I walked away from everything I'd done without looking back. Now, reading about Steve, I was surprised to discover that he'd made replicas of my guitars. Not only that, but he'd claimed to have designed them himself!

I was annoyed at first, but then I realized it was a kind of honor. I guess I feel the same way today when I see copies of my books pirated online, or in China. (Note to pirates: This does not mean I give you permission to reproduce my book. Random House's lawyers are vicious, and they will hunt you down.)

I'd ignored all the earlier queries about those guitars because I felt I'd moved on to other things. Between raising a kid and running a business, there was no time to start an electronics project. At least that's what I told myself.

Deep down, I knew the truth: I didn't think I could do it anymore. I look at my electronic creations from that period, and they seem totally unfamiliar. Someone else must have made them, I tell myself. Of course, I know that's not true; I really did design and build all those things. But I'm in a different space today.

This time, something clicked in my mind. *What about Cubby?* I thought about his work on microcontrollers, and all the other things he was doing. He was obviously brilliant and creative. *Could my son make a light guitar?* He'd never really shown interest in them, but of course that phase of my life was way before he was born. *Perhaps his mom would help.* I called her up, and she jumped on the idea immediately. Actually, they both did.

I talked to the fellow who wanted the guitar and told him Little Bear and our kid would be doing the work. He was thrilled because she had done the actual wiring of the original guitars, and Cubby was the next generation of me. After handing them his deposit check, I sat back to see what would happen.

Musing over what they might do, I found myself imagining the guitar-to-be in the mold of 1979. Back then we used incandescent lights, bipolar transistors, and a state-of-the-art Intel 8748 microcontroller. The whole thing was powered by a battery pack beefy enough to jump-start a Cadillac.

To their credit, they didn't let the past slow them down. With each of them leading the way in different areas, they designed a guitar for the twenty-first century. In the space of a few months, they developed a whole new approach to the problem of illuminating an electric guitar, beginning with the choice of LED lights—nearly ten times more efficient than the incandescent bulbs I'd used in the original. Little Bear selected a modern microprocessor to control it—an Arduino—and Cubby wrote the code to make it work.

New technology made everything better. The guitar Cubby and Little Bear built runs brighter, longer, and better than anything we could have done thirty years before. I'd worried about whether they could match what I'd designed before, but they surpassed it! *Maybe I underestimated that kid,* I thought.

The best moment was when I picked up and held their creation. At that moment, I knew how Ace Frehley, lead guitarist for KISS, must have felt, holding my original thirty-five years before. The new guitar was far lighter than the original. The original would run for just five minutes before the battery was exhausted, but the new one will play a whole set with energy to spare. When Ace played mine the lights used so much power that the whole guitar got hot, and you could hear the circuitry in the background while he played. The flashing of the lights had to be perfectly synced to the drums, because there was a pop every time the pattern changed. The new guitar is smooth and silent.

Before sending the guitar to its new owner, Cubby and Little Bear made a video of it in action and uploaded it to YouTube. In a matter of weeks, Ace Frehley's manager called. He'd lost track of us over the years, but Ace still played the instruments we built him all those years ago. After reconnecting, I drove to New Jersey and brought the original light guitar back for refurbishment. When I opened the back I had to smile. After all those years, it still had our names—John and Mary Robison—and phone number in permanent marker on the inside plate, along with our slogan: Thunder Lizards Rule the World!! Cubby and his mom are working on restoring that very guitar as I write this chapter. I can't wait to see his name on the inside plate alongside ours.

Right now, all over the world, several million young people are coming of age with Asperger's or some other form of autism. Many of them are wondering if they will be able to find love, friendship, and a good quality of life. Cubby's life shows that such a thing remains possible even today. I did it years ago, and he's doing it now.

I can't believe how far he's come.

AUTHOR'S NOTE

Nowadays one of the first questions people ask memoir writers is "How much of this is true?" The answer is, this story is all true, but it's my truth. Each of the scenes in this book happened as I describe them, but if you ask the other people who were there, they will have their own slightly different tellings of the story. Each of us remembers differently, and each paid attention to different things at the time. This is a story of family life, not news reporting. Notes were not kept as life unfolded, and few recordings were made.

For example, I watched Little Bear and Cubby complete a project together and wrote, "My son took the lead." His mom read the story and said, "That's not right! I designed it so I took the lead!" So I asked my son, and he said, "She's nuts! I did all the work!" With me watching and advising, and the two of them doing it, we ended up with three different interpretations.

But that's okay. This dichotomy of memory shapes life in any family—yours or mine. Anyone who has raised one or more kids has seen this phenomenon.

The passages of dialogue from Cubby's childhood are reconstructed as best we remember, over the span of his life. I certainly can't guarantee they are accurate word for word, but the essential elements—what we did, where we did it, and with whom—are all true and correct, as best I remember.

Places and dates from my son's childhood are described as accurately as possible. All are subject to limitations of recall. I reviewed many of these stories with friends and family, who were often able to fill gaps in my memory.

In depicting the raid and subsequent court action, I have relied on my own notes, our attorney's notes, media accounts, and available transcripts of court proceedings. Since I did not have a fully transcribed record of the various legal proceedings at hand, and there is no such record of the raid that I am aware of, much of the dialogue and some of the testimony have been reconstructed from memory and notes. However, dialogue and statements from the grand jury proceedings, my son's testimony, and the opening and closing statements of the trial are drawn from transcripts and are nearly verbatim. The only changes I have made to material from the transcript is to condense lengthy testimony and delete minor repetitions or filler phrases like "you know."

Most people in this book are identified by their real names. This isn't the kind of story where identities need to be hidden. In most cases, if I made up names for peripheral characters, it was simply because memory failed me. Julie Jones is the real name of Cubby's Montessori teacher, and I'm happy to say we are still in touch with her today. The same is true for Cubby's Scout leaders and many of his friends. In the case of Cubby's first girlfriend, I have changed her name and identifying traits to protect her privacy. It's possible I have described a few people from the past incorrectly. If you're one of those people, I apologize.

ACKNOWLEDGMENTS

Before closing, I'd like to thank the supporting cast who made this book possible.

The list begins with my great-grandfather, Albert G. "Dandy" Robison. Dandy was a lifelong farmer and county agent for the U.S. Department of Agriculture. He was the one who told me explosives are a farmer's best friends and showed me how to use them safely to split rocks, remove stumps, and dig ditches. Then there was Hank Schmel, pyro master for KISS. Together we delivered rock-and-roll thunder to thousands of concertgoers without a single mishap or injury. I guess those experiences set the stage for me to accept my son's interests.

Then there is my brother, Augusten. He's always liked Cubby, but he's lived far away from us almost all his life, so his role in our day-to-day lives has been limited. I wish he lived closer. Still, he's always been entertaining, even from a distance. Cubby will never forget the Sack-o-Knives his uncle sent him by FedEx on Christmas Eve, when he was nine. Fifty knives! Each one different! And then there was the time my brother said, "You're not getting a proper education! I'm going to take you away and send you to boarding school in England!" That never came to pass, but it did give Cubby something to ponder.

Next I must recognize my aunts, uncles, cousins, and friends. All have their own memories of Cubby and our family, and I apologize that space did not permit fitting all of you into this little book.

My father deserves a special mention, though he died before this book was written. My stepmother, Judy, is still with us, and I thank her for all she did to raise Cubby, especially for the times when she slept in the basement so he could be safe and warm upstairs, where the monsters could not get him.

Particular thanks is due to David Hoose, his law partner Luke Ryan, and the rest of their staff. Throughout the book—in the interest of brevity—I refer exclusively to David Hoose as "Cubby's lawyer." In fact, as David would be quick to point out, we could not have won the case without the assistance of his staff, and all of them together are the heroes of this story. The monsters Judy kept at bay were imaginary, but the ones Hoose and company defeated were all too real. As my late Uncle Bob would say, *They whupped 'em like dogs, and sent 'em out the door with their tails between their legs!*

Luke and David spent countless hours researching past cases and developing the strategies they used so successfully. A lesser pair of lawyers might well have folded under the state's onslaught, but Luke and David didn't. They sat together at my son's side every moment of the trial; you'll see them in photos if you search them out online. I thank you from the bottom of my heart, as does Cubby.

Now it's time to thank the people who actually helped create the work you are reading now. That starts with my literary agent, Christopher Schelling of Selectric Artists. Without him, there would be no book deal. I might even be a fugitive in some foreign country.

Then there are the folks at Crown, and elsewhere at Random House. The list begins with Molly Stern, my publisher, and her boss, Maya Mavjee, who heads the Crown Publishing Group. Both have been staunch supporters of this book from the beginning. Next are Jay Sones, Julie Cepler, and Danielle Crabtree in marketing, who together have devised creative ways to reach people who might not otherwise discover my writing. I mustn't forget the indefatigable Sarah Breivogel in publicity and Stephanie Chan in editorial. Thanks to production editor Robert Siek, who taught me when the names of judicial branches should be capitalized. The jacket and interior design of the book come to you courtesy of Chris Brand, Oliver Munday, Elizabeth Rendfleisch, and Lauren Dong. And if you're reading this in some faraway corner of the world, you can probably thank Linda Kaplan in subsidiary rights.

My editor, Rachel Klayman, put a tremendous amount of work into this project. I was going to say "and it shows," but you never saw the book before her editorial touch, so you'll have to take my word for it.

I have been kept on the straight and narrow by Matthew Martin of the Random House legal department. He's a stickler for accuracy and detail, and his considerable efforts substantially improved the last part of the book.

I'd like to thank the parents and readers who helped me shape the story. First is Lisa Greenman, a federal defense attorney who works tirelessly to help young people with disabilities charged with serious crimes. Monica Adler Werner of the Ivymount School in Rockville, Maryland, offered valuable advice about teaching kids on the spectrum. Lori Shery of ASPEN (the Asperger Syndrome Education Network) offered a parent's perspective and wrote the reader's group guide to this book. Pat Smith of Sewall Child Development Center in Boulder, Colorado, provided her perspective. Jan Anderson provided the valuable insights of a parent and is responsible for setting up my ongoing school events and work-shops.

Finally, I'd like to thank David Lavin and his staff at the Lavin Agency. It's their work promoting me on the lecture circuit and managing my speaking events that keeps me in the public eye be-tween books.

CLOSING THE CIRCLE

I'd like to close by recognizing two people who play a vital role in our lives but who are underrepresented in this book: my mother, Margaret, and my wife, Maripat.

Maripat and I married in the summer of 2011, which means she was not part of most of the stories you've just read. However, it is her kindness and consistent loving demeanor that have kept me on an even keel these past two years, while her gentle spirituality has brought our family together in a way we've never really known before. To a significant extent, that's what made this book possible.

After my last marriage ended in divorce, I found myself living alone in a residential suite of a Springfield Hotel. Glamorous as hotel life sounds to some, it was a formula for depression. The winter I spent there was in many ways the longest of my life. The following spring, I returned to the home I'd built here in Amherst. It was nice to be back, but everything was subtly different. The house felt empty, big, and scary. My son was with his girlfriend in Greenfield, and my mother was in an apartment an hour away. My brother had lived near me for a while, but now he'd moved back to New York. I really didn't feel I had anyone to turn to.

I tried dating, but the people I met were set in their ways and well established in their own lives. I felt too old to start again. It was hard to imagine any of the people I met living in my home, or me living with them somewhere else. I also couldn't see how the family who'd been part of my life up to now would stay connected if I moved on.

That was where things stood when Maripat arrived on the scene. I'd known her for many years from the business community and cars, but when I got divorced I didn't think of asking her out because I believed she had a long-term boyfriend. Likewise, she didn't think of me because she assumed I was married.

One chance conversation changed everything. She told me she'd broken up with her boyfriend. I volunteered that I'd gotten a divorce. "We should go out," we said, and we did. We were married within a year, and the past two years have been the best of my life.

We are very comfortable together, but Maripat and I together is not the most remarkable aspect of our relationship. The most magical thing is the way she brought our two little tribes together and reconnected me with my own family, especially Cubby, Little Bear, and my mother. Those were things I could never have done on my own. At the same time, she wove us into a family unit with her two sons and her daughter. I had great fear and insecurity about stepkids—would they instinctively hate me? To my great relief, they welcomed me. Even her Imperial War Pug liked me. Dog people who know War Pugs say that's rare and a sign of a good upbringing.

She began shaping us into a family with Sunday dinners. At first, the dinner group was just Maripat, her two sons, and me. Then the circle expanded to include Cubby and Kirsten, who were quick to return for tasty free food. For our first Christmas, she invited Little Bear, and they bonded right away. As the tradition developed, Maripat alternated the locations. Some weeks we'd eat in Amherst, other weeks we'd eat at her place. Everyone was welcome. Friends and neighbors joined us.

Today my relationship with Cubby is the best it's been since he was little and I was still Wondrous Dada. Getting together every Sunday, and the interest Maripat's shown in his life, have made all the difference.

When Maripat and her youngest son moved in with me in Amherst, things got better still. They've settled in, and the house has been transformed into a warm and friendly place. People notice and comment on the changes. There are flowers everywhere, and little rocks and statues. Keepsakes line the windowsills, and photos of our kids are on the mantels. Cubby's old room has become a meditation studio. Bird feeders ring the yard, and the calls of woodland creatures are audible day and night. It's a remarkable thing, the way she transformed this house.

Best of all, its superior engineering features remain fully intact, and the animals continue to recognize my dominion over the yard and grounds. You might say I made it functional and she made it peaceful.

Little Bear is now a regular too; she and Maripat have become best friends. I watched their relationship develop with a combination of wonder and unease, but it's turned out very well for all of us. Little Bear and I had our differences that led us to divorce, but we also have much in common; and I suppose I should not be surprised that Maripat shares many interests with her too—like target shooting and edgy television shows.

My mother was next on the list. I had become estranged from her in recent years, so we didn't have much to do with her at first. However, Maripat pushed me to be involved with her, and we tried inviting her to Sunday dinner. To my surprise, she came, and all of us had a good time. A few months later, we had dinner at a local restaurant. Strained as my relationship with her was, I could see everyone else was very happy at the new turn of events. Then my mother got sick and ended up in the hospital. Maripat went with me to see her and continued visiting on her own. As they got to know each other, they realized they shared interests in spirituality, poetry, and many other things. Little Bear also stood by my mother, and when my mother was recovering in a nursing home, she and Maripat cared for her together. It was as if they were meant to be friends, or perhaps Maripat and Little Bear are both the daughters my mother never had.

Maripat showed a tenderness and warmth while looking after my mother, something I have had a hard time doing because I'd become so alienated over the years. By her behavior she has reconnected my mother and me; that's a wonderful thing.

She's shown my son caring behaviors too, and I hope they help him in his life going forward.

Then there is my mother and Cubby. In the beginning chapters of this book I wrote about my mother and my son growing together twenty-some years ago. He was a toddler, learning to walk, and she was beginning to recover from her stroke. Afterward, when Cubby was self-propelled, he spent many enjoyable days helping Grand-Margaret at her house, next to the Bridge of Flowers in Shelburne Falls. Little Bear would leave him with her all day while she was at school. Like all things, that came to an end. Cubby started school. His mom and I got divorced. I moved. Cubby stopped seeing Grand-Margaret except on special occasions.

Then Cubby grew up, and something changed. He missed his grandmother. At the same time, she became more disabled as she got older. Now she needs help around the house every day, and Cubby answered the call. He began going there once a week, then twice, and finally three days a week.

Over the past year Cubby got to know his grandmother as an adult. It's been a good experience for both of them, especially my son. With her, he shows a kindness and consideration I've not seen him display with others. It's the first time he's had to take care of someone else. I guess that's one of those key transitions: When we're small, people take care of us, and when we get older, we take care of others.

With all the people Maripat has woven into the rich tapestry of our lives, it looks like all our kids will be there for us when we are old, but more important, we are here for one another now. That is a very special feeling that I've never known before.

Who knows what tomorrow will bring?

ABOUT THE AUTHOR

John Elder Robison lives with his family in western Massachusetts. His business, J E Robison Service, restores and services European motor vehicles. He has an active international speaking schedule and serves on many boards and committees, including the International Society for Autism Research, the Interagency Autism Coordinating Committee of the Department of Health and Human Services, and the science board of Autism Speaks. John is the author of two previous books, *Look Me in the Eye* and *Be Different,* which have been translated into many languages and are sold around the world. Find him online on Facebook, Twitter, and at www.johnrobison.com.

Find Jack Robison (Cubby) on Facebook or on the web at www .robison-industries.com.